P9-DDO-678

THE VICTORIAN POPULAR BALLAD

THE VICTORIAN POPULAR BALLAD

J. S. BRATTON

ROWMAN AND LITTLEFIELD
TOTOWA, NEW JERSEY

First published in the United States 1975 by
ROWMAN AND LITTLEFIELD,
Totowa, N.J.

First published in the United Kingdom 1975 by
THE MACMILLAN PRESS LTD

Library of Congress Cataloging in Publication Data
Bratton, Jacqueline S
The Victorian popular ballad.

Bibliography: p.
Includes index.
1. Ballads, English—History and criticism.
2. English poetry—19th century—History and criticism. 3. Folk-songs, English—History and criticism. I. Title.
PR507. B65 821'.04 75-20128
ISBN 0-87471-760-4

Printed in Great Britain

FOR JANE TRAIES

Contents

Acknowledgements viii

PART ONE: THE BACKGROUND

Introduction 3

1 The Literary Ballads 12

2 The Popular Background 23

PART TWO: THE BALLADS

3 The Heroic Ballads 37

4 Ballads of the Common Man 89

5 Propaganda 137

6 Comic Ballads in the Music Hall 155

7 Comic Ballads in the Drawing-Room 203

Conclusion 251

Notes 254

Bibliography 267

Index 271

Acknowledgements

I would like to thank all who have helped me in the writing and preparation of this book, particularly Dr C. M. Ing of St Hilda's College Oxford, for her assistance with the work from which it sprang; Frances Dann, for her advice about melodrama; Christine Webb, for reading and commenting upon the typescript; and Jane Traies, for everything she has done.

J. S. B.

PART ONE

The Background

Introduction

This book is an attempt to claim for the popular ballads of the Victorian period a place in the mainstream of the great ballad tradition. I do not mean by this that I have sought out the last rags of orally-transmitted rural balladry which survived in the nineteenth century, nor that I have pursued ancient tunes and texts into the unlikely corners which were their last resting-places after they had died out of the popular memory. Far from it; for while the remnants of the ancient conventions of ballad singing did undoubtedly survive into the Victorian period, and beyond it, they were not the most common nor, I would argue, the best folk-song and popular poetry it produced. The great urban communities of the nineteenth century did not know them; but these were not a people without a culture, and the habit of singing and of verse did not die out with the old songs. The remnants of the old ballads were submerged, and subsumed, in a new upsurge of poetry and song which expresses the feeling and is the creation of the Victorian people. It is this huge, unexplored though often denigrated body of verse which I wish to establish as the Victorian popular ballad. Departing from the critical practice of seeking genuine folk poetry only in rural, or at the least in closed, tightly-knit industrial communities, I have sought out that poetry of the Victorian period which had an audience of tens of thousands, in concert rooms, village halls and the streets of London, and examined it to see whether that may not be the 'folk-song' of the nineteenth century. I am convinced that it is; and in the following pages have endeavoured to point out the noble lineage of Little Billee and Mad Carew, and to establish that Marie Lloyd was the rightful heir of the medieval minstrel.

I am of course aware of the rashness of such an enterprise, and of the dangers of any sally into the recondite and fiercely disputed realm of ballad scholarship. In 1806 Sir Walter Scott commented for the *Edinburgh Review* on a work of criticism by Joseph Ritson which attacked Thomas Percy's ballad editing. In the course of his review he accused Ritson of being vindictive and acrimonious, and indulging in 'coarse and violent invective', and went on to call him, in regard to his own editorial activities, 'a mere collector of stones and rubbish', 'better qualified to assail the opinions of others, than to deduce from the facts which he produces a separate theory of his own'.[1] Differences of opinion about the English and Scottish ballads have been discussed with as much passion, if with less personal abuse, ever since, and I shall accordingly begin with a cautious appeal to any critical support that can be found; for my argument for the Victorian ballad tends to call into question the few critical assumptions about the ballad which have been generally made.

The most important of these assumptions is the division of ballads into types, a division which is not only descriptive, but also evaluative, so that the traditional ballad, collected from oral tradition and included in Professor Child's definitive edition,[2] is placed at the top of a scale in which late white-letter broadsides, drawing-room or 'royalty' ballads, and literary imitations, dispute the bottom place. These three forms make up a considerable proportion of the ballads of the Victorian period, and most of the others fall into categories not so far recognised as ballads at all. Any case which is to be made for the mid- and late nineteenth century as having contributed something of value to the ballad tradition must be founded upon the questioning of rigid divisions between kinds of ballad which is found in recent scholarly discussions of the origins and transmission of the earlier ballads.

This questioning begins with the recognition that when Sir Arthur Quiller-Couch asserted, in his introduction to *The Oxford Book of Ballads* in 1910, that the ballad had been dead for two hundred years, he was mistaken. From the realisation that the great traditional ballads do not belong to a distant past, sealed off from later times by an indistinct but impervious barrier, arise all later recognitions of the continuity both temporal and artistic which exists between the traditional ballad and other ballad forms. The notion has been stated and exemplified many times. Robert Graves, for example, envisaged as early as 1927 the possibility of true folk ballads even according to his own communalistic theory of ballad origins being created in modern times, if suitable social conditions should arise, and he included the broadside 'goodnight', 'The Night Before Larry was Stretched', in his collection as an example. He remarked that the 'distinctions between the song and the narrative ballad, and between the oral and the literary ballad . . . did not exist until recent times',[3] but it was left to M. J. C. Hodgart to use this fact to begin to break down the isolation of the Child ballads in a timeless limbo. He pointed out that the ballad is 'an artistic form, not a scientific category',[4] and like many other forms its precise limits are rather a matter of taste than of fact. The point in the continuous spectrum between lyric and narrative at which one marks off ballad from song is a personal choice; Professor Child's exclusion of over half the narrative popular poems he collected because they had complex plots of many incidents, rather than a single exposition beginning as if in the fifth act of a tragedy, was an aesthetic rather than a scientific judgement on his part. Professor Hodgart accordingly went on to replace the ballads within the current of ordinary literary history, and therefore to discuss the differences between them in terms of development and change, concluding that far from belonging exclusively to an unspecified period of communal creation and being influenced only by the forces of communal recreation in the process of oral transmission, the great ballads emerged at a late date, for 'the height of the ballad art is reached when this [fugitive and scattered] imaginative beauty of folk-tradition is caught and fixed by skilled poets, poets able to keep the essentials of tradition and unite them with the literary graces.'[5] He goes on to show the evidence for this in specific ballads collected in the eighteenth century, and to point out especially the parts played by Burns and Scott in the creation of famous examples of 'the height of ballad art'. David Fowler has subsequently taken Professor Hodgart's investigation of the literary history of the great ballads much further,[6] and his examination of the stages and hands through which the 'genuine' traditional ballads which Child admitted to his canon passed must call into question the use of this rigorously selected group of poems of a certain type as a definition of what all ballads should be, if not as an aesthetic standard by which others may be measured.

All these commentators have, indeed, stopped short of an attack upon the aesthetic supremacy of the Child ballads in general, and in particular of the handful of romantic ballads such as 'Edward' and 'Sir Patrick Spens' which were given their final shape by the eighteenth-century ballad masters. They have, explicitly or by assumption, retained the evaluative scale which placed these naturally and inevitably ahead of the rest, and even those critics who, following up the idea of continuity between all ballad forms, have concentrated their attention on the neglected broadsides or on literary ballads have still regarded their chosen objects of study as necessarily inferior to these. Vivian de Sola Pinto and Allan Rodway introduce their selection of street ballads, *The Common Muse*,[7] by deprecating absolute distinctions between types of ballads and appealing to aesthetic judgement alone to place their examples of patriotic ballads above those composed by Tennyson; but they also distinguish the broadside from the traditional ballad in aesthetic terms which clearly place the one below the other in poetic value and potentiality. R. Nettel,[8] who has been concerned to trace the history of all kinds of popular song and to defend that which is not necessarily rural and traditional, adopts the term 'vulgar' with all its pejorative overtones when he is speaking of the street ballads of the early nineteenth century; and in arguing for the scholarly reconsideration of the distinction between them and the Child ballads Professor Hodgart himself made use of the same descriptive word.[9]

It might well be argued that until a street ballad is put forward which will stand beside the best of traditional ballads it is correct to regard the differences of method and focus between the types as inevitably productive of qualitative difference; but the same assumption of the innate superiority of the traditional ballad lies behind discussion of the literary ballad, which can show several examples to dispute it. In *The Ballad Revival*[10] A. B. Friedman discusses at length the eighteenth- and nineteenth-century literary ballads, written by known, often famous, poets deliberately adopting ballad style, and assumes throughout that there is something false and unreal about them, using the assumption to explain, for instance, the tendency to ballad parody which grew up during the period, which he regards as arising from the writers' consciousness of this unreality. Anne Ehrenpreis, in her collection of literary ballads,[11] clearly regards her material as something innately lesser than the ballads of tradition, because the ballads influenced these poets to write these poems, a fact which she and most critics take to mean not that these poems are ballads, but rather that they are verses in which the major creative force is a literary one. Yet when the confusion which arises from regarding the ballad as a closed account, to which nothing can be added and from which no current coin can be drawn, is set aside, it must surely be obvious that many of the examples she includes in her selection, such as 'La Belle Dame Sans Merci' and 'The Ancient Mariner', more than challenge comparison with the best that Child's collection can offer. If it is now thoroughly accepted that the ballads belong in the main stream of literary history, and are not invested with some mysterious power by virtue of their origins and transmission, then it must follow that the qualities which belong to them, and distinguish them from other forms of poetry, are capable of being brought to a high standard under various circumstances. They can coexist with the conditions of ordinary literary composition; they are not necessarily destroyed by having a learned writer, nor by becoming current in an urban community, nor even by showing relationships with other literary forms. As Leslie Shepard has said, 'the essential quality of the ballad is an *attitude of mind* rather than a specific form. This attitude takes different forms at different periods of history.'[12]

It is necessary to stress this possibility of continuity and therefore of equality between the traditional and other ballads if there is to be any case made out for the ballads of the Victorians; for the great period of ballad collection, when dozens of scholars busied themselves salvaging verses from oral tradition throughout the British Isles, produced few new ballads of that kind. The Victorian ballads I wish to discuss are rarely confined to oral tradition, and have a multitude of different shapes and forms, perhaps the least common of which is that in which the majority of Child's ballads are written. This is not to be bewailed, however; for, if the essential feature of folk or popular art is not oral transmission or anonymity or antiquity but the fact that it represents the common denominator of feeling and experience in the community to which it belongs, it would be a decline indeed if the ballads of this rapidly-changing period of British history were the same as those of previous ages. If we measure them by their direct resemblance to the Child ballads we shall be disappointed; but if we review them without presuppositions as to the possibility of excellence in the various ballad forms, a clear and fertile tradition of popular narrative poetry can be discerned, and one which expressed a great deal about the people to whom it belonged.

Cecil Sharp was perhaps the first to discuss[13] the profound change which took place in the ballad in the mid-nineteenth century, and he noticed it but to express his regret. Collecting folk-songs around the turn of the twentieth century he found that nobody under sixty had in memory any of the kind of material which he sought. He concluded that around 1840 there was a dividing line, a point when something snapped, and songs ceased to be composed in the old tradition. It was the common experience of collectors,[14] and was remarked in other contexts too, for instance by Thomas Hardy,[15] who remembered a sharp change in country songs which was brought about by the coming of the railway to his village when he was a child, in the 1840s, when the new songs of the town suddenly became available. I wish to suggest that after this marked change (whatever it was, and whatever the reasons for it) there was not a complete disappearance of popular song rooted in the ballad of tradition, but rather that the coming together of many social, practical and literary changes resulted in the merging of the country folk tradition with other manifestations of the ballad, creating a spectrum of popular ballad which was distinctively Victorian. It included, at one end, the last of the old folk ballads, but the area I wish to discuss in relation to these covers a much wider range of popular audience, including music-hall songs and also much poetry hitherto regarded as an artistically poor part of the literary tradition rather than as popular writing. A new and very healthy lease of life was given to the ballad-singing tradition, a kind of narrative poetry was evolved which expressed the mores and the attitudes of the communities of England, and which was created by many writers, composers and performers, famous, anonymous and amateur. Its styles and conventions became indeed so strong that varieties of talent tend to be submerged in them, and differences between practitioners are discernible only in terms of relative expertise. This is of course true of all popular forms of art, which express the general rather than the particular, not intending to distinguish the individual who creates from the mass for whose benefit he does so. Far from there being a decline of this kind of composition in Victorian times, there was such an upsurge of it that many readers and writers who would in previous centuries have been either completely ignorant of popular poetry or contemptuous of it now devoted themselves to it exclusively, and regarded anything else as somehow effete.[16] Such an attitude might well indicate that there were drawbacks in the spread of the ballad revival, and indeed the Victorian ballads were, amongst other things, an outlet for the worst aspects of the culture, carrying for example its sentimentality and its jingoism to extremes excluded from the more esoteric areas of literature. For this reason a redrawing of the line which separates 'art' and 'popular' poetry, so that some of the work of many of the poets of the period from about 1840 to the First World War is removed to the area of popular writing, with which it has most in common, would seem to me to clarify our response to their work, and provide a fuller explanation and therefore a less distorted view of it by placing it in its proper context.

Before the strength of the Victorian revival can be demonstrated, and the role played in it by all the various sources of ballads and songs can be assessed, it is necessary to work out some form of definition which will make the new ballads recognisable and at the same time establish what they have in common with the old. One element of it has already been mentioned, and that is the impersonality of the ballad, which is related to the *sine qua non* that the ballad is a narrative. The Child ballads are 'anonymous, narrative poems . . . not only anonymous but also impersonal: the storyteller does not intrude his personality'.[17] Victorian ballads, having lost anonymity, are still impersonal, in that they are the utterances of the public voice, for public consumption, and reveal nothing of the individuality of their composers. The only personalities involved are the dramatic ones which in many cases are used by the writer or performer to reinforce the drama of the action narrated: a character steps out of the story and tells it in his own person. Technically, the device is a good substitute for the technique of 'montage', the narration by means of isolated action shots which the great eighteenth-century ballad transmitters used to achieve the intensity and compression characteristic of their poems, which few other balladeers were accomplished enough to achieve. The first-person narrator of the Victorian ballad does not violate the principle of impersonality because he is hardly ever an individual; rather he is a type, a representative of a class or group, and it is to that class or group, or a larger audience which is familiar with the stereotype, that he addresses himself. The Child ballads also make use of stereotypes – simple, emblematic roles and objects which have a certain fixed range of connotations and are manipulated by the storyteller in the confidence that the audience will understand by them exactly what he does, and not need, therefore, any elaboration or redefinition which would hold up the story. In that case they were roles such as those of brother, lover, king, or witch, and objects such as horse and hound and sword; for the Victorian tale-teller they are mother, child, wicked father, drunkard, soldier, and many more, a much longer, but still finite, list; and their world contains, for example, flowers, bar-rooms, the carriages of the rich, and the barrows of the poor. Both include, incidentally, the evil mother-in-law.

The immortal mother-in-law joke is also an element in and indication of the other major characteristic of the Victorian ballad by which it can be distinguished from 'art' poetry and which links it firmly to the ballad of previous ages: that characteristic is best described as a distinctive set of social attitudes. This peculiarity is far less concrete than the details of narrative technique, but far more important in understanding the essence of popular poetry and the function which gives it life and coherence. Literature is a way of assimilating life; it sets up patterns out of the raw material of experience to guide and to guard the reader, and to help him comprehend and therefore bear human existence. The complex and elaborate tradition of post-medieval poetry in English works with one such pattern; but popular poetry and song works with quite another.

They are of course not insulated from each other; but it is the recognisable difference of primary assumptions and attitudes to the world which marks out folk-song, and which is the basis of the instinctive recognition of true ballad which scholars have relied upon more firmly than any formal definition.[18] Its elements, in the form in which they exist in the Child ballads, are well described by many, including a comprehensive treatment by Gerould in *The Ballad of Tradition.*[19] They include notions of the function of human relationships, of the roles of women and of the dead, and of the balances between for instance passion and violence, or possession and right, and even ideas of the normal human reactions, all of which diverge from the equivalent assumptions of the mainstream of literature. The hostility of the mother to her child's spouse is an example of a phenomenon with fairly complex psychological roots and implications, which affects most people at some time and to some extent, which was noticed by the folk tradition at an early date, so that it is handled in a number of ballads and runs throughout the nineteenth century as a commonplace of popular entertainment, while it has for some reason slipped through the net of the other tradition. One effect of this accident has been the inclination of those whose perception is largely conditioned by the sophisticated tradition alone to regard the mother-in-law joke as a senseless vulgarity, and the motives of the evil mothers in such ballads as 'The Lass of Roch Royal' (*English and Scottish Popular Ballads,* no. 76) as mysterious, even supernatural. In dealing with larger matters, such as the role of woman, each of the traditions has a set of assumptions which is a selection from experience. The courtly basis of the sophisticated tradition gives it an inclination to emphasise the weakness of woman and her passivity, idealised until she becomes a helpless, motionless object of adoration whose chief functions are to inspire devotion and to spiritualise mankind. The folk tradition is complementary to this: it stresses instead the endurance and tenacity of the female, the strength of her life-preserving instincts, so that the beautiful woman is active, practical, and fertile, turning man's sexual urge not to spirituality but to procreation. The ballad heroine cast in this mould is a powerful figure in those Child ballads (about a third of the total) which are love stories; and, in the Victorian period, when the other stream of literature often turned the courtly lady into an angelically simpering doll, popular art did something to redress the balance by preserving in its stories at least some of the characteristics of the ballad woman. What is true of love stories is equally true in other areas: the popular ballad makes a different selection from experience, and the result has a different tone. It is tempting to call its distinguishing characteristic a greater realism than was to be found in sophisticated poetry, and it was certainly felt by a large contemporary audience that such verse was nearer to real life than were the effusions of high art; but it is not so, and the modern rejection of the way in which, for example, the wars of the nineteenth century were presented on the popular stage, is a reaction against a distorting selectivity in folk-art. Some recent critics, such as Edward Lee, have found the sentimentality and the chauvinism of the Victorian people so distasteful as to impel them to reject nineteenth-century ballads from the sphere of folk-art and to attribute them to the inferior taste of the middle class. Mr Lee describes the emergence of a separate bourgeois 'stream of taste'[20] in the nineteenth century. Later he discusses the decline, due to social changes, of the folk tradition in the same period; but he does not connect these two phenomena. When a new 'stream of taste' emerges as an older one dries up, it seems at least worth considering whether the new takes the place of the old and preserves from it what is still vital. Mr Lee uses the terms of class apologetically and with reservations; but he is not prepared to see the possible unity of taste between those whose sharing of national and urban environments is at least as significant as their class difference. Victorian ballads express the values and aspirations not only of the middle class but also of the urban working class.

I hope to show that the complex variety of narrative verse and song which appeared at every level in Victorian entertainment, from the boards of the music-hall to the publications of the Poet Laureate, includes much that can truly be regarded as belonging to a tradition of folk-art, and that that tradition had its roots in the common ground of popular poetry, which it shared with the ballad of tradition, while belonging quite distinctively to its own times.[21]

1 *The Literary Ballads*

The distinctively Victorian ballad is derived only indirectly, however, from those which preceded it. The unbroken tradition of the street ballad, which began in the sixteenth century and continued into the middle of the nineteenth, did not lead straight on to it, and indeed might be said to have existed for half a century beside the new Victorian popular verse without being wholly part of it. Between the broadside tradition and that of the music-halls and the drawing-room recitations there intervened two major circumstances which changed popular verse enormously. Popular poetry was taken up and used by poets of the literary tradition as an element in the formation of the high style and taste of the century, and fed back into popular use changed in its form and assumptions by the contact; and, equally influentially, the whole structure of popular entertainment, its organs of dissemination, the composition of its audiences, their tastes and their habits, underwent a series of changes dictated by social and practical developments ranging from the growth of the industrial towns to the diversification of the periodical press. The Victorian popular ballad grew out of the old common ground of popular poetry, but its form was partly dictated by its contact with the literary tradition, and its flourishing was the result of its being surrounded by peculiarly encouraging circumstances. Both these elements must be set beside the history of the ballad tradition itself before the Victorian mutation of it can be fully understood.

The rise of the literary ballad in the poetry of the Romantic and Victorian writers should be distinguished from the older phenomenon of the writing of broadside verses, for some specific satirical or political purpose, by poets of established literary reputation. This was a habit, not without its own influence on the formulation of Victorian ballad styles, which nineteenth-century poets inherited from previous generations, in its dying years. The use of the broadside as a weapon in social and political controversy was as old as the form itself, and greater and lesser poets had turned their hands to it throughout its life. Their efforts were not in any sense literary ballads, and continued quite unselfconsciously in the eighteenth century, when the division between popular and sophisticated poetry was strongest, and into the early part of the nineteenth century, with more consciousness, perhaps, but no sense of falsity or imitation. After Prior, Swift and Gay came ballads of social protest from Blake and Byron, Leigh Hunt, Coleridge and Southey, Shelley's *Mask of Anarchy*, and eventually a series of satires, the best of which is a version of 'The Fine Old English Gentleman', from Charles Dickens. All used the broadside stanzas and metres, as appropriate to their subjects and to their intended audience; but few nineteenth-century poets actually printed them on slips and had them sold for a penny. Most were intended for periodicals, which were bought by as wide a spectrum of the community as that which had once bought broadsides. A side-effect of this was the increase of the danger involved in the enterprise, for publishers of magazines are much more vulnerable to prosecution and suppression than fugitive operators of a single press selling their wares in the street; *The Mask of Anarchy*, indeed, was thought too risky to be published. The poets who dabbled in the political broadside naturally absorbed some of its formal and technical features into their other verse, and its influence is pervasive in *Songs of Innocence and Experience*, and quite clear in some of Shelley's poems, such as 'Arethusa', 'The Cloud', and 'The Sensitive Plant.'

The poet who drew most upon the broadsides did not, however, approach them from this direction, but adopted the form on artistic principles. Wordsworth's *Lyrical Ballads* are deliberately modelled on broadside themes and often set in broadside metres, as part of his attempt to strip away the artificialities of sophisticated poetry and return to writing of the simple passions of the natural man in language which he used and understood himself. It is not altogether a successful experiment, unless one argues that the extremes to which it is taken, while they are not in themselves acceptable as good poetry, were essential in order to make possible the re-establishment of a balance between artifice and simplicity in subsequent writing. Certainly the broadside influence is directly responsible for the worst features of those lyrical ballads which are modelled on them stylistically.

Wordsworth found white-letter broadsides all around him in the country and in London, and he, like most of his contemporaries, did not distinguish them from the traditional ballads which he read in Percy's *Reliques*.[1] Some broadside versions of Child ballads were still available well into the nineteenth century, but the predominant style of those Wordsworth saw must have been the stanzaic, metrical and verbal patterns which he reflects in his ballads. Characteristically, these are more complicated than the four-line stanzas of the Child ballads; often they have an extra line, or run two stanzas together and unite them with a rhyme pattern which attempts to find a rhyme at the end of every line (though rarely succeeding very convincingly) and takes particular pride in multi-syllabic chimes. The weak, often repetitious, five-line stanza of 'The Idiot Boy' is common on broadsides, and in 'Goody Blake and Harry Gill' and 'Simon Lee' Wordworth's greater technical skill enabled him to carry out the double rhyming, to which broadside hacks aspired, so much more regularly and efficiently than they did that it is almost unbearable. The old-established mannerism of the minstrel ballad, descended to the Irish 'Come-all-ye',[2] which addresses exhortations and asides to the audience to command attention, is turned into the irritating 'old sea-captain' narrator of 'The Thorn', and the mock-reportage of ballads about the latest murder, which were laced with circumstantial details to add authenticity, gave rise to the notorious 'Four foot long and two foot wide' pond in the same poem. Stylistically the broadsides are not so much simple as crudely decorative, and to reproduce their style is not to come very much nearer to ordinary speech than did Dryden or Gray. Many indeed had scraps of arch poetic diction embedded in them, from some contact with stage or glee club, and even these are reproduced in the *Lyrical Ballads*.

Wordsworth was more fortunate in the plots he took from the broadsides and from his other encounters with popular art, especially with the early melodramas. The themes, stories and attitudes of the old broadside ballads were largely unchanged, and Wordsworth helped their transmission from the dying form into the more 'respectable' areas of the Victorian ballad. The characters in the *Lyrical Ballads* are objects of contemplation, which Wordsworth explores for their psychological interest. Behind each of them, however, is a story. The chief business of the poem is to consider the people as they are after their particular story has ended, when they are reduced to the edge of human existence; but part of the exploration is made in terms of narrative of previous events. These events, the stories of his people, Wordsworth draws from popular sources, and they have the tone, attitudes of mind and of response to events, which belong to folk-art. Stated baldly some of them are unlikely, apparently unrealistic. The shepherd in 'The Last of the Flock' and the female vagrant have both been subject to such unrelenting series of misfortunes that they strain credulity: in a different context the successive loss of home, parents, husband and children which has fallen upon the vagrant, would seem but over-emphasised by the addition of her illness and vagrancy. The shepherd, in a realistic novel, would not have been given quite so many as six starving children, and even that figure was less than the one Wordsworth first thought of. Madness and murder and death, all kinds of extreme situation, are used by Wordsworth in bringing into being the extreme states of human nature which he wishes to study; and the stories in which they occur are all to be found in popular poetry and drama, where the extreme and the larger than life are habitually used. Tales of seduction and desertion, followed by infanticide and madness, were archetypal ballad stories before being used in 'The Thorn', and 'Ruth' is closely modelled on the commonest of broadside stories of the lost lover. Mad songs were also a speciality of broadside writers; and in the melodrama there are several examples of unfortunate children, dumb or blind, who are the centre of stories, as is the idiot boy. The driving emotional forces which are emphasised in Wordsworth's ballads are those emphasised by popular tradition, particularly the stress which he lays upon the maternal instinct of his female figures, and their strength and activity in protecting and providing for their children – indeed, their very fertility, with its often unhappy results, is part of the convention of ballad stories.

The general reader was not prepared for this uncompromising exposition of ideas and situations unfamiliar in polite literature, any more than he was for the use of the garish, jangling doggerel of the vulgar street ballad; but when other Romantic poetry, including that inspired by the revival of interest in the traditional ballad, had prepared the ground, and Wordsworth had become an established man of letters, readers and other writers did accept the *Lyrical Ballads*, and through them the broadsides exercised an influence upon Victorian taste. The iron pathos which Wordsworth had drawn from the desperate people and situations he used tended, certainly, to be weakened into sentimentality, and the harsh vulgar ring of his broadside diction was watered down into silliness and jingles; but then that is true to the popular tradition, for the grim psychological conclusion to the story of violence was a part of Wordsworth's personal response, imposed by him upon melodramatic and sensational stories which had more often been given a facile, even a happy, ending. Popular taste accepted the stories, sharpened and refreshed from his hand, but rejected the vision of humanity which it could not share and found unsatisfactory. Instead the more clear-cut, if less truthfully likely, death-or-glory conclusions of the popular tradition were restored.

Wordsworth's preference for the forms of broadside rather than of traditional ballads was unusual amongst those Romantic poets who were influenced by the ballad revival. A. B. Friedman has suggested[3] that the *Lyrical Ballads* are the last in a line of genteel verses derived from the street ballad and written by many minor eighteenth-century poets, such as Thomas Tickell. It is true that many eighteenth-century writers who took an interest in the ballad were apparently unable or unwilling to see any difference between the styles of ballad they came across, and tended to mix them all together in collection or imitation. Thomas Percy, the central figure of the eighteenth-century revival of ballad scholarship, was no exception, and the epoch-making *Reliques of Ancient Poetry* contains a confused mixture of popular styles and of poetic quality, along with much that is not popular at all. It was this book, however, which was the foundation of the huge burst of interest in ballad and romance which was a mainspring of Romantic poetry, and which was perhaps the most pervasive and powerful external element in the shaping of the Victorian ballad.

The description of the ballads as 'ancient poetry' is the key to the nature of the Romantic revival and imitation of ballad style. Wordsworth was chiefly interested in ballads as being the poetry of the people, as were Shelley and Byron when they used broadside styles. But the great Romantic ballads of Coleridge and Keats, and the work of the later poets who followed them, are chiefly inspired by a notion of the antiquity of the ballad form. The development and use of the Romantic ballad style went hand in hand with the development of ballad scholarship, and was aimed at creating poetry in a mould which was being gradually revealed and defined by academic research. The best examples, of course, use the technical characteristics described as belonging to the ancient ballad to frame the poets' personal responses, and are unmistakably literary rather than popular, expressing the reaction to life, literature, history and ideas which is peculiar to the individual writer. Through this kind of writing, however, and through the study of the ballads which were being collected from oral tradition, which became for some time a fashionable and busy area of scholarly activity, ideas of what ballads are like, the sort of stories they contain, and their significance in historical terms, became very widely disseminated. Thus the ballad revival affected popular poetry on at least two levels: it led to the complete acceptance of the reading and writing of ballads as once more a worthwhile, indeed a fashionable, activity; and it spread a familiarity with certain themes and attitudes which were either derived from, or in some cases read into, the ballad of tradition.

The first Romantic ballad-writer of the nineteenth century was by far the most influential. Sir Walter Scott combined in himself all the elements of the ballad revival: he was a lifelong ballad collector, an antiquarian with an overpowering love of and reverence for the historical associations of the Border ballads he edited, and a poet of unsurpassed popularity and reputation. Many later scholars have bemoaned this last characteristic, for it led him to play an active rather than a passive part in ballad transmission, handling material himself, as an editor, in the same way as a singer might, altering and improving, patching up texts to suit his ideas of good balladry.[4] The recognition of Scott as a great popular poet in his own right, for these very activities, which are after all what kept ballads in oral tradition alive, is not yet completely ungrudging. The feeling, paradoxically originating with Scott and his fellow pioneers, that the ballad texts are of great antiquity, so that historical value resides in every word which can possibly be preserved, has led critics until very recently to deprecate his editing because they admire so much the poems his editing produced. Most of the 'ancient' ballads for whose sake Percy and Scott have been attacked were partly their creations.

The ballad texts known to Victorian readers were those of the *Reliques* and of Scott's *Minstrelsy of the Scottish Border*, and the literary ballads they read were derived from them. The tone of the latter differed from that of contemporary popular poetry in several ways, all of which can be traced to the reverence the Romantic writers felt for the ballad's antiquity. To them the ballads were the product of the Middle Ages; and the medieval period was a golden age. In the ballad they could find a form and an excuse for rejecting modern ugliness and squalor, and write of human relationships in a context which endowed them with dignity, mystery and beauty, both physical and spiritual. For this reason successive poets, beginning with Scott himself, stressed the supernatural aspect of the ballads, and also imported into their ballad editing and composition elements of the supposed medieval world which belonged to the courtly rather than the popular tradition. These changes of stress, together with a steadily developing subtlety and variety in the use of the technical devices of the ballad, created a characteristic literary ballad form which was romantic in several senses, and which influenced, but formed no part of, the popular tradition.

Scott had certain precedents for his beginning of this trend. He derived his ballad style not only from the oral examples he collected, but also from the Gothic imitation ballads of Matthew Gregory Lewis.[5] These early products of the spread of German Romanticism to England were sensational tales of ghosts and fiends, erring priests and robber barons, couched in exclamatory language and heavily-rhymed anapaestic stanzas, which had a certain vogue before the turn of the century, and found their way into the early verses of Shelley and Southey as well as those of Scott. They are ludicrous, and were soon recognised as such, but they did much in establishing the range of characters, and the bias towards the supernatural in later and better Romantic ballads. The devil of the medieval mysteries, complete with horns and tail, gained a new lease of life, and all unearthly phenomena from spectres to country superstitions were made familiar to the ordinary reader, along with the stereotypes of the costume drama, the picture of olde times which is still not quite dead. The technical variety and complexity of stanza-forms which were used within the ballad genre in the nineteenth century also owe much to the work of Lewis and of those who drew upon it. Scott's best ballads, 'Proud Maisie' and 'Red Harlaw', for example, are confined to the simplest common measure, and he maintained traditional versification scrupulously when editing; but many of his other ballad poems have long, complicated stanzas, metrical intricacies and involved rhyme schemes, which became recognised as 'ballad metres' though they are unrelated to anything in popular poetry.

Lewis's ballads are extremely crude, based on little real knowledge of or interest in the form apart from its sensational possibilities. Scott was a sensitive and erudite scholar of the ballad, and improved greatly upon his literary model in his own ballad writing. Those who learned from him copied not only his edited texts and his own ballads, but also his romances, and from the elision of ballad and romance the great Romantic ballads were developed. Coleridge in his great ballad was perhaps less influenced by Scott than directly by Percy and the earlier Gothic ballad imitation: *The Ancient Mariner* continues the movement towards the use of the ballad as a vehicle and outward shape for the figuring forth of supernatural and psychological forces. The next generation of Romantic poets, however, accepted the ballad from Scott's hands. For Keats the value, and the urgency, of the medieval vision was perhaps even greater than for Scott, whose knowledge of the historical reality was so much wider, and balanced the idealisations of the literary influence. All Keats's shorter narrative poems (excluding, that is, *Hyperion* and *Lamia*) are more or less products of Romantic medievalism, most of them dominated by courtly rather than ballad models, but all owing much to the spreading influence of Scott. Keats's one great ballad, 'La Belle Dame Sans Merci', is the triumph of the Romantic literary ballad; on the purely literary level, all that came after it, the ballad writing of the Victorian romantics, was a decline.

The reasons for this are literary, and have no place in an examination of the popular poetry of the century. It must, however, be noticed that the verse of Rossetti and Morris was quite as useful as the finest flowers of Romantic medievalism in providing the popular balladeers, particularly the parodists, with stylistic models. The medieval settings, characters and vocabulary of Romantic poetry provided a groundwork and source of reference for ballad writing, and the progressive development of later literary ballads kept the aspects of it which had been transferred to the popular level by means of burlesque alive, by providing fresh absurdities. On the other hand, the aspects of the ballad revival which had been accepted seriously by the Victorian public, particularly its stress upon nationalism in poetry, were dropped from the literary ballad as it pulled further and further away from the popular level, and they became part of the popular ballad.

The split between popular and romantic is evident in the various ballads of Lord Tennyson, some of which must be reserved for later discussion as popular poetry, while others belong to the aspect of his writing which was his contribution to Victorian medievalism. His major contribution, of course, was his handling of the Matter of Britain. It added a body of material to the medieval revival whose frame of order was that of the metrical romance, and the *Idylls of the King* were perhaps the most powerful influence in the further assimilation of ballad and romance in Victorian poetry. Tennyson also wrote several poems which are primarily derived from the literary ballad convention, and indeed are early examples of its stylistic elaboration. In the volume of poems published in 1832, for instance, there is not only the title poem, 'The Lady of Shalott', but also 'The Sisters', in which the influence of Scott is very clear. 'The Lady of Shalott' is a good example of the combination of technical elaboration of ballad devices, clear, evocative description of the details of an idealised medieval landscape and characters, and a story whose events and implications are mistily imprecise and laden with sad suggestion, which is characteristic of the sophisticated literary ballad. 'The Sisters' is suggestive of the dangers inherent in the artificiality of the form. The story is horrific, with a gratuitous final twist which is clearly inspired by emulation of the climax of the ballad 'Edward', but which is groundless, and so ineffective; and the use of two chorus lines, woven into the stanzas, is derived from the same source, but fails in its intended function of building up atmosphere because it is too studied, and tips formality into artifice. There are instances of the same failing in other early poems, such as 'The Ballad of Oriana' and 'Lady Clara Vere de Vere'.

Tennyson had largely abandoned experiments in literary ballad technique before the next major exponent, Swinburne, began his. Swinburne was moved to an interest in the ballad, like most of his generation, by childhood enjoyment of Scott's *Minstrelsy*, and his sally into ballad editing was inspired by a nationalistic intention to assert the claims of the English border against the Scottish monopoly suggested by the title of Scott's collection. His edition (intended for a challenge both to the Gaelically biased rewriting of Scott and also to the tedious, pedantic setting down of unpoetic nonsense in vogue in modern editions like that of Professor Child which had just been published) was projected while he was a rash undergraduate, and never came to fruition.[6] But though the introduction on these lines was rather wild, the preparation of texts, such as the complicated case of the ballad of Tam Lin, was done with care and with poetic sensitivity which showed he was not by any means unlearned in traditional ballad techniques. It gave him materials and skills for the composition of his own literary ballads. Despite his avowed intention in the projected edition, the real attraction of ballad story for him was not nationalistic, for he edited very few Border ballads; it was rather the depth, and the darkness, of the passions expressed in some of the domestic ballads. His own compositions use such stories – they use them, that is, as far as the stories can be discerned at all, for most of the poetic energy goes into atmosphere, suggested by the use of intricate, fantastic verbal elaboration. The poems which result are structures displaying a technical virtuosity distantly derived from technical features of the traditional ballad, but no longer subordinated to or serving narrative purpose in any way.

In Swinburne's work the combination of the suggestion of corrupt, unmentionable events, and obscure complexities of expression, was precisely the opposite of the popular poetry of the 1860s, when the first series of *Poems and Ballads* was published. Verses like 'The King's Daughter', a glittering, sinister story, probably about incest, with an incomprehensible chiming burden and insidious, incantatory repetitions, was linked with similarly peculiar publications by William Morris and Dante Gabriel Rossetti in a wave of public hostility and contempt. All three of these poets were capable of producing exact copies of ballads with medieval settings, in the conventional stanza with simple, coherent stories: they were thoroughly familiar with their models, and the strange uses to which they preferred to put them were an assertion of artistic independence of the opinions of the conventional audience. They were not popular poets. They did not court the people, and they did not speak for them. Later in his life Morris changed his attitude to the uses of poetry, and did write some popular ballads; but *The Defence of Guenevere*, published in 1858, was a volume which emerged entirely from the dream-world of medievalism. The literary ballads it contains use the technical devices he selects from the ballad to erect a vivid personal symbolism. Like Swinburne, Morris found the way in which some ballads reveal the beginnings of their story indirectly, by means of a few selected details or phrases, an attractive device for emphasising the allusive, compressed quality of poetry. Combining this device with other elements to which he responded in medieval literature, particularly his delight in the visual excitement of heraldry, with its flat, primary colours and evocative formal patterns, he attempted to use elliptical narrative studded with colours and objects so that they developed, hopefully, the resonance of the bright brown swords and kirtles green in the traditional ballads. Unfortunately the potency of the symbols is almost always severely limited, for they belong only to his own experience or imagination, and the romantic narratives in which they are set are too vaguely or elliptically told to lend them significance, or to receive it in turn. The results – poems such as 'The Song of the Seven Towers', 'Golden Wings', 'Near Avalon' and 'Two Red Roses Across the Moon' – are unfathomably obscure without explanation, and convey little more than an intense mood of some kind, whether of exultation, despair or ennui. They never fulfil ballad purposes, and indeed are so obscurely esoteric as to have provoked popular anger and contempt. His technical manipulations of, for instance, the ballad chorus, are full of life and energy; but it is the life of a vivid personal fantasy. For Morris they were apparently very clear and concrete notions, but for the reader they create only an atmosphere of vague, mysterious beauty and dreamy enchantment punctuated by violence and picturesque corruption which is the final distillation of the other-world of literary medievalism.

Rossetti's ballad writing was similarly a personal blend of the elements of medieval literature which appealed to him most, and is also marked by the use of technical details of traditional ballad style in a sophisticated, highly literary way. 'Sister Helen', which Swinburne praised[7] as the best of modern ballads, is justly regarded as the typical pre-Raphaelite poem. It is a story of blood-feud and witchcraft which nicely represents the combination of real ballad motifs and the sensational supernaturalism imposed upon them by the Gothic ballads; it uses the most admired ballad narrative methods, the exchange of question and answer, and the indirect revelation of past events which lead to the climax of present action; and it carries a picturesque chorus or burden which punctuates and also contributes to the action. The highly-wrought, conscious, artistry with which these elements of a narrative form are made to express levels of psychological subtlety and a counter-point of emotional and moral forces within the characters is the opposite of popular writing.

These writers had some influence on the use of ballad formulae in serious poetry – chiefly, it is true, in preventing most of the poets who followed them from attempting to go any further in a style which they had more or less exhausted, and had certainly brought into contempt in some quarters. Their effect upon the upsurge of popular writing which was taking place at the time they wrote was quite considerable, continuing the effect of the Romantic ballads in making a wide range of ballad style familiar and available, both to those poets who were eager to transform even the most insubstantial new turn of phrase or rhythm to enrich their popular writing, and to the host of parodists and journalists who were just as eager for new mannerisms to mock. Popular poetry, however, while it made use of the Romantic ballad and its successors, had a separate life and a development of its own which parted from the literary ballad at the beginning of the century, in the heat of the ballad revival. The Victorian popular ballads have a complex and many-layered history, and the form was powerful enough to draw into itself much technical and stylistic support from many sources, creating a wide range of expression for what remained, basically, the concerns of a folk-art.

2 *The Popular Background*

Just as the new relation of polite literature to folk-song had an effect upon the development of popular poetry during the nineteenth century, so also the changing conditions of popular composition and communication affected the Victorian ballad profoundly. During the first half of the century there was in effect a growth and spreading out of the popular culture, which scattered the seeds of country folk-song into dozens of new, urban, nurseries, where it grew and proliferated in many different ways. Alongside the old broadside prints and the handing on of songs by oral tradition there grew up Glee Clubs, pleasure garden entertainments, Harmonics Meetings and ballad concerts, and minor theatres staging musical shows and melodramas, as well as the amateur singers and reciters who outnumbered all those who attended professional entertainments put together. This was a movement towards social unification, giving more people a share in the popular culture. The popular audience, sharing tastes and attitudes, embraced members of several social groups, who enjoyed the same songs, though often in quite different surroundings and without consciousness of sharing an experience with anyone outside their own immediate circle.

There was also, on the other hand, a stratification going on in these years. The reading public, of whose pursuits and tastes an eighteenth-century writer or publisher could be reasonably sure, split up, and became, from the point of view of someone wishing to sell his wares, a series of specialist markets. As many literary figures never tired of pointing out, cheaper printing, higher literacy and more publications did not mean more good books read by more people. A large section of the reading public divided itself off from the lovers of literature and became the audience of the popular writer. Many people, including once again members of most social groups, read a great deal without ever opening a book of any merit according to the standards of the literary tradition. These readers had verse, as well as prose, created for them; and there were many publications in which such verse could be sought without fear of confronting the obscurities and what many felt to be the moral dangers of the other kind of modern poetry. The two kinds of writing sometimes inadvertently overlapped: the qualities which sold thousands of copies of Tennyson's successive volumes were not on the whole the literary merits they possessed; they were the qualities of popular poetry, which could be found in different manifestations in the pages of journals and daily papers, in books compiled for the use of reciters, and selections of innocuous sentiments for the schoolroom. The attitudes and assumptions of the popular tradition, inflected for the modern reader, broke out of the moribund vehicle of the broadsides and invaded respectable publishing houses, becoming indeed the acceptable manner of writing verse for everyone from the readers of *Punch* to the scholars of the Sunday Schools. Some account of the various new ways in which a popular ballad could be communicated from its writer to the community for which he spoke is therefore the last preliminary step towards an examination of the Victorian ballad itself.

The broadside ballad continued in existence until at least the 1870s. The accumulated stock of W. S. Fortey, the last great entrepreneur of street printing, was sold at Sotheby's in 1901, and included ballad sheets printed by John Pitts and James Catnach, the rival leaders of the trade in the opening decades of the century. Fortey, however, had spent his latter years in rivalry with the Such press in printing and selling 'songsters', books of the words of music-hall songs. The single-sheet white-letter broadsides, giving one or two ballads and a woodcut for a penny, had first been replaced, in an effort to attract custom, by the triple columned sheets three feet long which offered three yards of ballads for one penny; and these were eventually superseded by the penny and twopenny songsters, booklets in a coloured paper cover reproducing songs composed for and circulated by the music-halls and sold in the places where they were sung. The patterers selling broadsides in the city streets had always sung their ballads, for the prospective buyers to learn the tune, which was not often printed; in the middle years of the nineteenth century they took to acting out their broadsides, even donning some sort of costume for the performance, in an attempt to compete with the full theatrical experience offered in the presentation of a song in a music hall.

The competition of the halls undermined the broadside ballads indirectly as well as by offering more for the customers' pennies. It also offered greater rewards and a better audience to the writers of songs; and the broadside presses, which had never paid more than a shilling or two for their material, found that the few shillings more a man might earn by selling to a music-hall singer, and the enormously greater reward he might reap by setting up to perform his own material, robbed them of all the versifying talent of the working classes. The area of experience handled in the broadside ballad narrowed, and its expression was impoverished. By sticking to certain lines, the ballad publishers could still sell, but at the cost of ceasing to represent what was best, and also what was newest and most exciting, in the popular inspiration. The still profitable lines were, briefly, what Mayhew[1] calls 'secret papers', sold without any advertisement in public-houses, and consisting chiefly of indecent songs – the last rags of the old bawdy invention which was a mainstay of earlier broadside writing – and topical ballads, about the latest crime or murder, real or invented. John Pitts, a man with a sense of history and a claim to his own place in it, reprinted many old ballads during his successful years as a broadside publisher which began in 1819. He found a market, probably chiefly in the country, for songs he collected from Irish immigrants living round his printing-works in Seven Dials, and for old favourites like 'Lord Bateman', 'Lord Thomas and Fair Eleanor' and 'An Excellent New Ballad entitled The Cripple of Cornwall . . .', first registered in 1624, which were amongst the songs he revived.[2] These became sufficiently well known to provide a recognisable reference for modern popular writers, who could begin a song with a burlesque of the first line of 'Lord Bateman', '——— was a noble lord, a noble lord of high degree . . .' For the rest, audiences were no longer satisfied with bawdy songs when all the life and wit had been worked out of them by generations of hacks relying on salaciousness rather than talent, and cheap newspapers soon took over the reporting of crime and provided authentic-looking pictures, and more reliable standards of veracity than a broadside printer who had to get his material written, printed and into circulation by the old, slow methods could ever hope to achieve.

The transfer of writers and audience from the broadside to the music hall carried with it very much of the spirit of the folk tradition, and indeed in the early years much of the material was unchanged, or only given a new angle to suit the latest movement of popular taste. A song such as 'Billy Taylor', sung by Jack Sharp, a popular performer in the 1840s in pleasure-garden and supper-room concerts, is clearly a broadside. It has been given an overlay of cockney, with the intention of adding to it a comic dimension, but without wishing to destroy thereby its other effects, of exciting narrative and suspense:

Four-and-twenty stout young fellers
(Clad they vere in blue array)
Came and press'd young Billy Taylor,
And forthvith sent him to sea.

Soon his true love follow'd arter,
Under the name of Richard Carr:
And her lily-white hands she daubed all over,
With the nasty pitch and tar.[3]

There is continuing life and growth in the tales thus transferred to a more sophisticated audience. But those writers who were left still attempting to produce new broadside ballads had only the hackneyed remains of a convention of expression with which to work, and though some were successful – A. L. Lloyd has found examples amongst provincially printed broadsides, where the tradition decayed less quickly, of vigorous new pieces written in the second half of the century – most were the victims of their own limitations, and those of the printers they worked for, and plunged into bathos and quite unintentional humour. Such for example is the fate of the writer of 'Pretty Little Sarah':

My heart is like a pumpkin, swollen with love;
For one of the fairest girl's that's in creation
She is too good for man – she ought to be above.
Such beauty is a credit to our nation.

The first time I met her was in the pouring rain,
I proffered her my arm and umbrella
She looked with a smile, I said I'd see her home,
She thanked me with a voice so low and melow.[4]

An instance of the continuity of inspiration amongst lesser talents is the resemblance to this broadside of a song composed by Charles Reeves, the father of Ada Reeve, for his daughter's use in her music-hall turn when she was about nine, in the early 1880s:

Strolling down a green, shady lane,
A pretty girl I chanced to me-heet.
She had light blue eyes – such a darling!
Such pretty, tiny little fe-heet.

As she picked her way through the gutter,
The rain kept on pouring so.
I offered her my arm and my um-be-rella,
But she gently answered No-ho![5]

Mr Reeves had the good sense not even to attempt two rhymes in a verse; but otherwise he is scarcely rising above the efforts of his predecessor.

A similar continuity can be observed at the other end of the scale, in the way in which material which was successful was transferred from one area of popular entertainment to another, finding its way to the lips of thousands of people. The musical stage in the early part of the nineteenth century was in a flourishing condition, with operas, operettas, burlettas, extravaganzas and plays with music of all kinds being produced in rapid succession at the many minor theatres which had sprung up to cater for the increasing population of London. Successful songs from these shows were being sung at other places by the singers with concert engagements, printed for sale to amateur performers at home and in social gatherings, and often pirated by the lesser printers. The mark of real success was for a song originating in an operetta to find its way into the repertoires of music-hall tenors and a concert soprano, on to the pianos of every drawing-room in the nation, and into a broadside printer's stock. Such was the fate of the songs from Balfe's *Bohemian Girl*, 1843, with 'I Dreamt I Dwelt in Marble Halls' topping the list of successes, but others also achieving a very wide popularity. Similarly the songs of Tom Moore (whose *Irish Melodies*, 1807–35, created a fashion for sentimental Irish laments like Mrs Crouch's 'Kathleen Mavourneen') moved out from the drawing-room to the broadside and the theatre. 'The Last Rose of Summer', for example, found its way into the repertoire of all sentimental singers, helped on its way by being inserted into the English version of F. Von Flotow's *Martha*, staged at Drury Lane in 1855. Another parlour poet, Thomas Haynes Bayly, had several such successes. His song 'The Soldier's Tear' found its way on to broadsides, and his unusually substantial ballad story based on legend, 'The Mistletoe Bough', had great popular circulation. It was even inserted into a play on the same subject at the Garrick, Whitechapel in 1834 – presumably at the end, or else it would have spoiled the suspenseful climax of the story in the drama.

Most of this various activity and talent came to centre, as the century progressed, in the Victorian music hall. The history of the growth of the music hall explains how all branches of popular entertainment came to be absorbed in it, and the material of the broadsides and of the musical theatre was transformed into the characteristic mould of the music-hall song. In the eighteenth and early nineteenth centuries there was a great variety of popular entertainment available, and those who sought it could all frequent many different places which catered for music and song. Folk material, in the form of broadside and traditional ballads and songs, became a fashionable pleasure for the middle classes as early as the 1720s. In 1725 Allan Ramsay, one of the most important eighteenth-century ballad collectors, put together a Scottish pastoral entertainment called *The Gentle Shepherd* from traditional tunes and verses. It was a success, and John Gay's *Beggar's Opera*, drawing its local colour from the songs of the London streets, was a phenomenal hit. The consequent steady stream of ballad operas, ballad concerts, and, later, other theatrical transformations of folk-song material into fashionable entertainment began a change which parallels the effect of the shift from rural to urban popular composition. An element of sophistication, manifest in several ways, was added to the basic folk tradition by professional, often theatrical, presentation. Audience participation, however, an essential part of folk technique, was by no means dead: rather it began once more to expand to embrace all classes. One of the attractions of ballad opera was the singable simplicity of the tunes, as opposed to the remote excellencies of Italian opera; and all kinds of people, not only those still possessed of the rural tradition of folk music, wished to sing and take part, either at home or in public. In coffee-houses and taverns the regulars formed their own 'Catch and Glee Clubs' and 'Harmonic Meetings', and they could seek models for their singing by visiting the various pleasure gardens, such as the New Spring Gardens which opened at Vauxhall in 1732, where, in between sporting fixtures, professional singers and actors performed. There were musical taverns peculiar to the lowest classes, such as those for the sailor ashore down the Radcliffe Highway, and in the 1830s and 1840s there were equally selective establishments at the other end of the social scale, tavern music halls like the Coal Hole and the Cyder Cellars which catered for fast young men, journalists and professional actors and the more daring gentry, and ran floorshows of a distinctly risqué kind; and there were also the rather more respectable, but still all-male, song and supper rooms. The most famous of these was Evans's in Covent Garden, where a chairman introduced the vocal offerings of soloists both amateur and professional, and all who felt inclined sang the choruses. Between the two extremes were the majority of taverns which offered facilities for singing, where the patrons were of the respectable working classes, and included many women.

The professional turns for such places came from the pleasure gardens and minor theatres, all of which provided work for singers and musicians because of the prohibition upon straight dramatic performances in any except the two Patent theatres. Their material, from theatrical sources often influenced by folk-song, or specially written for their singing engagements, mingled with the songs provided by the audience, which must have included all kinds and ages of popular song from many sources. This motley and obviously very productive situation was crystallised by the passing of the 1843 Theatres Act, which was intended to sort out the anomalies of theatrical licensing. The many suburban and East End theatres which had sprung up since the turn of the century wanted the right to perform dramatic works without inserting songs throughout the action and playing continuous music in the background, and the new Act gave them this by substituting a system of individual licences for the old monopoly patents. It was decided, however, that such new theatres as came into being must confine themselves to theatrical activities, and be separated from establishments whose primary function was to provide food and drink. These were to license themselves under the local magistracy, and were to be allowed to entertain their customers with variety turns and songs, but not to perform plays, and not to open before 5 p.m. The owners of the singing taverns with theatrical ambitions had to decide on which side of the line they fell, and, when they came to expand, to build their premises accordingly.

The earliest music-hall buildings, such as the Yorkshire Stingo's hall, the Apollo, the Surrey, and Charles Morton's Canterbury Hall built in 1852, were designed on the same pattern, a flat open space before a high, small stage, with a shallow gallery at the back or round three sides. They were all small, intimate buildings, and contact between the stage and the auditorium was close; they drew their patrons from their surrounding areas, Wilton's from Whitechapel, Macdonald's from Hoxton, Collins's from Islington, Deacon's from Clerkenwell, and so on. The purpose of such establishments was to provide a centre for communal enjoyment of singing, eating and drinking, and they were an integral part of the lives of their patrons. The regular customers knew each other, and the favourite entertainers; often the minor turns included local people trying their talents on the first step of the professional ladder, for almost all music-hall entertainers came from the working classes. The songs, written by professionals who were also from such a background or by the singers themselves to suit their own particular audience, were direct expressions of the feelings, hopes and aspirations of the people present, who took an active part in their performance. The professional theatrical overlay upon the community gathering was at first only thin, and came into existence to meet logistical and physical problems arising from the comparatively large size of the Victorian urban communities. It was, however, profitable, and the local halls were soon enlarged or superseded at last by less intimate organisations. Morton built the first West End hall, the Oxford, in 1861, and as they flourished and expanded the halls began to take on the regular auditorium plan, until by 1880 they were mostly large theatres run by syndicates rather than local concerns managed by the owner. In their last decades the music halls lost some of their closeness, therefore, but not necessarily their ability to represent the voice of the community at large, and to present it with its values and ideals on a local and even a national scale. T. S. Eliot's comment on Marie Lloyd, that

> In music-hall comedians they find the expression and dignity of their own lives . . . The working man who went to the music-hall and saw Marie Lloyd and joined in the chorus was himself performing part of the act; he was engaged in that collaboration of the audience with the artist which is necessary in all art and most obviously in dramatic art[6]

illustrates that.

Nor were the lower classes the only part of the popular audience to which the music-hall stars of the last years of the century catered; many, like Albert Chevalier, were welcome in the most august drawing-rooms and politest concert halls. Such exchanges had been part of the spreading influence of the music hall from its earliest years. At Wilton's, an early East End hall, with an entirely local audience of sailors, tradesmen and worse, a popular turn which might take up half an hour of the bill on any night in the 1850s or 1860s was a 'drawing room entertainment' performed by a small troupe in evening dress, with a piano, who recited and sang operatic and ballad numbers. Conversely the middle classes who did not frequent theatres of any kind were eager to be entertained by troupes of minstrels who might perform one night in a hall – there was always at least one 'negro delineator' on the Wilton's bill – and the next in a respectable room where ladies and gentlemen flocked to hear them. In the fifties and sixties the German Reed Entertainments were created specifically to bridge the gap between the respectable audience, who enjoyed popular song, and the theatres, where they could not go to hear it. These quasi-theatrical performances carried a cast-iron guarantee of respectability, a promise that nothing offensive could possibly occur, and gradually succeeded in wooing their patrons back into theatres. They presented musical entertainments which were often written by journalists whom the middle-class public knew from their work for the press and periodicals. W. S. Gilbert was one such writer, who moved from the comic papers to German Reed's and on to the theatre, drawing audiences after him. Many individuals functioned as links in this way, holding the broad network of popular entertainment together. The movement between the theatres and the press was particularly important and productive, since it not only carried attitudes and values from one section of the popular culture to another, but also enabled writers to draw upon a rich stock of comic models which became common to both, transferring the best of the music hall to the magazines, and vice versa.

The part played by the ever-expanding periodical press in the shaping of the Victorian popular ballad is the last of the interwoven strands of the background which remains to be traced. The newspapers took over from the broadsides not only the printing of reports on crimes and extraordinary events of all kinds, but also the publication of topical verses. Celebrations of heroic battles, rousing addresses to the nation, and effusions upon political events all found a place in the daily press. Tennyson's public poetry written in the 1850s often appeared first in *The Times*, the *Morning Chronicle*, or the *Examiner*, where 'The Charge of the Light Brigade' was published. Earlier in the century the trend had begun in the critical and political magazines, where it had become the fashion to make use of the ballad form for social and literary satire. From Baron Macdonald in *The Anti-Jacobin Review* to the *Examiner* in its early days in the hands of the brothers Hunt one may find squibs in ballad form which are directly descended from the political broadside.

It was, however, the birth of largely or exclusively comic magazines and annuals which fostered the development of less purposeful, and eventually simply humorous ballads which grew into a distinct comic form. These publications began to appear in the second and third decades of the nineteenth century; they were practically the invention of Thomas Hood. At the beginning of his career Hood, like Tennyson, was a frequent contributor to miscellanies and annuals, especially the kind of annual produced for the gift-buying public around Christmas, elegantly designed for the boudoir table. In, for instance, the *Gem* of 1829 one of his most important serious poems, 'The Dream of Eugene Aram' appeared for the first time. More often his contributions were comic, and several of his comic ballads appeared in such publications before being collected under the title of *Whims and Oddities*, the first series of which appeared in 1826. But in 1830 the first *Comic Annual* was produced, the contents of which, verse, prose and engravings, were entirely comic. Hood intended to edit contributions, and the first *Annual* does contain work from various hands, but in subsequent years he was obliged to write it all himself.

The idea, however, caught on, and imitations, often very close to the original, began to appear, under such titles as *The New Comic Annual*, and *The Comic Offering, or the Ladies' Mélange of Literary Mirth*. In many ways these were the successors of the polite miscellanies to which Hood had contributed previously, and their humour was dictated by the tastes of the public Hood had in mind, as well as being shaped by his sense of the comic. Its salient features were those of all popular comic verse, very often using burlesque ballad and closely following the popular emphasis upon the physical, even the violent, joke, with one important exception: for the politer audience, the restriction upon sexual reference (which filled the music-hall song with innuendo in place of the open bawdy of the broadsides) was much stronger, and the fascination with the comedy of the human body strictly excluded its sexual nature.

The mildness of comic magazines and annuals for the family circle also excluded the humour of topical reference and critical comment, and in the 1840s other periodicals for the same section of the public in its masculine, club-going, politically and socially *au fait* divisions began to appear, and to carry satirical ballads. The first and undoubtedly always the best of these was of course *Punch*, founded in 1841, and carrying a wide variety of popular ballad poetry from the beginning, using some aspect of the form for its lightest jokes and its most serious attacks upon corruption and injustice. *Fun*, a close imitation, had the same practice, and to *Punch*'s ballads by Thackeray was able to oppose W. S. Gilbert's *Bab Ballads*. So the rise of the comic magazines not only coincided with the development of the music hall, but also shared some important contributors, and also a portion of the audience, with the stage. This was particularly true of the fashionably Bohemian frequenters of such places as Evans's in the 1840s and 1850s, who were the readers, and often the writers, of the new magazines. Spielmann's *History of Punch* says 'Punch was born . . . upon the stage . . . from the first he proclaimed that Music and the Drama were to be amongst the most prominent features of his work . . . as a record of the London stage, the pages of *Punch* are fairly complete.'[7] Indeed *Punch* contributed its talent freely to the stage: each editor up to 1895 wrote an entertainment for German Reed, and Douglas Jerrold wrote his famous *Black-eyed Susan* before the magazine was born. Thackeray, Theodore Hook, and Percival Leigh were amongst the many who contributed their pieces to the magazines and their presence and occasional songs to music-hall society. Hook was especially noted as an *improvisatore*, which art seems to have been reborn in the enthusiastic atmosphere of the mid-century gatherings. Charles Sloman of Evans's practised it professionally, and F. C. Burnand has left a record[8] of its existence in gatherings of *Punch* contributors, especially at the famous *Punch* dinners. He says he had heard the single line 'We Went for to Catch the Whale, Brave Boys' (which is part of a folk-song still in oral circulation today) and 'when, on convivial occasions, I was "called upon", it suddenly occurred to me to invent the metrical form and the tune . . . to suit the idea of "The Whale" . . . anyone present was at liberty to suggest a word rhyming to "whale", which the singer had to fit, somehow or other, into his verse, and so the song lasted just as long as these suggestions might be forthcoming . . . the singer had the last rhyme and last verse in reserve.' Thackeray's 'Little Billee', he says, had a similar origin, and 'Married to a Mermaid', sung by Arthur Lloyd, was printed with the note 'Known among a select circle to be an impromptu of the late Mr. Thackeray.' One of Richard Doyle's best-known cartoons shows the famous W. G. Ross singing 'Sam Hall' and is entitled 'A Cydere Cellare Dvryng a Comick Song', having a commentary by Percival Leigh;[9] Henry S. Leigh wrote the popular music-hall song 'Shabby Genteel'. Later, connections between the magazines and the stage were just as strong, when both were becoming staid and respectable. Besides Gilbert, other important men of letters, such as Clement Scott and George Sims, had fingers in several pies. Scott's dramatic criticism was of course of the legitimate stage, though the sensibility he brought to it was hardly that of a member of the literary intelligentsia; he wrote both serious and jocular recitation ballads which *Punch* published. Sims, a recitation poet who considered himself 'a Bohemian', published his ballads in the popular press, frequented music halls for his own entertainment, and wrote popular plays.

Very many more strands could be traced in this web of association and interaction, which supported popular poetry with an audience and a fund of writing and performing talent drawn from it. The popular culture of the nineteenth century was enormously rich, often unanimous in feeling and in its values while it was multifarious in the forms it found in which to manifest itself. For the comic song and ballad, whether sung in the music hall or printed in *Punch*, this situation, with its wealth of familiar association and conventions, its powerful tradition and the constant refreshment of men of talent from all sections of society, was very fertile, and from it some of the best popular poetry in English was to emerge. For the serious forms of folk-song and ballad the conditions of metropolitan Victorian England were less than ideal. The rise of the huge and comparatively articulate popular audience of the nineteenth century, dictating how poets at every level of attainment should write and what they should write about, was not always, in this sphere, so artistically admirable.

PART TWO

The Ballads

3 *The Heroic Ballads*

Behind very much of the serious verse of the Victorian popular poets there lies a questionable, indeed a damaging, critical assumption: the assumption that a poem is to be judged primarily, if not exclusively, by the sentiments it expresses. It enabled the anthologist E. W. Cole to identify the 'dozen grand and noble poets of humanity' as 'Burns, Hood, Wordsworth, Mackay, Swain, Sims, Longfellow, Whittier, Lower, Carleton, Felicia Hemans and Letitia F. Landon.'[1] His inclination to judge the social value of the intentions, instead of the artistic validity of the achievements, of these writers was a common one, and it must be borne in mind when examining Victorian popular writing.

Consider these two examples:

Here upon Guard am I
Who dares to say that British pluck
Is somewhat on the wane,
That British valour never will
Be seen or known again.
The Crimean page will yet be read
And honest cheek will glow,
When learning how we nobly fought,
And thrashed the stubborn foe.

Chorus Here upon guard am I,
Willing to do or die,
Fighting for Queen and country too,
Fighting for home so dear.
Cannons are there in sight
Bayonets to left and right,
Hands true and steady are willing and ready,
And hearts which know no fear.

What matter tho' we lose an arm,
Through rifle shot or sword

'Tis for our country's good, and she
Will help us when we're old;
Will look with pride on us and say,
For conquering the foe,
You shall now end your days in peace,
And want shall never know.

Here upon guard am I
Bullets around me fly,
Something is creeping along the way,
Treachery there 'tis plain.
Steady my aim shall be;
Nearer it crawls to me,
My trigger I pull it,
It accepted my bullet,
He'll never more breathe again.

Up, up, they go, no faltering there,
Succeed they know they must,
You'd crush them, would you, not just yet,
Hurrah! they bite the dust.
I dare not leave my post, or I
Would not be in the rear,
Take heed – ah yes – at last, at last,
One's found its way in here.

Still upon guard am I
Is it I'm 'bout to die,
Heaven protect my darling wife,
And look to my children dear.
Darkness seems coming to me,
Still the bright flashes I see
Yes! at last they've done it,
The battle they have won it,
List, list to the loud ringing cheer.[2]

The Private of the Buffs

Last night, among his fellow roughs,
He jested, quaffed, and swore;
A drunken private of the Buffs,
Who never looked before.
Today, beneath the foeman's frown,
He stands in Elgin's place,
Ambassador from Britain's crown,

And type of all her race.

Poor, reckless, rude, low-born, untaught,
Bewildered, and alone,
A heart, with English instinct fraught,
He yet can call his own.
Aye, tear his body limb from limb,
Bring cord, or axe, or flame:
He only knows, that not through *him*
Shall England come to shame.

Far Kentish hop-fields round him seem'd,
Like dreams, to come and go;
Bright leagues of cherry-blossom gleam'd,
One sheet of living snow;
The smoke, above his father's door,
In grey soft eddyings hung:
Must he then watch it rise no more,
Doomed by himself, so young?

Yes, honour calls! – with strength like steel
He put the vision by.
Let dusky Indians whine and kneel;
An English lad must die.
And thus, with eyes that would not shrink,
With knee to man unbent,
Unfaltering on its dreadful brink,
To his red grave he went.

Vain, mightiest fleets, of iron framed;
Vain, those all-shattering guns;
Unless proud England keep, untamed,
The strong heart of her sons.
So, let his name through Europe ring –
A man of mean estate,
Who died, as firm as Sparta's king,
Because his soul was great.[3]

These two sets of verses are both products of the Victorian ballad tradition at its height, and show it in what perhaps modern taste would regard as its least appealing mood, that of aggressive and sentimental nationalism. Between them they show how widespread, and how uniform, that mood was. The first is a music-hall song written by Harry Adams, a South London hatter, to a tune of E. Jongmans, sung by a star of the early hey-day of the halls in the 1870s and 1880s called Charles

Godfrey. He was the original performer of the song 'After the Ball is Over', later made famous by Vesta Tilley, and he died of a week's excessive hospitality on a tour of Australia, at the age of forty-nine. The second example is the most famous and frequently anthologised work of Sir Francis Hastings Charles Doyle, fellow of All Souls and Professor of Poetry at Oxford. What differences there are between the two are such as arise from the difference of education between their composers, and the different circumstances of their performance. The second is more fluent and less naive in expression; the Professor's vocabulary is rather wider, and he cannot rely upon the music and the performer's dramatic skill to supply atmosphere and to eke out faltering lines, explaining what might otherwise be lost, so he has to work harder at the completeness and vividness of the verses themselves. If he uses fewer verbal clichés than Harry Adams does, however, he is no less reliant upon those of emotion and sentiment. The similarity between the two in this respect is far more striking than the slight differences of execution. Each relies upon the audience's response to certain sentiments – patriotism, the admiration of stoicism and military daring, with on the other hand tenderness for home and family, and belief in the superiority of British men and institutions to all others. The Professor of Poetry's sentiments would be acceptable – and perfectly familiar – to Charles Godfrey's audience. The only difference lies in a modulation of attitude to the hero of the episodes related. Both are examples of an important figure in the Victorian ballad, the idealised common man. In the serious songs of the halls he often appears as a soldier or sailor, and is treated as a hero; in recitation pieces like 'The Private of the Buffs' there is often an added dimension of class awareness, taking here the typical form of pointing out the weaknesses or dangerous qualities of the model before reassuringly affirming his goodness and loyalty: if a drunken private is also a strong-hearted son of England, all is well.

The unanimity of sentiment is reflected in resemblances in style. The two pieces are so similar partly because they are both consciously written as ballads, and there was a general agreement as to the style and content appropriate to the heroic ballad form. Only the music-hall song has a chorus, but both use the doubled version of the basic ballad stanza, with alternate rhyming, and both use, as a vehicle for the sentiments they express, a rather tenuous narrative thread. Doyle's verses are based upon an incident which was reported in *The Times* in 1860, in which a private, left behind by his fellows drinking with some natives, was surprised by the Chinese and killed because he, unlike his companions, refused to kowtow. The extract was usually printed with the verses, to make clear what is happening in the poem. The fictitious incident in the music-hall song would be clarified by the acting of the singer, and by his characterisation of the central figure in the story within a dramatic 'scena', which might well extend the narrative in the song. The use of such a device is characteristic of music-hall ballads: in almost all of them the first person is used in the narrative, and the singer represents the central figure in the story in costume and bearing. It is a natural development in storytelling when it is transferred to a theatrical setting, and does not in fact make the ballads any less the property of the public, for the 'I' is not the voice of the poet or the proper person of the singer, but an already-established character or type from the common stock, in this case the ideal soldier. The stock of types was shared by music-hall and drawing-room writers, and indeed their material became, especially towards the end of the century, to a large extent interchangeable.

For the beginnings of this confluence of taste, style and subject-matter we must look at the development of popular poetry in the first half of the nineteenth century. On the popular level expressions of patriotism and nationalistic fervour had been becoming more and more common throughout the previous century. The theatres had taken to public displays of loyalty in song at least as early as 1745, when Arne's *Masque of Alfred* had its first public performance at Drury Lane, and in the heated atmosphere of London facing possible invasion and insurrection the song 'Rule Brittania' which it contained became a great success. 'God Save the King', which had been around since at least 1688, was taken up in the same year when actors, first at Drury Lane and then at Covent Garden, took to stepping forward in a line at the end of their performances and singing it with solemn dedication. In 1759 another crisis in national affairs, this time in the Seven Years War, produced 'Hearts of Oak',[4] with words by David Garrick; and in the sustained excitement of the Napoleonic Wars around the turn of the century flourishing popular entertainment featured a figure of great national importance – the British sailor. The Jack Tar was the first manifestation of the idealised common man, and he was the creation of a public mood of anxiety, excitement and pride, which was turned to effect by writers like Charles Dibdin the elder and William Shields, both working closely with the popular stage, and singers like the ex-sailor Incledon, who performed Shields's songs. 'Jack' had not only a set of characteristics and attitudes, but a whole vocabulary, which was created for him by the men of the theatre. Willson Disher describes[5] the sailor created by Dibdin as exhibiting 'courage, generosity, simplicity of heart, unworldliness, warmth of affection, love of present enjoyment, and thoughtlessness of tomorrow'; it would be just to add to these admirable characteristics his xenophobia and pugnacious self-satisfaction in the matter of the number of foreigners he could take on single-handed. The use of nautical jargon in sea-songs was older than the Jack Tar stereotype, but the twisting of the terms of the sea into a metaphorical tangle of 'colourful' expression on all subjects is peculiar to the Dibdin tradition, and had a long life on the nineteenth-century stage. 'Tom Bowling' is the only song using this convention which is now remembered:

Here, a sheer hulk, lies poor Tom Bowling,
The darling of our crew;
No more he'll hear the tempest howling,
For Death has broach'd him to.[6]

Many were much thicker with local colour than this, especially when the sailor himself is supposed to speak, as in 'Poor Jack', also by Dibdin:

Go, patter to lubbers and swabs, do you see,
'Bout danger, and fear, and the like;
A tight-water boat and good sea-room give me,
And it a'nt to a little I'll strike.
Though the tempest top-gallant mast smack smooth should smite,
And shiver each splinter of wood,
Clear the deck, stow the yards, and bouse everything tight,
And under reefed foresail we'll scud:
Avast! nor don't think me a milksop so soft,
To be taken for trifles aback;
For they say there's a providence sits up aloft,
To keep watch for the life of poor Jack![7]

These nautical songs often introduced a narrative element into early nineteenth-century patriotic songs of the theatres. Dibdin and Shields wrote music for complete entertainments, operettas and extravaganzas, rather than for solo performance. Their work, and that of other theatrical writers, was taken from its context and sung by all kinds of popular entertainers and by amateurs at home. It was quite common for theatrical songs to find their way back to the broadsides, where they can appear oddly remote and rhetorical amidst the remains of the street ballad tradition. In for instance a Fortey songster of the mid-century,[8] one opening juxtaposes 'Velvet and Rags the World Over' and Leo Dryden's 'Going Home', both early music-hall songs showing considerable broadside influence, with 'The Fair Land of Poland', from Balfe's *Bohemian Girl*:

> When the fair land of Poland was plough'd by the hoof,
> Of the ruthless invader, when might
> With steel to the bosom and flame to the roof
> Completed her triumph o'er right . . .
> I fought and I fell by her side.

Successful stage borrowings were those which had enough story to survive as character songs and ballads, such as Prince Hoare's story of 'The Arethusa', which was set by William Shields. It tells of an engagement with the French in overwhelming numbers, using a light, dancing variation of the 'Come-all-ye' ballad stanza:

> Come, all ye jolly sailors bold,
> Whose hearts are cast in honour's mould,
> While English glory I unfold,
> Huzza for the Arethusa!
> She is a frigate tight and brave,
> As ever stemmed the dashing wave;
> Her men are staunch
> To their fav'rite launch,
> And when the foe shall meet our fire,
> Sooner than strike, we'll all expire
> On board of the Arethusa.[9]

There was also a strong influence in the direction of narrative which came from the old broadside ballads and songs which dealt with the sea and sailors. The broadside was fulfilling one of its oldest functions when it recorded long and circumstantial accounts of sea battles, such as the Battle of the Nile, and printed largely fictitious accounts of for example the last hours and the death of Lord Nelson. This was a favourite topic, and ballads about it were reprinted throughout the first half of the nineteenth century, each descanting on the various elements of what very rapidly became a national myth, and the printers pirating each other's versions and those of the minor poets. The tone of these works varies from the brisk to the lacrymose. A version printed in 'A Collection of New Songs', a garland which was printed in Newcastle, apparently in the 1840s or the early 1850s,[10] is set to Shields's tune 'The Storm', and stresses the successful side of the engagement:

Long our tars had kept their station,
Long insulting foes defied,
Spite of all the Gallic nation,
Dutch bravado, Spanish pride.

A version reprinted by Leslie Shepard[11] is, on the other hand, a song of mourning, with the chorus

Mourn, England, mourn, mourn and complain,
For the loss of Lord Nelson who died on the main.

The most famous version combines both approaches, and it belonged to the repertoire of every concert and amateur tenor. Braham's 'Death of Nelson', composed and sung by him as part of the opera *The Americans* in 1811, had a motley set of words by Samuel James Arnold, a nautical writer who also composed the original version of 'A Life on the Ocean Wave'. It recommended itself to the many audiences who applauded it by its sentiments rather than its graces of composition: the combination of mourning and pugnacity, while it gives scope to a dramatic performer, is very crude. Opening with recitative:

O'er Nelson's tomb, with silent grief oppress'd,
Brittannia mourns her Hero, now at rest:
But those bright laurels ne'er shall fade with years,
Whose leaves, whose leaves are water'd by a Nation's tears . . .

it swings suddenly into narrative and takes up the Jack Tar stance, defying the French:

'Twas in Trafalgar's bay
We saw the Frenchmen lay,
Each heart was bounding then,
We scorn'd the foreign yoke,
For our Ships were British Oak,
And hearts of oak our men!

The combination is topped off with a chorus containing a catch-phrase sufficient in itself to ensure the success of a popular song – 'For England, Home and Beauty!' There is no distinction of motive or execution between this drawing-room and concert-hall song and the broadsides; the songs and the sentiments were common to the whole nation over a long period.[12] In 1859 Wilton's music hall in Whitechapel opened its doors to the nautical population of the area with the confidence that 'Singing and sailors appear to be almost synonymous terms', and the new tenor there engaged (a performer with the unpromising name of W. Smith) was reported[13] to have selected appropriate songs, such as 'Stand to Your Guns' and 'The Anchor's Weighed'. On the other hand, G. K. Chesterton, born into a solid bourgeois family in 1874, recalled his grandfather as 'a fine-looking old man' who 'kept up the ancient Christian custom of singing at the dinner-table', and whose repertoire consisted of 'pompous songs of the period of Waterloo and Trafalgar'.[14]

Beside the songs of patriotic sentiment which originated in eighteenth-century theatrical response to popular feeling, there grew up a connected genre which expressed the same sentiments in spoken verse without music. The heroic recitation ballad was born in the early nineteenth century, an offspring of the Romantic ballad revival, and particularly of the work of Sir Walter Scott. It descended, therefore, from the literary level, to meet and merge with the sub-literary theatrical and broadside tradition. An outstanding feature of Scott's *Minstrelsy of the Scottish Border* was its nationalist flavour. Each ballad he printed was surrounded by introductory matter and explanatory notes which linked it with the period of Scottish history with which the editor felt it was associated, and told all the parallel and in any way relevant episodes in the factual history of the Borders. Scott dwelt with loving detail upon the extraordinary tales of the daring and the quixotic honour of the cattle raiders who might well be regarded by another historian – an English one – as petty thieves. His Scotticising of the language of the texts themselves was part of this transformation of the poems into documents of national importance, objects of loyal veneration for all true Scots. Sir Walter, more than any other British writer, gave rise to the feeling that ballad literature was directly connected with national pride, and the possession of such a body of verse essential to, and expressive of, the strength and loyalty of a nation.

In the early years of the nineteenth century this feeling was strong throughout Europe, each nation striving to gather up its folk-songs, particularly its heroic narratives, to lay claim to a healthy culture with a basis in popular song and historic lays. The Scandinavian countries, of course, did particularly well; Spain, with Latin carelessness, only just managed to rescue the great saga of *El Cid* in time. Lockhart translated the Spanish ballads for English admirers of the form; many British collectors published learned commentaries on their own and others' gleanings. The next step, after the collection of existing ballads and their recognition as vital records of national history, was to reverse the reasoning and to look upon history unsupported by ballads as incomplete. Scott had surrounded his texts with historical facts to elucidate them; subsequent writers took episodes of history and made ballads about them to teach and make memorable the events. The practice was given some colour of reason by stressing the mnemonic value of verse, and indeed the probable intentions of the old minstrel ballad composers when they turned events into memorable ballad form. The pattern of the *Minstrelsy* was closely followed, and newly-written ballads appeared embedded in enough annotation to clarify the most obscure and decayed casualty of an oral tradition hundreds of years long. The first practitioner, and the theorist, of this kind of writing was Lord Macaulay, who in 1842 published the *Lays of Ancient Rome*, containing four recitation pieces based on the early history of Rome, five more on miscellaneous incidents of British and European history, and a great deal of revealing annotation and explanation. In his preface he displays a sensitivity to the tone of his subject matter which deserts him in the verses, observing that the early books of Livy are clearly recording the stuff of legend rather than fact, discerning the ring of folk tradition about them. He goes on, however, to deduce from his observation that Livy must have been working from ballads or from earlier historians who worked from ballads, and that the loss of them, in their original ballad form, is a disaster in the history of Rome. He conveys the impression that the loss of its primitive ballad literature is a moral failing in a nation otherwise great and admirable, suggesting some reprehensible laxity on the part of its inhabitants who allowed a foreign culture derived from Greece to eclipse their national poetry. He even goes so far as to seem to reprimand Cicero as personally at fault, for confining himself to lamenting the loss of ancient poetry, when 'a search among the nooks of the Appenines, as active as the search which Sir Walter Scott made among the descendants of the moss troopers of Liddesdale, might have brought to light many fine remains of ancient minstrelsy.'[15] This whimsical notion is put forward with all seriousness, as are the versifications of incidents from Latin history which he creates to replace the lost ballads. Each is introduced with a discussion of all available versions of the story, and has, the writer assures us, been written from the point of view of a person who might be supposed to have written such a poem, in the correct temporal and social relation to the events described, and in an English equivalent of the verse forms and diction he might have used. Macaulay seems completely unaware of the ridiculous nature of this enterprise, the fact that the whole fabrication is without meaning as a scholarly endeavour, and makes nonsense of the painstaking procedures of explication which he goes through for each poem. He found several serious imitators, and the notion of the ballad as 'heroic lay', for the expression of patriotic sentiment and the inculcation of historical fact, was widely accepted. There were writers who did see the funny side of it, and the *Lays of Ancient Rome* and their elaborate apparatus became a stock-in-trade of parodists, but their use of it did not affect its position as the pattern of serious heroic ballads.

The originals were the more ridiculous in that the spurious antiquarian framework copied from Scott surrounded verses which were not only perfectly comprehensible without it, but which could never, even if they had not been written in modern English stanza-forms derived from the ballads, have been mistaken for anything but early Victorian. Macaulay's ability to imitate Scott did not extend to imaginative projection into the period about which he was writing, and his heroes do not act and feel like ancient Romans. The most famous of them, Horatius, turns from his heroic rearguard, not deigning to notice the odds against him nor stooping to address a word to Sextus 'who wrought the deed of shame', glances up at the 'white porch of his home', and plunges into the Tiber to come through to a hero's happy ending, far more like an English schoolboy nurtured on the values of clean living and excellence at games than a Roman soldier. Macaulay creates Virginia, in her ballad, in the image of the early-Victorian miss; and in 'The Battle of Lake Regillus' he shows the concern of a good master of foxhounds for the horses as well as the men involved.

In some ways the *Lays* are very successful. They not only established the nineteenth-century idea of the heroic ballad-lay, but also made use of some of its most effective technical devices. The least memorable of the metrical forms he tries is that of 'The Battle of Lake Regillus', which is nevertheless an easy, fairly accomplished version of the alternately-rhymed octosyllabics of Scott's romances. 'Virginia' is meant to suggest the formulae of the street ballad, and its long, rattling couplets, like those of the Irish broadsides, became a favourite method amongst drawing-room balladeers for indicating dramatically a touch of vulgarity in their tales or the tellers. 'The Prophecy of Capys' and 'Horatius' share the simple double ballad stanza; in the latter Macaulay rises to touches of rhetorical genius which set a standard for his followers. He fulfils admirably the mnemonic function of the balladeer which he stressed in his introduction: no one who has ever read 'Horatius' can possibly have failed to remember some of it, if only disjointed fragments such as the first few lines of the first stanza:

> 'Lars Porsena of Clusium
> By the nine gods he swore . . .

usually followed in memory by a blank, and then 'Shall suffer wrong no more.' There are touches of antithesis which are so simple as to be infinitely satisfactory, like

> But those behind cried 'Forward!'
> And those before cried 'Back!'

and there is the pleasure of isolated phrases such as

> 'Now who will stand on either hand,
> And keep the bridge with me?'

in which heart-stopping heroism is somehow conveyed by the internal rhyme. In telling a story which is strong in itself Macaulay has deployed a great deal of verbal skill, manipulating simple, basic metrical and technical devices derived from Romantic and traditional ballad writing to create a rhetorical impact of great force. The influence of his example was very wide, and apart from the writers of comic verse, who seized upon his neat formulae with glee, he was copied by many other writers of serious ballads, all convinced of the importance and usefulness of writing out historical incidents in a form which would make them comprehensible, memorable, and inspiring to the modern reader, especially to the young.

The closest follower of Macaulay's pattern for the *Lays* was a Scot, William Edmondstoune Aytoun. He published a collection of Scottish ballads in 1858, in the introduction to which he expressed exactly the same attitude as Macaulay to the possession of a body of ballad literature by a nation, suggesting that he was making good an omission on the part of his fellow Scots by publishing a comprehensive edition of the ballads of Scotland which would act as a clear statement of Scotland's claim to a ballad corpus worthy of comparison with those of the other countries of Europe. He would seem to have felt, however, that the poems he gathered together and cast into a definitive form in that publication were not enough, for he began to write further ballads on neglected but important incidents in Scottish history, publishing them one by one in *Blackwood's Magazine* during the 1840s, and finally collecting them into a volume entitled *Lays of the Scottish Cavaliers* in 1849. It was published complete with the apparatus of introduction, annotation and commentary which

Macaulay had used, and the best of Aytoun's lays show clearly that they are imitative of the *Lays of Ancient Rome*. In 'The Island of the Scots', for instance, apart from the resemblance of the heroic deeds performed by the Scottish soldiers serving with the French to the deeds of Horatius and his supporters, there is a distinct reminiscence of Macaulay's rhetorical style in stanzas such as

> The Rhine is running deep and red,
> The island lies before –
> 'Now is there one of all the host
> Will dare to venture o'er?
> For not alone the river's sweep
> Might make a brave man quail:
> The foe are on the further side,
> Their shot comes fast as hail.
> God help us, if the middle isle
> We may not hope to win!
> Now is there any of the host
> Will dare to venture in?'[16]

Aytoun was right in estimating that there was a place for modern heroic ballads on such topics, for the *Lays of the Scottish Cavaliers* joined the *Lays of Ancient Rome* and the *Minstrelsy* itself, from which they are both descended, as a universally approved and safe book of poetry, regarded as particularly useful and suitable for schools.

It was this appropriation to schoolroom use, as much as anything else, which converted the heroic historical ballad into the staple popular poetry of the middle classes, and imposed upon it the peculiarity of becoming as much oral as written poetry. Children were set to learn these instructive and inspiring pieces; and what is learned must be recited. The benefit of the recitation devolved originally upon the reciter, but was very soon to be extended to the audience, still with the admixture of edification in the entertainment which was expected in the schoolroom. Recitations are essentially improving and instructive for all concerned.

The distribution of the heroic ballads in print took the characteristic form of the 'Reciter'. Many public poets, like Aytoun, published their verses initially in periodicals or newspapers, and some of the more successful gathered up complete volumes to themselves, but they are most often to be met with in collected volumes compiled by one of the indefatigable editors of the day – Frederick Langbridge, for instance, or Alfred Miles – and served up specifically for the use of reciters or teachers. In this form, too, it is easiest to observe the distinction of the heroic, as opposed to the comic or the sentimental, recitation, which remain to be considered later, and which the editors usually hived off into separate volumes for publication.

The highest literary level of these publications is represented by W. E. Henley's *Lyra Heroica*, 1892, which is largely confined to poets of the literary tradition up to the point where, in its chronological arrangement, it reaches the nineteenth century. With considerable insight, he places his selection of traditional ballads as a barrier between his century and previous ages, dating their 'master influence' from Percy's *Reliques* and regarding it as the distinction between classic and romantic in English verse. After the ballads he includes not only the major Romantic poets, not always represented by what could be called their ballads, but also a sprinkling of theatrical ballads, 'The Arethusa' and two by Dibdin, as well as heroic recitation pieces by all the major and many of the minor Victorian poets who wrote them. His intention in compiling this selection of popular poetry is clearly stated in his preface: he says that he believes (in fact mistakenly, for several others had the idea before him) that there is no book of English poetry compiled for boys, and so his

> purpose has been to choose . . . a certain number of those achievements in verse which, as expressing the simpler sentiments and the more elemental emotions, might fitly be addressed to such boys – and men, for that matter – as are privileged to use our noble English tongue. To set forth, as only art can, the beauty and the joy of living, the beauty and the blessedness of death, the glory of battle and adventure, the nobility of devotion – to a cause, an ideal, a passion even – the dignity of resistance, the sacred quality of patriotism, that is my ambition here.

Henley stressed, in other words, the sentiments which he hoped his selected poems would convey, the sentiments of heroism and patriotism. Implicit in the tone of his explanation, moreover, is a suggestion which might well be construed as derogatory of the poetry which he did not select. The verses whose sentiments he approves are recommended as being 'fit' to be addressed to boys – 'and men, for that matter'. The inescapable implication is that some verse is unfit for boys and for men privileged to be English. Verse itself is suspect: only if it is used in the service of the sentiments which are the reverse of effete and enervating can it be safely given to growing and grown British males. Other ballad writers, compilers and editors expressed the same unconsciously Philistine[17] view more openly. Alfred Austin, the popular balladeer who was potentially a very appropriate, but in fact a rather disappointing, late-Victorian Poet

Laureate, showed a parallel distrust and distaste for high art in the dedication of his *Narrative Poems*, published in 1891. It is addressed to Millais, and praises his work for its Manliness and Britishness, congratulating the artist for liberating himself from the sway of the 'Aesthetic Revival', a negative achievement which Austin considered was his 'distinctive and abiding glory'. The implication, although unstated, is quite clearly of the British Manliness, and independence of any aesthetic pretensions, to be expected from his own narrative poetry. Alfred H. Miles, describing the ballad poetry of one of the most prolific parlour poets, William Cox Bennett, stressed the fact that 'His verse is characterised by hearty English sense and feeling. There is no obscurity of style to pass for profundity of thought, but all is written for the people in a manner easily to be understood.'[18]

There is an interesting transition here from stressing the educative power of ballads in directing the feelings of boys into the right channels to seeing them perform the same function for 'the people', but still self-justification, suggesting a fear of the corrupting effects of poetry, lies behind it. Bennett himself projected a history of England to be written entirely in ballads, by himself and other people, and published the plan, together with his first contributions to it, in 1868. In 'An appeal to the poets of England and America', which prefaces the volume, he explained the popularising and educational nature of the project: 'in the Ballad and Song we have a measureless power of weaving through the existence of the many, nobility in the knowledge of the achievements of our noblest.' He made clear the origins of his inspiration by including an ending to Macaulay's 'Armada' in the volume. His conviction that he was conducting a crusade to educate some rather undefined mass of popular feeling through his ballads extended to the practical, but probably not very effective, method of publishing many of his own poems upon small single sheets to be sold for one penny. Their genteel appearance, lack of pictures, and shortness as compared with other popular products for the same price cannot have endeared them to possible plebeian purchasers, and like other writers with similar ambitions to reach all the popular audience, he was probably only read by the upper half of it. When in 1889 Frederick Langbridge dedicated his anthology *Ballads of the Brave* to Bennett, he assumed that Bennett's chief audience was the one for which he intended his own work, the schoolboys of England.

The way in which the recitation poets did reach a wider audience than that of the school and drawing-room was through public performance. For each anthology which is directed to the use of the schoolchild, there is, especially in the 1890s and 1900s, another which purports to serve the needs of amateurs who 'give recitations'. Alfred H. Miles's *Ballads of Brave Women* (n.d., *c.* 1900) was 'designed to provide a repertoire of suitable pieces for recitation by women at women's meetings and at gatherings and entertainments of a more general character.' Many editors, like J. K. Tomalin, whose activities as a compiler around 1900 produced, among other volumes, *The World Wide Reciter, The Ludgate Reciter,* and *The Twentieth Century Reciter*, included hints for the public performer in standing gracefully on the platform, adapting one's movements to the piece, avoiding solecisms of pronunciation, and preserving the voice from damage. Many books cover all the possible uses of the contents in the sub-title: 'A popular book of Recitations for Home, school and public platform' or 'for Guild, School, Home, and Public Entertainment'. Heroic recitation was not of course excluded from the music halls: working men flocked to hear blood-curdling temperance ballads recited by philanthropic society ladies at least partly because of their similarity to tales of action and disaster familiar from the music hall. Bransby Williams found that all levels of the popular audience responded to 'The Green Eye of the Little Yellow God', 'How we Saved the Barge', 'For a Woman's Sake' and 'The Yogi's Curse', just as a singer could command a hearing anywhere for 'The Death of Nelson' or 'Hearts of Oak'.

The audience for heroic popular poetry expressive of a martial spirit and nationalist fervour was in fact enormous, and its demands were directed rather towards correctness of sentiment than accomplishment in execution. It was not discriminating about the poetic or musical form which the ballads took. Certain techniques and conventions, however, came into being, and rapidly found favour as conveniently easy to use and ideally adapted to the purpose in hand. The oldest and most universally successful convention was that of the rousing chorus. If a song, and in some cases even a recitation piece without musical support, was supplied with a recurring phrase which could be remembered and repeated by the audience, and embodied the heroic tenor of the whole, then its success was assured. The rest of the lyric need not be of any distinction, and indeed many chorus songs of the music halls and the drawing-room have verses which are feeble to the point of idiocy: the verses stayed in the song-sheet, and the choruses were carried away to be sung in snatches in the streets and shops and public houses. The process was a kind of instant oral tradition, by which pieces created for the sake of a single catchy phrase of music and the vital words which it carried were stripped of all superfluities in the single transition from the original performer to a thousand humming and whistling members of the general public. The staying power of some of the best-known catch-phrases was prodigious, as a collection of choruses from such songs, written in the last two hundred years, makes plain. 'Rule Britannia', dating from 1745, has perhaps an unfair advantage in the uses to which it has been put, but 'Hearts of Oak' has made its way on the strength of the chorus

Hearts of Oak are our ships, jolly tars are our men,
We always are ready,
Steady, boys, steady
We'll fight and we'll conquer again and again

since 1759. Somewhere in the latter part of the eighteenth century the anonymous 'British Grenadiers', with the simplest chorus of all – 'With a tow, row row, row row, row row, for the British Grenadiers' – came into being; Thomas Campbell's 'Ye Mariners of England', having a variable chorus of which the memorable lines are

And sweep through the deep
While the stormy winds do blow

was written in 1800. By 1836 the deterioration of the rest of the song when a catchy couplet becomes its *raison d'être* can already be seen, in 'A Life on the Ocean Wave', by Epes Sargent after a brief lyric by S. J. Arnold. Here the exclamation

A life on the ocean wave!
A home on the rolling deep!

is made to support three empty verses. Even the other, rarely remembered half of the chorus is clumsy. Only the strong beat and the easy melody keep it afloat. In the case of songs which have a more immediate and concrete heroic or rather nationalistic point to make, the sentiment can sometimes be enough to make a chorus catch on, and carry not only bad verses but also an uninteresting tune. Such is the notorious case of Macdermott's 'War Song' – the 'Jingo' song composed by G. W. Hunt, a music-hall hack, in response to the public uproar about the Russo-Turkish war in 1878. The verses are a farrago of bombast and pseudo-literary language, every line betraying the ill-educated hack writer struggling with a subject he feels is of solemn importance, but the chorus breaks into colloquial expression in the vein of understated pugnacity beloved of the British Patriot, and for which a word was obviously needed, for 'Jingoism' passed immediately and usefully into the language:

> We don't want to fight, but by Jingo if we do,
> We've got the men, we've got the ships, we've got the money too;
> We've fought the Bear before, and while we're Britons true,
> The Russians shall not have Constantinople!

Even this chorus is not free of the fustian which constitutes the rest of the song, but the single word ensured its abiding remembrance. By the end of the century such songs and verses had little pretence to more than one memorable line, whether constructed in careful dialect by Sir Henry Newbolt ('Capten, art tha' sleepin' there below?') or thrown off to capture the patriotic fashion of the moment by successful music-hall writers like Leslie Stuart, who wrote 'Soldiers of the Queen' (with the simplest possible chorus – 'We're soldiers of the Queen, my lads') as well as sentimental songs such as 'Lily of Laguna' for the black-face performer Eugene Stratton.

These are examples of the successful choruses, in which the combination of words and music, even occasionally the words alone, found the niche in the public mind which preserved them indefinitely as the perfect expression of the moment. Very many more verses were written, and recited, published or sung, intended to crystallise or influence the mood of the public, which had as much or as little intrinsic value as the songs from which these are taken, but which were forgotten as soon as they appeared. The exhortatory verse of Tennyson (pieces such as 'Riflemen Form!', published in *The Times*, 9 May 1859, 'The War', in response to the outbreak of the Franco-Prussian war, and 'Britains, Guard Your Own', published in the *Examiner*, 31 January 1852, in response to the *coup d'état* of Louis Napoleon) are the tip of an iceberg of such work, remembered only for the sake of their author. Cox Bennett and Martin Farquar Tupper produced many such pieces, deservedly submerged for ever, and the music-hall writers' daily patriotic gestures are similarly lost. Only the preserving power of the right formula at the right moment, catching the mood of a day in a chorus-line remembered whenever the mood might come again, rescued a handful out of hundreds of songs from oblivion.

The power of the chorus to lift a topical sentiment into permanent remembrance was paralleled by the power of the old broadside ballad formulae to lend strength and staying power to the inspiration of the moment. Those writers of the halls, and the newspapers and periodicals, who based their work upon a sturdy foundation of old narrative styles, instead of relying upon their own original gifts – which were often very slight – were occasionally capable of producing a powerful piece, worthy of respect as a poem as well as for the sentiments it expressed. Authors who have left one or two ballads, the only poems which are still remembered from a large body of work, or the only examples of their composition, have generally written their isolated successes firmly within the broadside tradition. Mrs Hemans's 'Casabianca' tells the story of an incident taken from a press report, in a plain four-line ballad stanza:

> The boy stood on the burning deck
> Whence all but he had fled;
> The flame that lit the battle's wreck
> Shone round him o'er the dead.[19]

The Rev. R. S. Hawker claimed that his 'Song of the Western Men' was actually based upon a traditional fragment, 'And shall Trelawney die? Here's twenty thousand Cornish men Will know the reason why!' It is certainly imitative of the ballad tradition. Another isolated success of this kind is 'The Burial of Sir John Moore' by the Rev. Charles Wolfe, published anonymously in the *Newry Telegraph* in 1817, which passed into the common stock of broadsides, pirated and parodied over and over again, and, after its discovery by Byron, claimed by many popular poets as their own. The basic pattern is drawn from the Irish street ballad, a part of the broadside tradition still thriving and capable of subtle effects when Wolfe made use of it. His masterly regularisation of the lines, using alternately masculine and feminine rhymes to give a dying, elegaic fall to each stanza, is derived from the literary ballad revival, however, and the rhetorical perfection of for example the last stanza:

> Slowly and sadly we laid him down,
> From the field of his fame fresh and gory;
> We carved not a line, and we raised not a stone,
> But we left him alone in his glory[20]

anticipates the combination of popular and literary inspiration into resonant, simple and emotionally loaded heroic phrases which Macaulay and his followers made their hallmark.

Many writers were not capable of refining their models, and used the broadside stanzas and narrative and rhetorical techniques with a crude vigour which is their only claim to artistic consideration. Their sentiments and chosen subjects are often recognisably peculiar to the Victorian heroic tradition, while their techniques are developed or taken unchanged from earlier and cruder popular composition. They may fall into the broadside inclination to bathos, as in Douglas Sladen's 'A Queensland Heroine', which amongst other unintentional comicalities has a stanza which asserts

> The woman was born of a nation of freemen –
> Their birthright to dare and to die on the wave;
> Yet, even to Britain's adventurous seamen,
> 'Twere hardly disgrace if they seemed not as brave.
> What wonder if Gilbert, who sank in the 'Squirrel',
> Or Davis, or Baffin, or Frobisher shrank
> From facing the strange, supernatural peril
> Of crossing the sea in a worn water-tank?[21]

They may, on the other hand, achieve a certain force, even dignity, from the simplicity of their statement of beliefs and values, as William Cox Bennett does on some occasions, or as a song of Charles Godfrey's for example, might. The Bennett piece on 'How they won the Victoria Cross at the Delhi Magazine, May 11th, 1857', is a good example:

> And in a moment rose the roar and the white clouds of smoke,
> That told to still-struck Delhi, butchering Britons was no joke;
> For that earthquake-shock sent up a rush of riven flesh and bones,
> And, where a thousand Sepoys yelled, there were only limbs and groans.[22]

The stanza form in use here, however, is very like that which developed in the work of G. R. Sims (discussed in the next chapter) and which became the typical Victorian recitation ballad stanza. Unimproved broadside techniques were wearing very thin and successes in that form were rare after the 1850s. The spark had gone out of broadside composition, and the powerful Victorian heroic ballad which emerged in the second half of the century incorporated new techniques which developed from the merging of popular and literary styles.

The verses with exclusively literary models which can be discerned in popular heroic writing are often no more effective than those which have relied too heavily on the outworn popular traditions. Fragments of the kind of pounding metre and exaggerated vocabulary which were characteristic of Matthew Lewis and his followers turn up as a sort of 'horseman's verse': rattling, galloping long lines whipping up physical excitement in the poem, not for the purposes of supernatural horror, as it was previously used, but employed by minor poets such as G. J. Whyte-Melville, the bard of the hunting field, in verses such as 'The Galloping Squire', for stirring effects. The pre-Raphaelite poets, the most unlikely models for the deliberately Philistine popular poet, were nevertheless raided for stylistic techniques which might be turned to the purpose of strong impact upon the emotions. A clear example is to be found in 'The Grey Lady of Blackstone Chad' by Frederick Langbridge, a drawing-room poet whose usual style may be inferred from the title of his most popular volume, *Sent Back By the Angels and other ballads of homely life*. 'The Grey Lady' begins

> 'Twas in the dusk of Lady Day
> The apparition came;
> The year crept on and the year crept out
> And all was just the same.
>
> 'Twas on the eve of Lady Day
> They found him in his bed,
> The kind squire, the gentle squire,
> Sitting stone dead.[23]

The mating of the literary and popular models could produce extraordinarily clumsy monsters, the ugliness of which seems to match the deformity of the attitudes revealed. The recitation ballads of Clement Scott include several horrific examples of this, such as his very popular and often printed 'Lay of the Lifeboat'. Sentiment here overrides the story upon which it is imposed; the metrical pattern is one peculiar to recitation ballads. The ballad rhymes in couplets, although it is divided into stanzas, and runs to enormous length of line:

> Gentlemen all, are your glasses charged? for I've a toast for the winter weather.
> Answer it, then, with a three times three; voice and heart, if you please, together.
> It is not a sorrowful theme I sing, though the red leaves rot in the winter garden,
> And east winds meet the embrace of the north, our throats to scourge and muscles to harden.
> Come far away from the weary fogs, those winding-sheets of our London life;

> Away from the prowl of the burglar-sneak, and the thud of the brute who has kicked his wife.
> I'd tell today of the rock bound coast, the screaming surf, and the sea-blown sand;
> And drink to the men who are off to sea, when the sailors shout that the Lifeboat's manned.[24]

In this jumble of popular attitudes and prejudices the technical oddity is striking. There seems to be a meeting between the Irish 'Come-all-ye' ballad and a sub-Swinburnian poeticising, both of which suggested sources the writer would no doubt consider insultingly disreputable. In places the attempt to strike as many chords of emotion as possible results again in the bathos endemic in bad broadside writing, which is also a patchwork of unrelated phrases. Most of Clement Scott's work, put together under journalistic pressures of topicality and speed, suffers from this tendency towards flatness and blatant appeals to the lowest common denominator of taste, interspersed with unintended comedy; he is sometimes not far behind his fellow drawing-room balladeer William McGonagal in the perpetration of ludicrous pomposities. On the other hand a similar stanza handled skilfully by Sims (see page 126) was a staple of heroic and sentimental writing, and one of the successful vehicles for the late Victorian heroic ballad, taking its place alongside the chorus song and the simple ballad stanza in supplying the framework for many powerful narratives.

The most common narrative stanza in the hey-day of the recitation ballad was, however, the eight-line, doubled ballad stanza made popular in 'Horatius'. To the followers of the convention, intent upon using its established effects upon their chosen bits of real or apocryphal history of the British Empire, this seemed the most compendious model of the heroic ballad. Sir Francis Doyle used it in 'The Private of the Buffs', and alternated it with stanzas of four longer lines in his other favoured recitation, 'The Red Thread of Honour'. Sir Henry Newbolt turned it, in 'Vitai Lampada', into the creed of the Victorian ballad hero, culminating in the exhortation, 'Play up! play up! and play the game!' which rings for ever in his ears. A typical example of the use of this stanza, and one which survives on the strength of its narrative to this day, is Phoebe Cary's 'The Leak in the Dyke'. She works her own variation upon the model by adding a third and even a fourth four-line unit to some stanzas – a process which in fact weakens them by relaxing their compression – but she is clearly holding Macaulay's ringing tones in mind, and using as far as she can the trenchant simplicity and the sensational appeal of his diction. These are obviously the model for the repetition and the cumulative effect in this stanza, leading up to the all-important lesson to be learnt:

> So, faintly calling and crying
> Till the sun is under the sea!
> Crying and moaning till the stars
> Come out for company;
> He thinks of his brother and sister,
> Asleep in their safe warm bed;
> He thinks of his father and mother,
> Of himself as dying – and dead;
> And of how, when the night is over,
> They must come and find him at last;
> But he never thinks he can leave the place
> Where duty holds him fast.[25]

Phoebe Cary is one of the many writers who apparently exhausted their efforts with one successful heroic ballad, and her humble contribution to the stock of the reciter is no better than a typical sample of the thousands that were written. But great writers lent themselves and their talents to the form, and they too took Macaulay's pattern as a model, and added to it enrichments and variations from the enormous stock of available ballad techniques with much more effect than she was able to achieve. Outstanding among these was Tennyson, who threw his whole effort into popular poetry when the occasion seemed to him to demand it, and invested his work with all his technical brilliance, while accepting wholeheartedly the values and assumptions of the form. He wrote a variety of drawing-room ballads over a long period, and the heroic examples improve upon the *Lays of Ancient Rome*. Besides the exhortatory verses already mentioned, they include powerful narratives much nearer to Macaulay in form and effect; 'The Charge of the Light Brigade', 'The Charge of the Heavy Brigade at Balaclava', 'The Revenge', and 'The Defence of Lucknow'. There were at least three ballads on this last theme, and Tennyson's was perhaps the least popular, being very long. Some of his heroic ballads are, however, the best of their kind. Wholehearted belief in such verse reinforced his gift for its creation, and indeed Alexander Macmillan recognised this and urged him to give up his Arthurian writing and stick to such ballads 'further down the stream of British life'.[26]

Tennyson's alteration of the common stanza in 'The Charge of the

Light Brigade' stresses the effects of heavy repetition, basic vocabulary, and strong antithesis proper to the heroic tone. Its unique character was his own invention, based upon the suggestive fall of the phrase 'someone had blundered' taken from the article in *The Times* which inspired the poem. The nearest equivalent for it which critics have found is, interestingly, the form of Chatterton's 'Song of Aella', which hints at a touch of Romantic medievalism carried over into the poem, but the important quality of the verse is its immediacy of effect, rather than its remoter connections. The dactyls thud upon the ear, driving home the effect of horror with which Tennyson invests the narrative by means of the slow, deliberate unfolding of events, studded stanza by stanza with vivid impressionistic pictures:

> Flashed all their sabres bare,
> Flashed as they turned in air
> Sabring the gunners there,
> Charging an army, while
> All the world wondered:
> Plunged in the battery smoke
> Right through the line they broke;
> Cossack and Russian
> Reeled from the sabre stroke
> Shattered and sundered.
> Then they rode back, but not
> Not the six hundred.[27]

The stanza of 'The Revenge' is hardly less powerful; it skilfully merges the characteristic shapes of two of the most common heroic ballad measures, the long four-stress lines of the 'Come-all-ye' type and the doubled quatrain, and uses the trick of internal rhyme, developed as a major rhetorical weapon by Tennyson's predecessors, as a structural device, adding greatly to its emotional force:

> And the stately Spanish men to their flagship bore him then,
> Where they laid him by the mast, old Sir Richard caught at last,
> And they praised him to his face with their courtly foreign grace;
> But he rose upon their decks, and he cried:
> 'I have fought for Queen and Faith like a valiant man and true;
> I have only done my duty as a man is bound to do:
> With a joyful spirit I Sir Richard Grenville die!'
> And he fell upon their decks, and he died.[28]

The colourful rhetoric, the broad effects and the assumptions of this are all developed directly from Lord Macaulay, and are expressive of the popular ideal of heroic poetry. As in 'The Charge of the Light Brigade', the larger shape of the poem is also ideally adapted to the purposes of recitation, slowly unfolding the story of a single, simple event, easy to be followed, in a series of vivid and evocative pictures, descriptions of Lord Howard's five ships, that 'melted like a cloud in the silent summer heaven', of the 'pinnace, like a fluttered bird', the 'little Revenge' and the 'mountain-like San Philip', and the dawn in which 'the Spanish fleet with broken sides lay round us in a ring'.

Adaptation to the purposes of recitation, like the use of the chorus in songs and other rhetorical and narrative devices discussed, is a reminder that the technical strengths of the heroic ballad are those of the oral poem, written to please the ear before the eye and moreover written to be transmitted direct from memory to memory, with all the disciplines and devices of diction that implies. Often they appear crude, either in the simplicity which they draw from the folk tradition or in the obvious oral devices they derive from Romantic poetry via the work of Scott and Macaulay; but an oral tradition, whether of song or of chanted verses, must always seek the immediate effect of the emotion distilled to its essence rather than attempting to convey intellectually satisfying analysis. Poetic subtlety is not possible in a smoky, beer-swigging assembly of two thousand people having a night out, and it was not considered desirable in the education of young sensibilities destined for the trials and glories of an Englishman's life. The techniques and conventions of this kind of oral poetry were also ideally suited to the powerful transmission of certain attitudes and beliefs. In such a medium the writer does not question ideas, nor submit them to the standards or values of high art, he simply gives them direct and memorable expression.

If, for the sake of better understanding, we fall in with the writers' own view of the value and purpose of the heroic ballads of the nineteenth century, and so direct our attention simply to the sentiments they express, we find in them a kind of mythology of the Victorian Empire. Most ballad writers derived from Scott and Macaulay the theory that all ballads past and present were written to immortalise the heroic deeds of the nation, providing a standard of comparison for each individual to measure himself against, a source of pride for the passive members of society, a lesson for the young in the honour and traditions of the race, and when performed an active source of inspiration to further efforts. The transformation of raw news of messy current events, whether reported as a line or two on the death of an obscure man or blazoned as headlines of national interest, into glorious ideals and inspiring narrative, was a function of all levels of popular culture. The music halls played their part with vigour, as the effect of Macdermott's 'War Song' shows. Much of the energy of the ballad writers went into producing versions of incidents in the various wars of the Empire, which were then published as soon after the event as possible in the daily or periodical press; and, as a secondary activity, into recounting incidents from older British history in such a way as to show them in the same light and to the same effect.

The most interesting aspects of these ballads are the heroic figures and the types of story which were most often selected for treatment, which met with the greatest popular success, and which can therefore be presumed to have best fulfilled their function in the popular culture. The crudest form of patriotism and an intention to stir the audience to pugnacious action are all that can be deduced from most of the simpler songs of the music halls, such as 'Soldiers of the Queen' or 'Sons of the Sea'. The narratives, however, both those sung by such men as Godfrey and the far larger number of recitation ballads without music, do yield an interesting consensus of ideas, a code of belief and behaviour characteristically expressed by certain metaphors and embodied in a remarkably narrow range of story patterns.

One might expect the heroes selected by the popular imagination to be some of the remarkable soldiers and sailors of the nineteenth century. But the mania for Nelson mentioned earlier in the chapter was not equalled in subsequent years, and those public figures who did achieve popular acclaim in the form of ballads were few, and apparently rather quixotically selected. The two people who figure most frequently are Florence Nightingale, about whom there is a very unusual broadside poem, adorned with a new, purpose-designed woodcut, as well as several recitation pieces and mentions in music-hall songs, and General Gordon of Khartoum. Gordon's seizure of that city and gallant resistance to the siege of the Mahdi, while British ministers delayed in sending Wolseley to relieve him until it was just too late, was a story which might have been made expressly for the balladeers. It has in common with the story of Florence Nightingale an aspect of desperation, the lone Britisher saving the country's honour in the face of neglect, even stupidity, which has left a tiny force unsupported in the midst of the foe. The fact that Gordon was supposed to be arranging a peace treaty, and probably precipitated his own disaster, was completely overlooked: the gallant and hopeless deed itself was the focus of attention, and the rescue coming just too late. The best known music-hall song on the subject was called 'Too Late', and dwelt on this aspect of the story, while Ernest Myers, a very obscure balladeer, drew from it the conclusion that Gordon was

> The crown of Being, an heroic soul.
> Beyond the weltering tides of worldly change
> He saw invisible things,
> The eternal forms of Beauty and of Right

which were, we learn, imbibed from

> The liberal air of England, thy loved home . . .
> With all of good or great
> For aye incorporate,
> That rears her race to faith and generous shame,
> To high-aspiring awe,
> To hate implacable of thick-thronging lies,
> To scorn of gold and gauds and clamorous fame.[29]

The few public figures who found a place in ballad lore were, then, individualists, people whose solitary and extreme exploits embodied a spirit which made them in some way representatives of the popular idea of heroism, rather than those who in sober truth won the country's battles and painstakingly maintained her position in the world. In fact this was the case even with Nelson, in that he was admired for personal qualities of daring and stubbornness and a refusal to know when he was beaten, none of which charismatic attributes endeared him to his political masters. The figures selected by the people were those who fitted a certain conception of the hero, as Englishman. Those who qualified were by no means all great or famous. The real people who fitted the heroic ideal, and the fictional characters created expressly to fulfil it, were most usually lowly individuals who had on one occasion – the occasion described in the ballad – been called upon to display extraordinary qualities, which they possessed simply because they were English. The ballads quoted at the beginning of this chapter, 'Here upon Guard am I' and 'The Private of the Buffs', are both good examples. The lone sentry, with nothing to keep him to his post but a sense of duty, and the man or small group of men cut off from their fellows without hope of survival, are favourite heroes. Joseph Malins, extending honorary citizenship of England to the people of ancient Rome, as was the custom since Lord Macaulay, wrote about 'The Sentinel of Pompeii':

> What of the faithful sentinel?
> Undaunted still is he!
> There, lava pours, 'midst thunderous roars,
> Into the boiling sea;
> Here, clouds of burning ashes fall,
> And all in terror flee –
> Save one, whose grave doth round him rise;
> He stands unmoved; and standing – dies![30]

Parallels to 'The Private of the Buffs' are sometimes very close; Lieut. S. S. Sugden, R.N., claims a separate and true incident in China as the basis of his ballad 'The Royal Marine', which heightens the refusal to kowtow by the fact that the Marines have the distinction of standing covered before the Queen. It seems a coarsening imitation of Doyle's ballad, but the very fact that Sugden felt it worthwhile to lay claim to the story for the navy emphasises its appeal. The Marine, like the private of the Buffs, dies for his intransigence.

The doomed isolation of the hero is often heightened or replaced by some other handicap which renders his adherence to duty and continued obedience even more remarkable. This is sometimes social inferiority: there are a number of ballads about heroism on the railways, usually by humble employees, whose low rank is stressed to emphasise how far they have to rise to the occasion. Alexander Anderson, said to be 'the well-known "Surfaceman" poet', wrote about an incident taken by the editor of *The World Wide Reciter* to be true, in which Jack Chiddy, a plate-layer, saw a block of stone fall into the path of the *Flying Dutchman*, and leapt down and moved it, losing his own life in the process. The poem begins with an introduction which twice stresses Chiddy's name, as being ludicrously 'common and plain', coming back to it at the end to assert that, despite his station, 'Jack had the soul of a man in his breast'. A favoured railway story, an anonymous version of which was first printed in *Good Words* as 'a fact'[31] was versified by G. R. Sims as 'In the Signal Box' and by at least two other poets. It was the account of the signalman who suddenly saw his own child on the line, in the path of an express, and was faced with the choice of switching the express to another track, where it would collide with a stationary local train and hundreds of lives would be lost, or directing it down the main line and killing his baby. He chooses the latter, but at least in Sims's version his wife leaps from the local train and scoops the child in as the express rushes through: had the father not done his duty, but sacrificed the express, they would both have been killed in the collision. In Robert Walker's 'The Level Crossing' the child-rescuing hero is Joe Smith, a man 'as rough as rough could be':

> There wasn't much of the saint in him,
> Only he never lied,
> And few who've lived a better life
> A nobler death have died.[32]

Willingness to die for the sake of a child is part of the hero's code; but children themselves are not exempt from the demands of heroism, and often figure as protagonists. The boy in 'Casabianca' is of course the most famous example:

> Yet beautiful and bright he stood,
> As born to rule the storm;
> A creature of heroic blood,
> A proud, though childlike form

waiting, like the sentry at Pompeii, quite pointlessly obedient, to be overwhelmed. The public schoolboy is not regarded by the balladeer as handicapped, but rather the reverse: his youthful training is regarded as the ideal preparation for heroism, and he is exhorted to manifest it at all stages of his life. 'Vitai Lampada'[33] is the epitome of this belief, taking the common image of the game, particularly the game of cricket, and the virtues of team spirit (not letting the side down), adherence to the rules, being an honorable opponent and if necessary a good loser, as an explicit parallel to the game of life, and indeed of war:

> And England's far, and Honour a name,
> But the voice of a schoolboy rallies the ranks
> Play up! play up! and play the game!

In these games, amateur status is preserved by the true hero: he is modest and does not fight for gain, whether in gold or in a specious kind of glory which is somehow distinguished from the true 'honour' which he is defending; but he is allowed to be proud of his membership of the team of Englishmen. He is inspired in his endeavours by the memory of the home for which he is fighting. A note of sentimental reminiscence is common in heroic ballads: the doughty soldier is moved and sustained by a tender recollection which represents the values he is fighting to preserve, and the occurrence of which proves his personal possession of the heroic virtue. Both of my introductory examples contain a moment evoking England, home and family; all the ballads which use the hero's boyhood (past or present) to intensify his bravery also dwell upon the picture of the old school, the beloved faces and the familiar fields. One of Sir Henry Newbolt's pieces, 'He Fell Among Thieves',[34] which is a compendium of heroic attitudes, takes this moment of memory and bases the whole ballad upon it. It is an indirectly related story of an ambush and a fight against impossible odds on the North-West Frontier, which begins, in a self-consciously dramatic ballad-like manner, after the hero has been overpowered. We deduce the foregoing events from his speech and actions. He speaks defiantly to his treacherous captors, who demand 'Blood for our blood', but allow him to live until dawn, in acknowledgement, it seems, of his prowess in killing five of them before he was overpowered. This settled, 'He flung his empty revolver down the slope', and sitting on the hilltop, 'clasping his knees' (a gesture presumably included to indicate his youth) recalls 'The April noon on his books aglow, The wisteria trailing in at the window wide' and other tokens of his ancestral home, his father, his horses, and his Norman ancestors in the church; then 'The School Close, sunny and green' and a race he won; and the long tables of his college dining-hall. Thus fortified, he faces the dawn, and with a vaguely pantheistic prayer to the life dwelling in earth and sun, dies by the sword.

The public-school hero has to be prepared to lay down the life so carefully nurtured and trained as soon as he ventures into the world; many other heroic children, without his advantages, meet their ends as soon as they are old enough to be conscious of the demands of duty. They include, for example, Phoebe Cary's boy with his hand in the leak in the dyke and Frederick Langbridge's blind boy making a dangerous cross-country journey for his father, and even the captain's daughter in 'The Wreck of the *Hesperus*'. She indeed does nothing very heroic, besides dying, but her American nationality may account for that. There is, however, a division of handicapped heroes peculiar to America, or rather perhaps to the sentimental English view of America, in that they are slaves who prove themselves men. They appear as 'The Black Regiment' in a ballad by G. H. Boker, which copies the metre of 'The Charge of the Light Brigade', and as the individual young man who climbs the spire of St Michael's, Charleston, to pluck away a burning brand, in a ballad by Mary A. P. Stansbury. He fulfils the heroic code expressed by Ernest Myers by rejecting payment,

'Ye may keep your gold – I scorn it! But answer me, ye who can,
If the deed I have done before you be not the deed of a *man*!'[35]

Heroic women are most usually concerned with rescues and survival, rather than daring deeds, but like the heroines of melodrama they are as active and enduring as their male counterparts. Few women soldiers survive from the old broadside ballad tradition, which allowed deserted wives and sweethearts to follow their men into battle by sea and land, successfully disguised; a truncated and in fact maimed version of such a story appears in Austin's 'The Last Redoubt', where the fair warrior fights on when all have given up, undiscovered until the enemy find her body, and bury her with honour. We have no intimation of why she is there, and no hint of the happy, often fertile, ending which traditionally belongs to the story, an affirmation of the power of life over death. Victorian popular heroines do affirm life, however, by the selection from the heroic character which is given to them. Many are nurses, after the pattern of Florence Nightingale, enduring pitiless hardship in their calling. Others are rescuers, like Grace Darling, or the Queensland lady who spent 'Eight days on the waves in a rust-eaten boiler' to preserve her children's lives, in the ballad by Douglas Sladen and also, apparently, in fact.

Fulfilment of the conditions of action and motive promotes not only women, children, foreigners and slaves to the rank of hero, but even dumb beasts. Most ballads about animals fall into the group of sentimental pieces discussed in the next chapter, but the horse, beloved of the Victorian boy and gentleman, is often dignified with tales of heroism. Horses may die to save their masters, like Bay Ruric in the ballad of that name by B. Montgomerie Ranking, or their desperate rides to the death may be simply in response to the demand that they should do their duty for the sake of carrying unspecified good news, fetching help to a wreck (in 'From the Wreck' by the Australian bushranger poet, A. L. Gordon) or even winning a trotting race, in the sentimental and comic song 'Down the Road' sung by Gus Elen. Bay Billy, in the ballad by F. H. Gassoway, does better than these: his rider, the colonel, is dead, and the demoralised troops have no schoolboy voice to rally them to the charge; the old horse steps out, and leads them on to victory by himself. Any creature which conforms to the standard of duty, obedience, and self-sacrifice in its allotted sphere is accorded the accolade.

If one turns from the pattern of heroism to the typical stories in which it is displayed, as clear and as narrowly-defined a picture can be established. Certain stories, usually drawn from the news of the day, or imitative of incidents which have occurred and passed into the mythology, are repeatedly used, as representing an ideal of conduct. The flux of daily event, at home and in the almost ceaseless round of colonial wars, was scrutinised by the balladeers, and certain kinds of incident picked out. After these had been dealt with, English, and also Roman and Greek, history were examined for events which could inculcate the same ideas and values in their readers. Events commemorated, like the heroes chosen, were rarely vital in the history of the nation; obscure actions in corners of the globe by insignificant men were chosen and great battles ignored. Large-scale, efficient and victorious operations were uninteresting, even sometimes treated with irony, the popular voice raised in protest against the inhuman treatment of the individual: Southey's 'Battle of Blenheim' was very popular and much anthologised. The most popular stories of all are the stories of rescue; children snatched from death under trains, sailors saved from the deep by Grace Darling or by the efforts of the lifeboat crews, whose praises are sung again and again, garrisons holding out hopelessly to whom relief unlooked for comes. 'The Relief of Lucknow' is the archetype of these. Its details passed rapidly into ballad mythology, and many hands worked over the starving women and children, the thinning ranks of defenders, the march of Havelock and his men, dying all the way, and the corporal's wife within the defences who heard the slogan of the Highlanders and the tune of 'The Campbells are Comin'' far off, before anyone else could believe that they were fighting for anything but their honour. Gerald Massey adds quite gratuitously an unnamed hero who is sacrificed for the sake of the relief:

> Stabbed by mistake, one native cries with the last breath he draws,
> 'Welcome, my friends, never you mind, it's all for the good cause.'[36]

While the rescue stories were the most popular of all, in terms of the success of individual stories, they were considerably outnumbered by ballads which do not have a happy ending. The heroes had to be prepared, like Massey's native, to die for the cause: the more likely the death, the more glorious the adherence to the cause. Acts of suicide, in obedience either to orders or to the standing orders of duty and love of country, are most highly praised. Many ballads already cited are obviously examples of this: the introductory stories, 'The Charge of the Light Brigade', the railway heroes, the defenders of the Delhi Magazine who blew themselves up to keep the powder from enemy hands.

These all fought, like the defenders of Rorke's drift in the ballad by Doyle,

> 'For victory! – no, all hope is gone; for life! let that go too;
> But for the colours still work on – the chance is left to you.'[37]

Suicidal gallantry is occasionally represented as stemming from bravado or misplaced romanticism, as in the case of Mad Carew's theft of the green eye of the little yellow god, an inflammatory disregard of native sensitivity for which he expected and duly received rough justice. He had done it to meet the demands of a silly woman, and there is a sense in the ballad of the feeling contained in the traditional story of the lady who threw her glove in the lion pit to test her knight: he does what he has been challenged to do, but the demand is felt to be wrong, and the lady falls in his regard and ours. Carew's death is also her punishment. The situations in which true heroism is able to show itself to good effect are those in which one man dies for his comrades. In the ballad 'Rake Windermere' (the punning title of which suggests its origin was in the music hall) for instance, the hero had brought 'a smirch on an honoured crest' by his life, but redeemed himself by his death, volunteering to be killed by a Moorish band who surrounded the party of tourists to which he belonged, demanding vengeance for a man accidentally shot. A man may also give his life heroically in the strict interpretation of the duties of his job, like the captain of a merchant ship in 'The Story of a Stowaway' by Clement Scott, who bound his own lifebelt round a Liverpool urchin who was discovered, as the ship sank, to have stowed away. He dies, and the child survives, showing a proper sense of gratitude by kneeling to kiss the captain's hand before leaping overboard. Death by drowning, to enable others to survive, was a favourite theme, and the story of the loss of the *Birkenhead*, a troopship which went down in 1852 off Simon's Bay, South Africa, was so popular as to inspire several ballads and the further tribute of an invented story based upon the incident in which men spur each other on to heroism by recalling the *Birkenhead*. Two versions of the disaster are interestingly contrasted: in *Lyra Heroica* Henley includes a rather pretentious poem by Yule,[38] beginning with a rhetorical challenge to the bragging French and those who regard England as corrupt, and continuing to tell the story stressing that the men who died were not 'Veterans steeled', but

> Far other: weavers from the stocking frame;
> Boys from the plough; cornets with beardless chin,
> But steeped in honour and discipline!

The ring of Doyle's reassuring treatment of the private is here; but the whole popular audience was excited by the story, and the version by John A. Goodchild[39] includes practical and sentimental details which link it with broadside writing. He imagines the scene, the striking of the rock, the activity of the crew, the five hundred troops swarming up on deck, sixty called for to man the pumps; then the lowering of the boats, three of which survive, and those overloaded with women and children; and then

> . . . four hundred redcoats stand to their ranks on either hand,
> Watching Death draw nearer, nearer, whilst they eye him face to face

until they go down, in unbroken parade order.

Success against heavy odds has always been particularly admired by the English people, presumably because the size and isolation of the country has always made it likely that any fighting force she could put in the field would be smaller than that of the opposing side; so Jack Tar was always represented as worth half a dozen foreigners, and music-hall and recitation poets seized upon those engagements in whatever conflict was going forward in which a small band defied the might of other nations. Tennyson's ballads often stress this facet of heroism, for instance 'The Revenge'; and the Crimean war gave balladeers a series of examples, of which they made full use: Alma was solemnly commemorated from stage and platform, Balaclava was of course the scene of the charge of the Light Brigade, and Inkerman, a soldiers' battle in which a few regiments of British soldiers kept the whole Russian line in check unaided, was almost as celebrated. The incompetence with which the whole campaign was conducted went unremarked by the bards, or rather was regarded, fatalistically, as an unremarkable act of God or of government only worthy of comment in that it gave the opportunity for the heroic acts of the common man. The rest of the nation's history, from Agincourt to the victory of a band of volunteers serving in the liberation army of Bolivar in Venezuela in 1821, was searched for similar incidents.

Victory under these circumstances is not a requirement of heroism; an equally good story may be made of a defeat, just as the individual may be called upon simply to die for the cause. The essential victory is over one's own fear and instinct for self-preservation, and so it came to be regarded as actually more heroic to take on the impossible, and deliberately die, than to conquer in unlikely circumstances. The metaphor of the game enters very often when this tenet is expressed: one should keep a straight bat, play according to the rules and to the best of one's ability, and it becomes almost bad form in one's enemy to make use of weapons or numbers greater than one's own. Indeed the enemy's admiration for and inability to comprehend the capacity the Englishman has for fighting on when hope is gone, is often the hero's posthumous reward. It occurs in 'The Revenge', and is the subject of Doyle's ballad 'The Red Thread of Honour', a story he claimed to have heard from Sir Charles Napier of an incident in India, in the Scinde desert:

> Eleven men of England
> A breast-work charged in vain;
> Eleven men of England
> Lay stripped, and gashed, and slain . . .
>
> These missed the glen to which their steps were bent,
> Mistook a mandate, from afar half heard,
> And, in that glorious error, calmly went
> To death without a word.

The chief of the robbers they are attacking finds the bodies, and judges their motives:

> 'These were not stirred by anger,
> Nor yet lust made them bold;
> Renown they thought above them,
> Nor did they look for gold.
> To them the leader's signal
> Was as the voice of God:
> Unmoved, and uncomplaining,
> The path it showed they trod.'[40]

The hillmen have a burial custom, whereby the wrist of a brave man is bound with green, and of a hero, with red. This warrior buries his dead followers, the defenders, with the green token, and although he intends to leave the Englishmen, as enemies, to the birds and beasts of prey, he accords them the red thread. Then, not satisfied, he decides they should be doubly honoured – and when Napier finds them, he finds the hero's token on both wrists of each corpse.

The way in which the values indicated by these stories developed from popular attitudes, and the reason why they took this form in Victorian England, remain to be reviewed. It is quite typical, indeed axiomatic, that in all folk poetry the stress should fall upon the feelings and exploits of the individual, rather than upon politics and the outcome of campaigns. From sixteenth-century tales of moss-trooping borderers to broadside laments for press-ganged lovers, the stress falls upon the one who is realistically acknowledged to be very likely to suffer and die if he is involved in fighting, but who is also idealised into the perfect pattern of manhood. His bravery, stoicism, daring and regard to his honour are chiefly important, therefore, as personal attributes: the ideal of behaviour is held for its own sake, not for the sake of the nation, which might well derive greater benefit from less spectacular behaviour. Patriotism is one of the hero's virtues, one of the things which raises him to the heroic level by prompting him to valour, but it is not the only reason that heroism is valued. The admiration expressed is for the qualities displayed by the individual in the face of danger which might be the result of his country's demands, or, alternatively, of his superiors' incompetence. His responsibility in both cases is not to betray himself, as a member of his race or as a man. A man like Jock o' the Side (*E.S.P.B.* no. 187) is shown as deliberately seeking danger and adventure, and his behaviour held up as a model; the same spirit is found in Billy, parted from his Susan, in one of the many ballads of the press-gang and the recruiting officer which were in circulation at the turn of the nineteenth century. They are laments, often from the point of view of the girl who is left behind, but they make no protest against the war or against the inhuman demands made upon the people in order to furnish men: if the impersonal tide of war carries a man away, he is thought all the better if he proves an heroic as well as a tragic figure:

> Sweet Susan I come to take my leave,
> My dearest I pray don't sigh and grieve,
> A letter of absence I have receiv'd,
> So my dearest Susan do not grieve;
> All on the main I will maintain
> King George's right, with sword in hand,
> My blood I'll spill e'er France shall have her will,
> All for the honour of my native land.[41]

The writers of this kind of broadside, and their successors writing patriotic songs for the stage, were concerned not to make a social protest, but to present the men who suffered such experiences, and their families and lovers, with an acceptable and comforting picture of themselves cast in an heroic role. The idealised Jack Tar was recognised as a good recruiting weapon for the Navy, the brutalities and hardships of which were well enough known to make the press-gang necessary until as late as 1832; but he was also an acceptable, indeed a glamorous, model for the ordinary seaman or even the adventurous landsman to adopt for himself. He gained from it a sense of importance, of playing a part in the life of his country, and the unthinking adulation with which the audience showered the singers of patriotic songs also rubbed off on the men who turned their boasts into bloody realities. It is a distortion to look upon such songs as these as being in any way imposed upon the people, in order to exploit them, for the emotions they expressed were those of the great majority of nineteenth-century Englishmen of every rank, and the image of the heroic common man which they project is one which he himself aspired to and enjoyed.

The extra dimension which it took on in the Victorian popular ballad, where individual achievement and devotion to the cause were demanded of everyone from the deserted sentry to General Gordon, was, it seems fair to assume, a reaction to the peculiar circumstances of the Empire, where the common soldier and the junior civil servant had to be relied upon to stick to their posts with the ever-present consciousness that they were quite hopelessly outnumbered. Only confidence in the right of the Englishman and unthinking, automatic adherence to the code, bred in from the public-school playing field or the song learnt at his mother's knee, could keep a man unquestioningly obedient and swift in his response to the call of duty. The popular poets, even the music-hall singers, played a part in the creation of the self-image which such Englishmen had to sustain them, and also, of course, in the image of them which was fostered to comfort the folks at home.

While the glory of being an Englishman is insisted upon, the reality of the hero's likely death is also stressed. In the folk view, while a hero's death is not without its compensations, and makes an inspiring song, it is still regarded as tragic before it is glorious. The press-gang song is a lament; the event is regarded as tantamount to the loss of the beloved. To take a tragic view of the death of soldiers and sailors is part of the popular stress upon the individual: no one is written off as a casualty, an inevitable part of the larger scheme, and each death is more important than the reason for it. The inevitability of death is perhaps one reason why mismanagement and mistaken orders are taken so calmly and fatalistically. While this is an established part of the popular attitude, the mortality rate of the Victorian ballads is nevertheless peculiarly high. It is also part of the older popular tradition to celebrate escapes from death, to accept the return of the hero as a bonus and an affirmation of the strength of life to be sung about as enthusiastically as his noble death would have been: a conventional ending to the broadside lament for the pressed sailor is his unexpected return. While the Victorian popular audience did enjoy happy endings, stories of rescue and escape, it also enjoyed the deaths. The gusto with which the drawing-room balladeer in particular killed off the protagonists of his stories is peculiar to mid- and late-nineteenth-century popular poetry. In this, as in the stress which falls sometimes too insistently upon the lowly rank or the youth of the dying Englishman, the Victorian heroic ballad diminishes itself, cheapens the strong and unanimous feelings to which it gives expression, and veers towards sentimentality and false emotion.

The explanation for this is partly the lack of artistic standards which I mentioned at the beginning of this chapter, and which has no doubt been adequately demonstrated by the examples quoted: formula writing for strong effects within an established convention is bound sooner or later to be exploited without skill or taste by bad writers, whose work may gain acceptance if the standard of judgement is moral rather than poetic. The problem is also, however, one of the division of the popular audience, inevitable because of its very size and because of its social range. The feelings of patriotism and so on to which the heroic ballads gave expression were common to all; but the relation of the individual listening to the ballad to the heroic figure presented in it varied greatly. One result of this was that writers, particularly towards the end of the century when the popular audience numbered millions, found themselves writing within the heroic convention but for particular purposes, selecting a narrower range of the emotions it touched upon to achieve a particular effect, with a particular audience. Thus the immediacy of personal identification and involvement with the hero was lost in the deliberate manipulation of emotion, and the divisions which that set up between writer and audience, and writer and subject, vitiated the ballads and songs in which it occurred. In for instance Kipling's 'The Absent-minded Beggar', which was published in the *Daily Mail* a few days after the outbreak of the Boer War, set to music by Elgar, and generally printed and sung thereafter, the intention of raising money for the families of soldiers leads to a sentimentality and a coyness of diction which is insidiously distasteful, and quite unfit to stand beside Kipling's *Barrack-Room Ballads*. The distinct and separate roles assigned to writer, audience and hero, and the consequent relationships between them, result in the condescension, superiority, aggressiveness and mawkish sentimentality which come together in the tone of the first verse:

> When you've shouted 'Rule Britannia,' when you've sung 'God save the Queen',
> When you've finished killing Kruger with your mouth,
> Will you kindly drop a shilling in my little tambourine
> For a gentleman in khaki ordered South?
> He's an absent-minded beggar, and his weaknesses are great –
> But we and Paul must take him as we find him –
> He is out on active service, wiping something off a slate –
> And he's left a lot of little things behind him![42]

This is an example of one of the worst sides of the Victorian heroic ballad; but Kipling's work also includes examples of the form which are some of the best popular poems the century produced. As the case of 'The Absent-minded Beggar' makes clear, Kipling occupied a place as popular poet which can be seen as the crown and the epitome of the Victorian popular tradition, taking in all levels of the popular audience and uniting in his work all that is most expressive of the music-hall and drawing-room poetic conventions. It is largely because he wrote strictly public poetry of this kind that his verse has often been undervalued. In an age to which we look for poetry of introspection and personal revelation, and whose public values we deprecate, a poet creating his artistic statements exclusively in the popular tradition, deliberately attempting to voice the responses of the average citizen, is very difficult to evaluate. The difficulty is most apparent in the lack of appropriate terminology: the standards and the vocabulary of current criticism do not seem to apply. T. S. Eliot recognised the difficulty when he described[43] Kipling's metrical composition as verse rather than poetry, and recognised his verse as ballad: 'The starting point for Kipling's verse is the motive of the ballad-maker; and the modern ballad is a type of verse for the appreciation of which we are not provided with the proper critical tools.' He did not, however, attempt to follow up this recognition by providing us with the critical tools, by connecting Kipling in more than a casual manner with the stream of 'modern ballad' by comparison with which his intentions and achievements can be defined. George Orwell, on the other hand, pointed out[44] the context in which Kipling's poetry must be seen, but in recognising it gave it a misleading name which makes an evaluation of it by inapplicable standards: 'one can, perhaps, place Kipling . . . if one describes him simply as a good bad poet . . . there is a great deal of good bad poetry in English, all of it, I should say, subsequent to 1790.' He then gives eight examples, which include six nineteenth-century ballads. He has, in other words, strayed into a literary evaluation of the popular stream of nineteenth-century writing. Both critics go on to mention Kipling's mass popularity, his connection with the music hall, and the obvious, universally available nature of his poetry, but neither has realised the context of his work sufficiently to appreciate that the peculiarities in his writing which they are striving to describe belong to and are explained by the popular tradition.

More recently, assessment of the best of Kipling's poetry in a different context has been begun. Charles Carrington's edition of the *Barrack-Room Ballads*[45] brings together all the poems he regards as falling into a special category of popular writing, though without a critical analysis which justifies his extension of Kipling's title to so many other poems. P. J. Keating[46] has gone some way towards a just estimate of Kipling's essential connection with Victorian popular poetry, but he has seen the music-hall song and Kipling's attitude to it entirely in terms of class, rather than as a more complex identification on Kipling's part with folk attitudes older than class awareness, and rooted in ballad poetry, still finding expression in its Victorian manifestation. His verse is distinguished not by standing alone and unique amongst the poetry of the literary tradition, but by being the best of popular poetry, drawing the Victorian heroic ballad into a unity by strong personal identification with the ideals and methods of the tradition. His best poetry is not self-expression, or rather, not simply self-expression, but public affirmation and expression of his belief in the values of his times. He was intensely proud of his position as a nineteenth-century Englishman. It required no falsification, scarcely any effort, on his part to make his own voice the public voice, saying what all felt about the contemporary world in language and forms that were common possessions of all, whether they listened to them in music hall, public recitation or drawing-room. He shared the values of those of all classes who subscribed to the glorification of 'hearty English sense and feeling'; where he did not do so wholeheartedly he strove to suppress, and would never have revealed, his doubts. He believed in the Empire and all the complicated web of observed emotions both admirable and, to the modern eye, less admirable, that went to support it; and perhaps more important than this, he had no desire to be different, to disagree or surpass. His chief need was to be accepted, and to belong. So he did not retreat into his writing, but rather tried to use it to connect him more closely with the countries and the times he loved: he even, most significantly, loved and wrote about the machine, to other poets the hated symbol of modern ugliness. He wished to be distinguished from the people about and for whom he wrote only by his ability to do so, a distinction shared by every singer of ballads from the beginning; and he became a public poet through his mastery of all the forms of the Victorian ballad.

There is an obvious artistic danger in the ease with which he wrote within the established forms: the propagandist 'Absent-minded Beggar' is one example of its consequences, and mastery of the drawing-room ballad and identification with its feeling led him, as it had led Tennyson, to produce a number of pieces distinguished only by their technical excellence, accepting too easily and superficially the assumptions of the form. In almost every variety of ballad he made some examples which transcend and justify the form, but he was repeatedly tempted to relax the truly communal voice which he achieved in the *Barrack-Room Ballads*, and the truly creative historical imagination he used in some poems, into the less acutely realised role of the Englishman, or simply the teller of tales. The later continuation of the barrack-room ballads, the songs about the soldiers of the Boer war, have a false ring of poems about, rather than poems for and expressive of, the spirit of the common soldier. The verbal mastery is there, in for instance the pattern of 'Boots', but the emotions are falsified or over-simplified towards the non-combatants' picture of the brave and patriotic army, in for example the coy 'Back to the Army'. Similarly the evocation of the landscape and the feeling of the war put into the mouths of the troops, in for example 'The Return', is that which only an observer, and an educated and artistically inclined observer, would have felt. Kipling found the heroic ballad a fluent vehicle for all kinds of stories that stir the easier emotions. Such a piece as 'The Ballad of Boh da Thone', for example, is nothing more than an efficient drawing-room cliché, for all its exotically sensational detail requires no depth of response and comes from no depth of feeling:

> Boh da Thone was a warrior bold:
> His sword and his Snider were bossed with gold,
>
> And the Peacock Banner his henchmen bore
> Was stiff with bullion, but stiffer with gore . . .
>
> He crucified noble, he sacrificed mean,
> He filled old ladies with kerosene.[47]

The bouncy ebullience of this more than cushions the apparent horror of the details, and the fantasy with which the story is worked out confirms the slightness of the intended effect.

If one turns to the first volume of Kipling's verse, the *Departmental Ditties*, 1886, there are examples of this superficial use of a talent for reproduction and parody, which span the whole range of ballad effects from the burlesque of traditional ballads to Gothic horror. One of his best parodies is 'The Ballad of the Clamperdown', which is a mock-serious drawing-room heroic piece written in response to an old-fashioned view of the Navy expressed in a newspaper, which the paper and its readers, showing even less critical judgement in the face of patriotic sentiment than usual, received with solemn approval. Elsewhere one can find Kipling using broadside forms in the old way, for political harangue, in 'Cleared' and 'The Ballad of the Red Earl', the most advanced literary medievalism in 'A St. Helena Lullaby' and 'Heriot's Ford', and romantic archaic diction in 'Henry VII and the Shipwrights'. There is direct imitation of traditional forms, the ballad 'The Wife of Usher's Well' in 'The Sea-wife' and the old folk-elegiac colloquy between a woman and the wind in 'My Boy Jock', and example upon example of straightforward recitation pieces. Few of these are of any distinction, but they are no reason at all for condemning Kipling as a bad poet without seriousness of intention. The lesser works of another kind of poet, working to find expression for his personal vision in personal terms, are treated with respect and read for anything they might contribute to an understanding of his major works; and these efficient public poems are simply Kipling's equivalent trial runs and lesser achievements. That they may appear complete and self-satisfied is a false impression which arises from a peculiarity of the form, which demands that the poet should master efficient communication first of all, and then find a way to bend it to say what he wishes, instead of the more obviously exploratory procedure by which the other kind of poet seeks for personal expressions to embody his concepts, closing the gap between thought and word from the other direction.

Kipling closes the gap completely, and achieves major poetry, in ballads which cover the whole range of Victorian popular writing. On the one hand he drew on his vital feeling for the contemporary world and its characteristic emotions, vocabulary and popular verse forms, to create the *Barrack-Room Ballads* out of the songs of the music hall. On the other, he was able to make poetry in the form of the heroic ballad which had descended from Scott's *Minstrelsy* because he also possessed an historical imagination as powerful and creative as that of Scott himself. The feeling for the common people and the feeling for the past, a combination which played a great part in the creation of the Romantic ballads, came together again at the end of the nineteenth century in Kipling, and they enabled him to draw together in his work all the developments of the ballad over ninety years.

If we consider only the poems which appeared scattered throughout his prose works, we find a range of examples of this masterly objective poetry which makes use of the poet's peculiar talents but is confined to public, immediately available expression. In 'A Truthful Song', for example, the sense of the substantive reality of past ages, lacking in verses like Macaulay's *Lays*, is grasped effortlessly by Kipling, and combined with his sense of the conventions of popular song and with his personal feeling for the in-group: a complicated exercise. He achieved a very similar effect with the strenuous simplicity of 'Tarrant Moss' and 'The Ballad of Minepit Shaw', both ballads using traditional techniques and telling ballad stories. The former is a mysteriously tragic narrative of love, and the latter makes a completely unselfconscious combination of mundane drunkenness and supernatural events. Poachers fleeing from the keeper's dogs are precipitated into a pit, and hold this exchange with their rough rescuer, whom they cannot see in the dark:

> 'And why's our bed so hard to the bones
> Excepting where it's cold?'
> 'Oh, that's because it's precious stones
> Excepting where 'tis gold.
>
> 'Think it over as you stand,
> For I tell you without fail,
> If you haven't got into Fairyland
> You're not in Lewes Gaol.'[48]

In other places the historical imagination is reinforced by Kipling's often-remarked feeling for England, which is near enough to the chauvinism of the ordinary Victorian ballad to pass as such without question, but has in effect a magical strength which is very near to a Wordsworthian pantheism. As always, the complexity of these drives is left implicit in the narrative and descriptive poems like 'Merrow Down', 'The Road through the Woods' and 'Puck's Song'. There are also poems in which the historical evocation stands by itself and pure, and they are valid, and indeed important, artistic achievements because of its simplicity and clarity. Kipling, like Scott, was able to convey the period of which he wrote without throwing the shadow of his own times across the verses. His ancient Rome is not Victorian, as Macaulay's is, but a city where

> A shiftless, westward-wandering tramp,
> Checked by the Tiber flood,
> He reared a wall around his camp
> Of uninspired mud.[49]

It is a camp, not a home, and has a mud wall, not a white porch. In 'A Smuggler's Song' the gentlemen who go by really seem to belong to the eighteenth century, and Kipling's song has the spirit and air of the period it describes; and even the 'Song of the Men's Side', an attempt to do the impossible by reconstructing the feeling of a period of prehistory, does not seem to strike a false note. Kipling draws on another aspect of his knowledge of people, his acquaintance with non-European races and manners, for the vividness of his picture of the neolithic tribe on the English downs, and so fills the Victorian ballad stanzas with alien life:

> Our women and our little ones may walk upon the Chalk,
> As far as we can see them and beyond.
> We shall not be anxious for our sheep when we keep
> Tally at the shearing-pond.
> We can eat with both our elbows on our knees, if we please,
> We can sleep after meals in the sun,
> For Shepherd-of-the-Twilight is dismayed at the Blade,
> Feet-in-the-Night have run!
> Dog-without-a-Master goes away (Hai, Tyr, aie!)
> Devil-in-the-Dusk has run!
>
> Room for his shadow on the grass – let it pass!
> To left and right – stand clear!
> This is the Buyer of the Blade – be afraid!
> This is the great god Tyr![50]

These are examples of the poetry which rose out of the long and, by then, hackneyed tradition of the heroic recitation ballad when it was placed under imaginative pressure. Kipling used his facility in conventional form for the purpose of self-expression, and the convention is both justified and transcended. It was possible for him to use it in this way because he consciously subscribed to the values celebrated by the convention; he differed from the audiences he addressed and the reciters who used his work in the intensity of his experience, not its nature. No other kind of poetry was possible for him, perhaps because of the very nature of these values; and the discrepancies between his personal feeling for his country, the Empire, history, loyalty, degree, and responsibility, and the cruder versions of these things purveyed by less committed and sensitive ballad writers passed unnoticed. They only affect the best of his heroic ballad lays, and those, unfortunately, are comparatively few.

The difference of attitude which elevates the *Barrack-Room Ballads* above the mass of similar writing is much more striking; but it too passed unnoticed except by the few critics who rejected the common run of popular ballads but found something genuinely poetic in Kipling's version of the same thing. The difference, unnoticed by those who did not in any case detect the crudity and condescension in the works of writers like Alfred Austin, lies in the way in which Kipling was able to identify as completely and unreservedly with the possessors of the music-hall song as he did with the audience of the drawing-room ballad. He did not write down to the people, or make use of the music hall; rather he found in music-hall songs another flexible mould for his sense of excited participation in the lives of modern people, with their vivid peculiarity of feeling, experience and expression.

This feeling is the transforming influence that fused the diverse forms of which Kipling was master into the *Barrack-Room Ballads*, a unique and immensely powerful unity. He acknowledged[51] that the ballads were inspired by the music hall. The 'observed and compelling songs' which he saw the 'Lion' and 'Mammoth' Comiques perform at Gatti's, together with the barmaid there and the English and Indian soldiers in the audience, 'set' for him 'the scheme for a certain sort of song.' His interest was attracted as much by the audience as by the songs, and he valued the form as an expression of the feelings of the people for whom it was performed. The particular songs he mentions, the character songs of the 1860s and 1870s, were ideal for this purpose. The 'comique' singers were men like Macdermott, who assumed a role or persona for their stage appearances which the audience recognised as representing a certain type of man. The commonest was that of the 'heavy swell', the rich man-about-town who sang about his life, his exploits with drink and with women, and generally provided a fantasy of pleasure and success which represented the working man's idea of what he would do if he were rich, and the music-hall patron's idea of the sort of enjoyment he was seeking at that very moment. Other roles were sometimes adopted for particular songs, each one recognisable as a type, and each song adding further layers of characterisation to the total effect which each evocation of the type would have. The songs were largely expositions of small incidents which illustrate the character, and typically took the form of a catchy chorus with a few, less memorable, stanzas leading up to it. The songs about drink, composed and sung in competition by the leading 'comique' singers and culminating in George Leybourne's 'Champagne Charlie', are examples of this type. Other 'heavy swell' songs include such titles as 'Walking in the Zoo', 'Up in a Balloon', 'Visiting the Aq.', and 'After the Opera'.

The stanza and chorus pattern of character song had already found its way into some recitation pieces, and the ballads Kipling wrote on the same plan bridged the gap completely. The *Barrack-Room Ballads* are predominantly various kinds of chorus-based character song built upon and illustrating the character of the common soldier serving in India, whom Kipling calls Tommy. Being without tunes, they are perforce recitation pieces, and indeed were widely used as such, but they have a frankness and naturalism more common in the halls than in the drawing-room, and they take an attitude to the idealisation of the common man which is both more realistic than that of much heroic music-hall song, and without the condescension of many drawing-room ballads. Kipling admires his ideal soldier, but knows him better than the drawing-room poet dares to or the music-hall singer wishes to. He does not ignore his faults, nor his grievances, as Charles Godfrey's songs do, but neither does he assure his respectable dependants that with all his faults and ill-treatment he is nevertheless a reliable and grateful subordinate. Instead he uses a cycle of character songs or ballads to create a vivid picture of the experiences, feelings and aspirations of the men in India which is both realistic and ideal, and out of which 'Tommy' emerges as the embodiment of the Victorian hero. He is eager to return home –

> Troopin', troopin', troopin' to the sea:
> 'Ere's September come again – the six-year men are free.
> O leave the dead be'ind us, for they cannot come away
> To where the ship's a-coalin' up that takes us 'ome today.[52]

On his return he is likely to find himself delivering the age-old message of the returning soldier:

> 'Soldier, soldier, come from the wars,
> Do you bring no sign from my true love?'
> 'I bring a lock of 'air that 'e allus used to wear,
> An' you'd best go look for a new love.'[53]

But if he is identified with the warrior of all folk-song by the form Kipling adopts here, he is singled out as a soldier of Victoria, a man sharing at a personal level in the ideal of empire, in 'The Widow's Party', which also uses a traditional ballad style and tells first the old story of the hardships of war from the soldier's point of view:

> 'They called us out of the barrack-yard
> To Gawd knows where from Gosport Hard,
> And you can't refuse when you get the card . . .'

but ends, after the tale of the food that was 'tough as a board', the campaign on which 'some were gutted and some were starved' and the narrator wounded, with

> 'What was the end of all the show,
> Johnnie, Johnnie?'
> Ask my Colonel, for I don't know,
> Johnnie, my Johnnie, aha!
> We broke a King and we built a road –
> A court-house stands where the reg'ment goed.
> And the river's clean where the raw blood flowed
> When the Widow give the party.[54]

He has also gained from his experience in foreign parts a love for the beauties of the place, expressed in 'Mandalay', and a slightly comic pride in his familiarity with them, which emerges in his self-conscious use of scraps of the native lingo and semi-defiant commendation of the bravery of some non-English, whether serving with him, like Gunga Din, or against him, like the Fuzzy-Wuzzies. All these reactions are finely observed and precisely expressed, representing the deeply insular values of the uneducated Englishman whose grudging sensitivity and self-commending honesty force from him vehement statements of the obvious.

The highlights of Tommy's life are experienced as a member of a tight community, with unique experience, whether of pride in the murderous screw-guns, comic despair over the commissariat camels, or horror at the loss of comrades, who die in bungled operations:

> Kabul town's by Kabul river –
> Blow the bugle, draw the sword –
> There I lef' my mate for ever,
> Wet and dripping by the ford . . .[55]

or heroically in action, as in 'Snarleyow', or even, most traumatic and yet most necessary of all to the community, to the sound of the Dead March in the barrack square, in 'Danny Deever'. Here Kipling turns the most literary of developments of the ballad style, the stanza form, and the question-and-answer pattern, of Rossetti's 'Sister Helen', back to popular use:

> ''Is cot was right-'and cot to mine,' said Files-on-Parade.
> ''E's sleepin' out an' far to-night,' the Colour-Sergeant said.
> 'I've drunk 'is beer a score o' times,' said Files-on-Parade.
> ''E's drinkin' bitter beer alone,' the Colour-Sergeant said.'[56]

The community of the army, held together internally by the shared 'mystery' of the trades and skills and experiences peculiar to their situation, and from outside by the threat of the hostile land which will overwhelm them if they break faith with each other, is an ideal setting and breeding-ground for the ballad, crystallising into myth and story the facts and precepts upon which the discipline of the group, and therefore its survival, rest. Within the accepted value of the shared experience described, the individual Tommy has freedom to display his less commendable and acceptable characteristics: he may be drunken, as in 'Cells', which uses the music-hall song pattern more or less unchanged to explore the wandering recollections of a soldier in the cells after a drunken attack upon the military police. Gradually, stanza by stanza, he recollects his offence, and uses the chorus, a jaunty off-hand reiteration of the official charge and penalty against him, 'So it's pack-drill for me and a fortnight's C.B.,/For drunk and resisting the guard', to bolster his flagging self-confidence. Kipling does not excuse him in conventional terms. At the end of the ballad he squashes his remorse about his children and wife by the reflection that he is bound to do it again. Instead he presents the offence to the audience, by the use of the official phrases about charge and punishment, as an expected, inevitable part of the role of a soldier. A similar device is at work in the ballad 'Belts'. This is cast in the form of an Irish 'Come-all-ye', and is about the habit, much disapproved by citizens who were endangered or outraged by it, of brawling in the streets, 'for fun', between rival regiments, using the heavy uniform belt as a weapon. Kipling fully accepts and enjoys the soldier-narrator's view of the proceedings which were just 'a row in Silver Street', until 'someone drew his side-arm clear', 'and so we all was murderers that started out in fun', so now ''Tis all a merricle to me as in the Clink I lie.' He is not blamed, even implicitly or indirectly: he is a soldier, in whose life such things happen. There is even a ranting, defiant ballad about 'Loot', an entirely unmentionable part of the soldier's activities as far as the armchair imperialist was concerned, vividly described in detail by a narrator who purports to be instructing the new recruit in an activity which he acknowledges 'with English morals does not suit'. He is in this case excused by an aside in the last stanza about his own inability to hang on to his 'pickin's', but Kipling rarely conceded so much to the sensibilities of his audience. Soldiers complaining in 'Tommy' and 'Shillin' a Day', the first and last ballads in the collection, of the official and civilian attitude to them as useful for the duration but to be put aside as uncouth in peacetime and paid a derisory pension when no longer serviceable, speak out bitterly and without compromise. There is perhaps a propaganda function in this, but in the *Barrack-Room Ballads* Kipling's consciousness of presenting the Tommy to the rest of the country does not predominate over his fascination with the man himself, and his desire to express his admiration of the ideal he feels him to represent, for its own sake. The impression of Tommy from the ballads is that he is human, hard-pressed and imperfect but admirable and even enviable, and that the life and philosophy learnt from the unique experience Kipling evokes are embodiments of the heroic.

All the aspects of this idea are expressed in 'The Young British Soldier'. The voice that speaks has the oracular tone of the experienced man giving the benefit of his wisdom to the youngster. He describes the recruit, and his expectations, and tells him the truth of the matter which he is about to discover. Nothing is left out, from the perils of the grog-shop, native women, disease, the climate, the sergeant, and marriage, to the way to behave when he finds himself terrified under fire, or left to the mercies of the enemy, wounded on the field. The advice the senior gives, and the experience and attitudes it reflects, have a ring of complete authenticity: if the recruit does as he is told here, he will behave like an ideal fighting unit, the pattern of discipline envisaged by the officers and the folks back home; but he will do so in each particular out of the soldier's basic and only motive, that of self-preservation. Even dying a hero's death, fighting to the last and choosing death before surrender, he will be preserving himself from a worse fate at the hands of the Afghan women. The succinct lesson of each verse is ironically driven home by the chorus, the beat of which is the marching chant of the parade-ground – 'Left, left, left-right-left' – so that the real and the unofficial training of the recruit is framed by a parody of the one, useless, thing that he has been taught officially to do:

If the wife should go wrong with a comrade, be loth
To shoot when you catch 'em – you'll swing, on my oath! –
Make 'im take 'er and keep 'er: that's Hell for them both,
An' you're shut o' the curse of a soldier.

Curse, curse, curse of a soldier,
Curse, curse, curse of a soldier,
Curse, curse, curse of a soldier,
So-oldier *of* the Queen! . . .

If your officer's dead and the sergeants look white,
Remember it's ruin to run from a fight:
So take open order, lie down, and sit tight,
And wait for supports like a soldier.

Wait, wait, wait like a soldier,
Wait, wait, wait like a soldier,
Wait, wait, wait like a soldier,
So-oldier *of* the Queen![57]

There is real knowledge and love here, so that Kipling's idealisation is neither condescending nor self-indulgent, but powerful and challenging. It is rooted in the people it is about and partly for, and speaks to them as equals while seeing them clearly as objects of admiration and even amusement. It does not compromise with the delicacy of the superior half of its audience, nor with common brutality, but honestly seeks truth to an experience and to an ideal. Kipling's ballads have the universality of application which arises out of truth to the specific situation in the best of folk-art, and they were accepted by the whole range of popular audiences of his time.

The tradition of the Victorian heroic ballad which went to produce them was itself a century long, and, as I hope I have shown, was so rooted in the popular tradition of ballad writing, and in the view of the world which that had always reflected, as to extend back indefinitely, via its connection with the mainstream of popular poetry. It dealt with the ideal hero of the common man, manifested as Jack Tar or as the private of the Buffs, but connected with the archetypes of folk-song, the warrior who was also the noble duke and the victorious moss-trooper of the traditional ballads. It stressed his often irrational sense of personal honour, and his usually tragic experience of life and death, while turning the stuff of Victorian colonial policy into popular legend. It sought to convey not so much a moral, but a view of the world and a set of assumptions which formed a code of belief and behaviour for imitation which is not completely separate from that of the ballads collected by Child. The ballad view of, for instance, the woman, as being strong and active in defence of her children and home, is preserved in it; and its assertion of its own values, and suspicion of those of the literary tradition, is that of all folk-art. The Victorian ballad departs from earlier assumptions of popular writing just as the Victorian community was changed by its environmental and social repatterning; in these particular examples, the crudity of the emotional effects, the extremes which were felt to be necessary and acceptable, and particularly the stress upon pathos and sentimentality, are reflections of changed popular taste.

Kipling in his best ballads transcended some of the limitations by which the artistic achievement of other poets in the tradition was confined to the level of effective rather than good writing. The chief of these was the stress upon the importance of the sentiments expressed, rather than upon the quality of the expression, which led to the pursuit of strong effects uninhibited by considerations of good taste. Kipling escaped this snare by the depth of his personal identification with the motives of the ballad-maker and the feelings of the common man which he expresses: his patriotism, historicism, superstition, and pugnacity, his sensitivity to rhythm, to exotic and homely beauty, to atmosphere and to the childlike excitement of exploration and adventure, and his very emotional commonness, and lack of intellectual profundity and discrimination, all fitted him for the role he adopted and gave his public ballad poetry the dimension of completeness which arises from the commitment of everything he possessed. This element poems like Tennyson's heroic ballads lack, for all their skill and conviction.

Kipling's other gift as an heroic ballad writer is of course his command of the web of interrelated technical developments which belonged to the form by the end of the century. He could draw upon country folk-song, Irish street ballads, Romantic and pre-Raphaelite literary ballads, to add effects to the mainstream of heroic popular ballad. In the recitation ballad he could surpass the originators, Scott and Macaulay, by the force of his historical imagination and the skill of his handling of the rhetorical patterns they established; and in the chorus song he understood and extended the incantatory power of the refrain which captures the imagination of the audience, and the possibilities of characterisation which lie in the use of stereotypes like his Tommy, who appear over and over again and add further episodes to the story of their many lives. Most important of all, the roots of his gift lie beneath the superficial divisions of class and distinctions of audience, so that the strength of his ballads is not confined to any section of the ballad varieties which he wrote, but is expressive of the unity which lay beneath them all and fed them from the same communal experiences and emotions.

4 *Ballads of the Common Man*

There is no sharp division between the ballads to be discussed here and the heroic pieces considered in the last chapter. The themes and situations of the heroic ballad are used in many of these examples; but here the ballads differ from those already discussed in two important ways. They embody a larger range of social attitudes, which distinguish one ballad from another with regard to the audience for which it was intended; while they are on the other hand united by an overriding uniformity of emotional tone. They all concern the life and ways of the ordinary citizen of the nineteenth century, and tend to idealise him, as did the heroic treatments of him as soldier or sailor; but while the imperialist, patriotic motive behind the heroic ballads was common to all classes, only occasionally touched and not materially altered by elements of class consciousness, these domestic ballads can be divided quite clearly, by the modern reader if not by the people for whom they were written, into ideal pictures made to suit the working man himself, and images of him cast into a mould which was intended to please a higher social group. The line between these two attitudes is clearer to us than it was in the nineteenth century, but it is by no means exactly where one would expect it; some writers and performers who were undeniably of working-class background wrote in a tone which resembles very closely that of the middle-class poets; and while many working-class audiences were led by their education and aspirations to reject all popular art in favour of the productions of the courtly tradition in music and poetry,[1] there was an appetite in the drawing-rooms of the respectable for more and more circumstantial accounts of lower-class life which was as remote from their own experience as grand opera was from the Welsh miners who loved it. All such stories, whether they dwell upon horrors, idealise the working man's skills and recreations, set him up as an invincible criminal or a model artizan, can be classed roughly together by the nature of the emotional reaction which they are designed to create. Where the songs and ballads of the last chapter strove to offer models and myths of bravery and heroic sacrifice, these seek to play upon sentiment and pathos. There are several motives behind the evocation of these responses, and other ingredients, such as sensational horror and comedy, may be added to them in various ways, but the overriding intention is to start a tear.

The first intimations of the emotional shading of the Victorian sentimental ballad are to be found in the drawing-room songs which were culled from opera and operetta on the London stage during the palmy days of musical theatre which began with the nineteenth century. The drawing-room or Royalty 'ballad', at its worst a few meaningless commonplaces of a vaguely pastoral tendency, set to a piano accompaniment simple enough for the least skilled performer, was a hybrid offshoot of declining romanticism, theatrical craftsmanship cut down for the amateur, and the beginnings of the entertainment industry. It catered for idle women. In the course of the century it developed a highly stylised pattern, devoid of artistic merit, but astonishingly economic and effective in its embodiment of the emotional keys of sentimentality. The archetype is 'Home Sweet Home', which is characteristic in its origin and exploitation as well as in its content. Its wailing, tear-laden tune was composed by Sir Henry Rowley Bishop, a man of the theatre who received his knighthood on the strength of this tune and others like it. The words were by John Howard Payne, and it first appeared in *Clari, or, The Maid of Milan* put on at Covent Garden in 1823. Its universal popularity was created largely by its later adoption by the soprano Adelina Patti, who sang it at Royalty ballad concerts, and indeed on every other occasion, until the end of her career. It illustrates the lack of any but the most primitive emotional connection between the words and images which is common in these songs:

> Mid pleasures and Palaces
> though we may roam,
> Be it ever so humble
> there's no place like home!
> A charm from the skies
> seems to hallow us there,
> Which seek through the world,
> is ne'er met with elsewhere.[2]

The 'palaces' of the first line are alliterative and emblematic, and there is a rhetorical suggestion of opulence beyond common experience, and indeed beyond morality, in using the word in the plural. The humility of the home is also an enjoyable idea, when it suggests modest comfort which is both moral and secure; and the vaguely religious 'charm from the skies' is really very considerate to 'hallow us there', and not demand that we venture out to 'seek through the world', or even take notice of its existence. By a slight extension of the idea we can also feel comfort in the conviction that other people's homes are equally desirable for them, and hallowed by such a name need not be improved by civic expenditure. There is room for such a drift of associations because there is scarcely even the barest logical framework to connect the notions. None but the music is needed: like 'Hearts of Oak' or 'Vitai Lampada', the song is an assemblage of talismanic words. It concentrates the emotional force of the sentimental ballad into lyric expression, in which shape it was universally popular. Its audiences and performers included both the lachrymose drunken navvy and the overfed and sentimental family circle.

'Home Sweet Home' uses in a vague and emotional way the impulse to idealise ordinary, everyday life which appears much more robustly in the early music-hall songs about urban society. These catered for the working-class section of the popular audience more or less exclusively. Their superiority to sentimental drawing-room songs is obvious. The quality of the words, in particular, has attracted the attention of critics who mention them in several different contexts, connecting them with the broadsides and with folk ballads, as well as with earlier theatrical songs. Reginald Nettel notes[3] that 'the music-halls idealized the working-class in the nineteenth century as the theatrical composers had idealized the sailor in the eighteenth'; E. D. Mackerness also points out[4] that one category of the early nineteenth-century broadside subject-matter was the song celebrating working-class people themselves, and their sports and pastimes. A. L. Lloyd, pursuing the development of the country folk-song into the flowering of the industrial folk-song in the nineteenth century, finds in it 'a synthesis of professional and traditional folk culture'. He discusses songs and ballads 'made and sung by men who are identical with their audience in standing, in occupation, in attitude to life, in daily experience', who wrote and sang about the work of the district in pit or mill, and about 'off-work scenes – ironic, hilarious or pathetic', in the northern music halls. The work songs came first, and the more general celebration of the local way of life followed, after about 1850.[5] In the next decade a note of protest was added to the ballads about such things as mining disasters, and it strengthened as the workers became conscious of themselves as members of their class and of a union. In London too the first flush of music-hall songs about the working man, which Willson Disher called[6] songs of life 'down our street', were celebratory, proud and often boisterous boasts of local prowess. There was, as in the north of England, a development of tone and focus in the 1860s, simple descriptions of life which were often meticulously and lovingly accurate, often comic and lighthearted, giving way to more serious, pathetic or protesting denunciation of living and working conditions.

At first, however, the stress was entirely upon enjoyment of identification with the group, through the description of it and the telling of stories about it. The songs were written by men whose professional status was little more than a modernisation of the ballad-maker's role in the community gathering, they were performed in the intimate, familiar atmosphere of the local musical tavern, and deliberately made use of local customs and in-jokes, and of the local dialect. The consideration of dialect in the Victorian ballad is by no means a straightforward matter, and one which must be considered in connection with these songs, and again in other contexts. M. J. C. Hodgart mentions it[7] as a characteristic of folk or popular art, of 'the little tradition', as he calls it, and cites it as one indication of the essentially multiple, fragmented nature of that tradition. But throughout the eighteenth century and the early part of the nineteenth the broadsides, which were one of the major organs for its dissemination on national and on local levels, were carefully set up to exclude dialect. They strove, often not quite successfully, to reach the level of literary English and avoid 'bad grammar' and illiterate spelling. Of the early miners' broadside ballads written between 1830 and 1860 when 'semi-professional musical performances in . . . beerhalls' were taking over from the broadsides, A. L. Lloyd quotes[8] seven famous examples, and only one of them is deliberately written in something other than standard English. Broadsides and very early music-hall songs printed in London about London life also tended to use standard English in their sardonic or celebratory descriptions of the cockney. Good examples are the popular and much-varied 'Twenty-five Shillings', and the charming 'The Way to Live', both of which catalogue with the true Victorian delight in detail the minute everyday circumstances of the urban poor. Such broadsides often betray that the writer and the printers thought and spoke another idiom, not only in that they are obliged to use local words for local trade and domestic objects which have no other names, but often also in spelling mistakes and rhymes which are not true in standard pronunciation. The collier ballads talk about pitprops, tubs and firedamp; and in 'The Way to Live'[9] there is the London rhyme 'Frills/eels' and whelks spelt phonetically as 'wilks'.

The songs used by performers in the music halls gradually discard the pretence to standard English, and move deliberately into the appropriate language. The proud use of local speech can be seen in the 'pitmatic' written and sung by the printer and comedian Joe Wilson, who died in 1874, and by Tommy Armstrong 'the pitman's poet', whose most prolific years were the last two decades of the century.[10] It also appears as the Lancashire vernacular, which had itself pretensions to literary beauties in the work of local poets like Ben Preston, Ben Brierley and Samuel Laycock, all textile workers; and of course the cockney character songs of the London stage. Although in print the cockney dialect may be not much more than an indication of what the singer will make of it, and in the very skilful songs of Gus Elen and Albert Chevalier, a careful ordering of sentence structure and word order, its coming was an indication of the assertion of pride in itself by the community who spoke it just as clearly as the movement into 'pitmatic' was in the north of England. In London printers were less convinced of the propriety of cockney than were the singers, and one can often find broadside and song-book printings of cockney music-hall songs which attempt to regularise the language, as if uncertain of its deliberateness or its validity. The northern songs much more obviously revel in the use of language and reference which is so peculiar to its locality as to mystify outsiders, thus reinforcing the pleasure of those who do understand. A. L. Lloyd quotes[11] a song called 'Little Chance' which has connections with ancient folk customs, in that it was used as the processional song by boys of the Tow Law area in County Durham when parading their Christmas-time 'tup', and has accretions of all sorts of local reference and jokes, about exhausted and impotent young husbands who work too hard at the pit, about boasters discomfited, even about mothers-in-law, but which is basically a song of praise for the pit pony whose name it bears:

> Noo, me nyem is Jackie Robinson, me nyem aa do advance.
> Aa drive a little gallowa', they call him Little Chance.
> Chancy hes two greasy feet, likewise a kittley back,
> An' gannin alang the gannin board, he myeks the chum 'uns knack.
>
> Aa was comin aroond the torn, titty fa la, titty fa lay.
> Chancy wadn't haad on, titty fa la, titty fa lay.
> The tubs they gie a click, aw got off the way at the switch,
> (Ye bugger!) Aa smashed the depitty's kist, titty fa la, titty fa lay.
> Tra la, lalalala, ower the wall's oot!

Equally firmly set in the dialect, though perhaps with more aspiration to the picturesque than to the esoteric, is the work of Samuel Laycock. He was a powerloom weaver, son of a handloom weaver, who took to the writing of songs and ballads to keep himself and his family when he was laid off during the cotton famine in the 1860s. A piece such as 'Bowton's Yard'[12] shows the same enjoyment of the language and life of the people it describes to themselves, though in a less carefree mood, since it was written in time of depression:

> At number two lives widow Burns – hoo weshes clooas for folk;
> Their Billy, that's her son, goes reawnd a beggin' wi' a poke;
> They sen hoo cooarts wi' Sam o' Neds, as lives at number three –
> It may be so, aw canno' tell, it matters nowt to me.
>
> At number three, reet facin' th' pump, Ned Grimshaw keeps a shop;
> He's Eccles-cakes, an' gingerbread, an' treacle beer, an' pop;
> He sells oat-cakes an' o, does Ned, he has boath soft an' hard,
> An' everybody buys of him 'at lives i' Bowton's yard . . .
>
> At number five aw live mysel', wi' owd Susannah Grimes,
> But dunno' loike so very weel, hoo turns me eawt sometimes;
> An' when aw'm in there's ne'er no leet, aw have to ceawer i' th' dark;
> Aw conno pay mi lodgin' brass, becose aw'm eawt o' wark.

Laycock's own gentle character seems often to show through his poems, but the stoic sentiments he expresses are always those of his audience. He was enormously popular as the voice of their distress, and also of their pride in their work when they had any to do.

The London songs seem on the whole to have a much stronger veneer of sophistication, although there are many which are as direct and simple as 'Bowton's Yard', such as Alfred Vance's 'Costermonger Joe':

> I'm Costermonger Joe, no money do I owe,
> For not a crust is had on trust by Costermonger Joe;
> But yes to barely live, why I must credit give,
> Or none would deal or grease the wheel with Costermonger Joe.
> I'm Costermonger Joe, and tho' I'm rather slow,
> I find the fast don't longer last than Costermonger Joe,
> The steady going pace just suits the human race,
> It's better to stop than gallop and drop, says Costermonger Joe.[13]

More often quoted and remembered, however, is a song like Sam Cowell's 'Ratcatcher's Daughter' (written by the Rev. Edward Bradley,

'Cuthbert Bede') where the enjoyment of the details of life narrated is only one element, and the characteristic slant of humorous exaggeration and sardonic irony can be seen:

> Not long ago, in Vestminstier,
> There liv'd a Ratcatcher's daughter,
> She didn't quite live in Vestministier,
> But t'other side of the vater.
> Her father caught rats, and she sold sprats,
> All round and about that quarter;
> And the gentlefolks all did lift there hats
> To the ratcatcher's pretty little daughter.[14]

The main joke in this first stanza is one for the locals, very funny for the inhabitants of Lambeth who frequented the Canterbury, where it was sung in the 1850s, but not making much sense to those who could not be tickled by calling an inhabitant of that rough area one who lived 'not quite in Westminster'.

Some odd things have been said about Sam Cowell's cockney songs, suggesting that the song quoted here, and his two other tragi-comic ballads, 'Villikins and his Dinah' and 'Lord Lovel', were 'a conscious imitation of the crudities of broadside and ballad-sheet songs . . . though the broadsheet itself, for the most part, did no more than reproduce the popular songs and verses of the moment. A circular movement.'[15] The intercourse between the broadsides and music-hall performance was indeed reciprocal, but the derivation of these songs from ballads extant on broadsides cannot possibly be described as 'imitation of the crudities' therein. Both 'Villikins and his Dinah' and 'Lord Lovel' are derived, unusually, from the country folk-song tradition, but their manifestations as broadsides and music-hall songs is not merely a mocking burlesque. Rather it is a conversion of old material to new tastes and settings, which serves chiefly to confirm the continuity of the old and new traditions. For the taste of the townspeople there is a superimposed layer of comedy, as well as the cockney accent; but the intention is not to destroy the tragic force of the old stories, but rather to include it in the blend of sentiment edged with humour and irony which is the characteristic tone of the cockney character-song and ballad. New material which uses the London scene as its setting, such as 'The Ratcatcher's Daughter' and Harry Clifton's 'Polly Perkins', has the same blend, which Leslie Shepard describes as 'irrepressible high spirits in dealing with tragedy . . . a curious warm-hearted sentimentality under the hardness and vulgarity.'[16] I would rather put the weight upon the restraint which the humour and the hardness place upon the sentiment, often adding greatly to its force. Other critics have picked up the apparent lack of feeling in cockney songs which joke about hardships, and have seen them either as a snobbish attack upon those who speak with a London accent, or as evidence of their brutishness. Edward Lee, following Willson Disher,[17] quotes as evidence of this trait Sam Cowell's singing of 'The Lost Child', in which a female who sells red herrings is bewailing the loss of her obviously very nasty and undesirable son Billy, and showing her blindness to the implied sensibilities of respectable folk – that is, by a further implication, of the audience:

> 'Why should he leave the court, where he was better off
> Than all the other boys?
> With two bricks, an odd shoe, nine oyster shells,
> And a dead kitten by way of toys?'

Mr Lee fails to point out the vital fact, which Willson Disher did make clear, that this is a version of Thomas Hood's comic poem 'The Lost Heir', and that Cowell sang it at Evans's song and supper rooms, to an audience of men-about-town far removed from that of the Canterbury in Lambeth. Both writer and audience were in a position to laugh at the common man rather than idealise him, and their humour has little to do with the tradition of cockney song in which Sam Cowell shared on other occasions. The sophistication of comic ballad-writers like Hood, and their exploitation of the cockney music-hall models, is discussed later, and does not invalidate the real relationship of the originals to the life of their audiences. Peter Davidson makes an important point when he comments in *Songs of the British Music Hall* upon 'Villikins and his Dinah'.[18] He takes the two-sided, serio-comic nature of the song, especially as originally sung by Frederick Robson before Sam Cowell took it up, as pinpointing an essential characteristic of music-hall song, the ability of the performer and the audience to accept equally the pathos, even tragedy, of the story, and the humour of the burlesque which is presented almost simultaneously. 'Robsonian' changes of mood within one song, irony and sympathy perpetually undercutting each other, are vital in the enriching vividness of the performance of these pieces, which Mr Davidson relates to modern theatrical techniques.

The cockney songs of the music halls moved easily from the description of life 'down our street' to picking out certain individuals and types for special treatment. The style of performance, in which the singer impersonated the hero of his song, led naturally to such a development. Some singers, looking primarily for comic material, featured in their acts songs about certain trades, like Arthur Lloyd's 'The Street Musician' and 'The Organ Grinder', and Leybourne's 'The Mousetrap Man'. Other singers, and these same men on other occasions, added songs and characterisations to older and more complex legendary figures, who represent human aspirations and obsessions of several kinds. One cockney hero whose many manifestations are clearly an expression of real admiration and vicarious pleasure through self-identification is the successful, self-assured criminal. The criminal hero has of course a long history in popular mythology in London and elsewhere, in story and song and broadsides.[19] At his mildest he is just the city man who is sharper in his wits than the country bumpkin and so runs rings round him for fun or profit; and this figure is associated in turn with the shrewd commoner who outwits authority in many ancient ballads, such as the tanner of Tamworth in *E.S.P.B.* no. 273. Many songs make fun of the convention by turning it round, and letting the countryman discomfit the cockney, as in Gus Elen's 'A Cove Wot's Lived in London all his Life!' Far more blend in a little humour with a characterisation which is basically admiring, and which raises the sharp man, the one who gets away with it, to the status of an idol. In broadside and melodrama the prototype is Jack Sheppard, closely followed by Dick Turpin; but the famous criminal of the music halls is Sam Hall.[20] This murderous chimney-sweep was based on the broadside character Jack All, which can be traced back to older broadsides about the pirate Captain Kidd, where the unusual stanza-form is already established. Sam Hall was created by an ex-compositor, W. G. Ross, at Vauxhall and in the Cyder Cellars and the Coal Hole, in the 1840s. He became so famous in the role that he was never able to succeed in any other. The song was not a typical nor an ordinary production, and indeed became a legend expressive of the corruption and immorality which attached to the fashionable Caves of Harmony in the minds of writers who knew only the relative respectability of the later music hall. The extant versions of the song hardly justify their horror, or their inclination to associate it exclusively with debauched gentlemen rather than with the patrons of the less fashionable halls, where it was also sung. Its strength and fascination lies in its combination of unmitigated realism, such as is common in the early lower-class songs, with the power and the intention of shocking. The intention to shock was important in later songs which developed out of these. In 'Sam Hall' the condemned murderer baldly and blasphemously tells his story, with a chilling directness and detail:

> They've shut me up in quod
> For killing of a sod,

and they are going to hang him:

> The Sherriff he'll come too
> With all his ghastly crew,
> Their bloody work to do,
> Damn their eyes!

He is not, however, repentant:

> And now I'm going to hell, going to hell!
> And now I'm going to hell, going to hell!
> And now I'm going to hell,
> But what a bloody sell
> If you all go there as well!
> Damn your eyes!

The pleasure of identification here is not only the thrill of enjoying something we would never do ourselves, but also the admiration of his careless strength and defiance of the worst that can happen, defiance also of those who seek to judge and put themselves above him. It is psychologically truthful and satisfactory, and its exaggeration, the distillation of experience into a drama of black and white, is an ancient ballad technique, no more unreal in the Victorian context than it is in 'Edward' or 'Lambkin'.

Later songs of the criminal hero which belong primarily to the working-class patrons of the music halls are less extreme than 'Sam Hall', and give the hero the more tangible success in his battle against society of not being caught out. He is 'fly', he wears the smart clothes of the 'high mob' rather than Sam Hall's chimney-sweep's tatters, and his crimes are chiefly concerned with other people's property. He struts and grins and winks, is laughed at and tolerated and acts as a release for impulses which, if less extreme than those of Sam Hall, are nevertheless dangerous. The Lions Comiques had several songs of this kind: G. W. Hunt, who wrote 'We Don't Want to Fight', produced 'A Good Job Too! Serve Him Right' for Herbert Campbell, and 'Bloomsbury Square' for Leybourne, while The Great Vance had 'Chickaleary Cove', which also incidentally demonstrates that the cockney dialect was sometimes as deliberately and thickly laid on, in the songs of the sixties, as an assertion of local solidarity and pride, as any of the northern dialects:

I'm a Chickaleary bloke with my one-two-three
Vitechapel was the willage I was born in;
To catch me on the hop,
Or on my tibby drop,
You must vake up wery early in the mornin'.
I've got a rorty gal, also a knowing pal,
And merrily together we jog on.
And I doesn't care a flatch
So long as I've a tach,
Some pannum in my chest – and a tog on![21]

The song which hinges on a catchy chorus-line is ideal for this character, who makes great play with new legalistic phrases such as 'Allowed to be drunk on the premises', or with his own outraged innocence as he repeatedly explains that he is 'Looking for the owner', or openly praises his own dubious skills with 'Gently does the trick!'

The successful bender of the laws in his own direction is often, in the 1860s and 1870s, an aspect of the costermonger, for he held an anomalous position in lower-class society. The costers were a very tight-knit group who were always living on the very edge of respectability, not exactly part of the underworld, but not exactly honest either, and if successful they presented the image of prosperous independence and freedom from care to every hard-up apprentice who envied their flash talk and clothes. By the end of the century, when the criminal heroes had largely died out as the music hall became more and more staid, respectable, family entertainment, the coster had lost his dangerous, raffish dimension and become the representative of a working-class way of life which was somewhat remote from reality, and was viewed not only idealistically, but through a subtle veil of nostalgia. The mixture of pathos and sentiment with the humour became ever stronger, in the work of the two great coster singers, Albert Chevalier and Gus Elen, although their better songs did retain to the end some of the toughness and restraint which the admixture of humour gave. Both rose to fame in the 1890s. Max Beerbohm indicated the difference between them when he complained that 'the homely humour of James Fawn and Bessie Belwood was superseded, ere long, by Chevalier, with his new and romantic method; by Gus Elen, with his realistic psychology and his admirably written songs.'[22] Chevalier's romanticism sprang from his not belonging to the world which he describes: he was an actor who sang his own cockney songs at private parties until his friends, and lack of work, persuaded him on to the halls in 1891, when he made such a success with

'The Coster's Serenade' that he could not escape again. His best coster songs were all produced before he first appeared or in the next few years, including 'The Future Mrs. 'Awkins', for which he wrote the words and music himself, 'Knocked 'em in the Old Kent Road' with a tune by Charles Ingle, his brother, then in 1892 two more to Ingle's tunes, 'Our Little Nipper' and 'My Old Dutch', and in 1894 'Wot's the Good of Annyfink?' and 'It ain't exactly wot 'e says'. The character he assumes is usually crossed in love:

> The coster, wot yer 'ears about in songs
> As allus talks about 'is gal, 'er beauty and 'is wrongs

is how A. Ellis describes him in a song sung by Gus Elen, which also mentions Chevalier's appearing in a blaze of 'pearlies' and limelight. His theatricality in such songs was obvious: they retained only as much contact with reality as was necessary to make it possible for the audience to identify with the figure on the stage, dazzlingly transforming themselves into creatures of glamour, whose miseries and awkwardnesses were quaint and pathetic, releasing a flood of warm easy emotion: nostalgia over fictional trips in donkey shays to 'the Welsh 'Arp, which is 'Endon way', or pride over the precocious child who 'stands so 'igh, that's all', or whatever self-consciously simple pleasure he was recounting. His best song was probably 'My Old Dutch', for which the characterisation was of an old man around whom he afterwards created a play, illustrating the way in which there is an understood story behind many of these songs which have little apparent narrative content but which draw upon tradition and convention for their context. The song itself is not tragic or dramatic; its mood is sentimental, and the effect is created rather by quietness and understatement than by exaggeration, or any suggestion of stress or danger to the speaker. A tradition reported by Colin MacInnes[23] has it, however, that the staging of the song added this element by reference to an ancient grievance of the poor: Chevalier appeared as an old man about to be separated from his wife as they entered the workhouse. In the song he makes only one point – that his wife is and has been his friend, his 'pal'. The only humour he uses is to maintain the evenness of tone and understatement, balancing the stanza which proclaims her a 'sweet fine old gal . . . An' wot a *pal*!' with one which allows she is not an angel, being inclined to 'A-jawin' till it makes yer smart.' He dedicated the song to 'my old friend and brother actor, William Macintosh', and clearly intended it to be taken very seriously.

Gus Elen, working with better lyrics and from a personally intimate knowledge of the ways of life he is talking about, was able to go much further in this direction, making indirect use of the humorous side of the cockney figure without the traces of condescension which mar most of Chevalier's jokes, and avoiding the glamorous and overstated characterisation in more of his numbers. His characters were not simply realistic representations of ordinary people, but their distancing from the commonplace was more subtle than Chevalier's hammy glamorisations. His song of married life is superior to 'My Old Dutch':

> We treads this parf o' life as every married couple ought,
> Me and 'er – 'er and me;
> In fact we're looked on as the 'appiest couple down the court,
> Me and 'er – 'er and me.
> I must acknowledge that she 'as a black eye now and then,
> But she don't care a little bit, not she;
> It's a token of affection – yuss, in fact that is love
> Wiv me and 'er – 'er and me.
>
> For she's a lady – yuss, and I'm a gentleman,
> We're boaf looked up to, and deserves ter be;
> For she's a lady – yuss, and I'm a toff –
> Me and 'er – 'er and me.
>
> 'Cos we keeps straight, we 'as to put up wiv some sneers and slurs,
> Me and 'er – 'er and me;
> Our 'oneymoon ain't over yet, though we've been married years,
> Me and 'er – 'er and me.
> We don't purfess to be no better than the rest o' folks,
> But the wife's a bit pertickler, don't yer see,
> So we goes to church on Sunday, like the village blacksmith did,
> Me and 'er – 'er and me.[24]

Any trace of condescension or insincerity would turn this idyll into an insult; but as it is there is respect and affection and precise observation in the song, all expressed in cliché and commonplace phrase, according to character.

Willson Disher, seeing Elen perform in a special revival presentation of the old stars of the halls, shortly before he died in 1940, said he performed 'exactly as he had always performed, the clothes he wore as a market porter or a dustman were such as had never been seen in our streets within ordinary memory. Yet there was such an air of authenticity about him that you felt sure these were what he had faithfully observed in his early, his very early, childhood.'[25] He turned his characters into heroes by seeking to evoke the smile of sympathy and recognition for them as suffering the unheroic, indeed the ignominious, tribulations of everyday life on an heroic scale: physically tiny, with a rasping little voice and a real cockney accent, and a solemn, straight-faced manner and presence, he presented potentially funny songs about all the standard vulgar jokes, such as the hen-pecked husband and the jilted lover, so as to bring out and thus to relieve the real pain from which they sprang. The lyrics of Edgar Bateman and Fred Gilbert, old-fashioned cockney writers, and the tunes of George Le Brunn, became in his hands haunted stories of men struggling for their self-respect and dignity in the press of working-class London life, and finding it just about possible to survive, and even occasionally to smile. 'Never Introduce Your Donah to a Pal', the song which begins by glancing at the Chevalier image of a costermonger, goes on to tell a sad story of betrayal, in which the coster represented by the singer tells of his desertion by his business partner and his girl, whom he trustingly introduced to each other, with the result that they went off together to marry and set up in business, cutting him out with the finally insulting gift of a large piece of their wedding cake. The story is funny, but the figure in it who would normally be laughed at is pathetically present as the story-teller. A similar tension is used in all his best songs, whether the character is the postman who recounts a day out with his family which was a series of disasters and slights, but who touchingly maintains 'I'm glad we 'ad a nice quiet day', or the equally stubbornly unrealistic, funny and sad townee who extols the country views he would have from his back yard 'if it wasn't for the 'ouses in between.' Even in 'It's a Great Big Shame', and ''Arf a Pint of Ale', which lean more heavily on humour, and 'Down the road', more openly sentimental, the exaggeration is not a distortion, and affection and concern are present in the singer's and the audience's attitude to the characters more strongly than is superiority. The strength of these songs, apart from some good tunes, is their adherence to the realistic detail which was enjoyed in the earliest cockney songs.[26] The suffering husband Jim, the object of the singer's worried account in 'It's a Great Big Shame', is described in vivid detail, both before and after his defeat by his wife:

> Now, Jim was class – 'e could sing a decent song,
> And at scrappin' 'e 'ad won some great renown;
> It took two coppers for ter make 'im move along,
> An' annuver six to 'old the feller dahn.

But today when I axes would 'e come an' 'ave some beer,
To the doorstep on tip-toe 'e arrives;
'I daresn't,' says 'e – 'Don't shout, cos she'll 'ear –
I've got ter clean the windows an' the knives.'

On a Sunday morn, wiv a dozen pals or more,
'E'd play at pitch and toss along the Lea;
But now she bullies 'im a-scrubbin' o' the floor –
Such a change, well, I never did see.
Wiv a apron on 'im, I twigged 'im on 'is knees
A-rubbin' up the old 'arf-stone;
Wot wiv emptyin' the ashes and a-shellin' o' the peas,
I'm blowed if 'e can call 'isself 'is own![27]

At the revival performance in the 1930s which Willson Disher saw was an enterprising film-maker who took all the stars he could persuade to a studio and recorded some of their songs. Gus Elen went through several favourites of his old repertoire, including this one, and the film clip shows vividly the powerful feeling with which he invested these apparently simple jokes. His movements are stiff and stylised, but not from age or awkwardness, for they exactly match the poses in which he appears on the cover of the song printed in the 1890s. The gestures seem to contain a violence which is barely controlled, and breaks out at the high points of the song in motions of frustration and anger: he holds a stubby claw hammer, with which he threatens and just prevents himself from attacking the infuriating little woman whom he vividly conjures up. The inarticulate conflict of the sexes, and the wounded jealousy of the discarded best friend, are much more than a joke for him and for his audience. The humour serves a strengthening purpose, and allows the strong feeling to be implicit, giving expression to emotions neither the character nor the audience could analyse or state directly.

Other singers were working in the same, still very fruitful, convention of reference, language and characterisation, and like Gus Elen were maintaining the toughness and tension of contact with everyday life, and with the motifs of the folk tradition, in their songs. Just as much of the tradition of country folk-song belonged to and was passed on by women, so there were several women among the cockney singers. The first was Bessie Bellwood, who had a range of coster and cockney female characters to match those of the men; in 1887, for instance, her great success was with a roistering flash song called 'What Cheer 'Ria!' about a cockney girl who is thrown out of the pit of a music hall; but she was equally successful with Joseph Tabrar's song 'He's going to marry Mary

Ann', in the character of a wide-eyed bride-to-be who gleefully lists the anticipated delights of her married life in a manner intended to provoke a sentimental smile of sympathy and recognition:

> He's bought a bed and a table too,
> A big tin dish for making stew,
> A large flat-iron to iron his shirt,
> And a flannel, and a scrubbing brush to wash away the dirt.
> And he's bought a pail and basins three,
> A coffee-pot, a kettle, and a teapot for the tea,
> And a soup-bowl and a ladle,
> And a gridiron and a cradle,
> And he's going to marry Mary Ann, that's *me*!
> He's going to marry Mary Ann![28]

Jenny Hill's blend of humour and sentiment leant more strongly towards the pathetic, possibly because, like Elen, she could make good use of her tiny stature in such roles, often appearing as a little boy or girl of the streets, but also as a sluttish 'Coffee Shop Gal' and as the ill-treated wife who sings a beautifully poised tragi-comic song:

> He's out on the fuddle, with lots of his pals,
> Out on the fuddle, along with other gals;
> He's always on the fuddle,
> While I'm in such a muddle –
> But I mean to have a legal separation.'[29]

The latest, and to most commentators the greatest, of the female cockney singers was Marie Lloyd, though all admit that her pre-eminence cannot be demonstrated from surviving evidence. Peter Davidson's comments[30] on her appeal seem the most convincing and apposite: he cites T. S. Eliot's claim that she had a 'capacity for expressing the soul of the people' and of 'giving expression to the life of that audience', but goes on to point out that in her case it is necessary to notice the difference in response between the audiences of the West End music halls, who enjoyed her 'blue' qualities, and those of the working-class halls, where she had to moderate her suggestiveness considerably because she was 'regarded virtually as the epitome of what the East End audience considered to be best in itself.' To the working people she represented an ideal, which did not include smuttiness, while to the more sophisticated West End the cockney characters she portrayed were part of the enjoyable naughtiness of a visit to the music hall. Chevalier similarly played the cockney differently for different audiences, and indeed Sam Cowell had done so forty years before.

A different kind of tension between singer and audience operated in the male impersonators' performances, and their songs invite a rather more complicated response than either identification or amusement. Vesta Tilley had a series of character songs which subtly played off audiences' expectations of amusement from the basic unreality of her masculine disguise against characterisations and stories which were funny, but which also recognised the pathos in the poses and pretences of the young men she imitated. Even such an apparently slight, hard song as Ella Shields's 'Burlington Bertie from Bow' has implicit a story of tragedy, and in the stoically maintained lightness of its telling there is a moving comment upon the character. The song is in its way as extreme and shocking as the story of Sam Hall, and the hero who emerges is as socially undesirable: the nonchalant beggar, Bert, 'So long without food, I've forgot where my face is', who always gets his cigars in the Strand, but has to be careful while he's about it that people don't tread on his hand, is as defiant, irreclaimable and damaging to good order as the murdering sweep, and his story is told just as firmly from the popular, anti-authoritarian point of view. The cast of pathos which replaces the profane relish of 'Sam Hall' indicates a change of taste rather than of point of view.

In these character-songs the changing taste of the audience was not necessarily damaging, artistically: the coster songs, and all the cockney characterisations, kept in touch with the sources of strength in popular art, and kept the healthy balance of scepticism and self-sufficiency through taking a comic view of the pathetic and tragic events of everyday life they recounted. They tended, however, to neglect the narrative patterns of early music-hall songs and move rather towards a simpler character presentation, keeping pace with the development of the comic music-hall songs of less specialised kinds, which concentrated more and more upon the impact of a catchy chorus and used fewer and fewer verses, losing all pretence of a story or indeed coherent words of any kind. The sentimental and pathetic ballads which dominated the music hall in the later decades of the century were of a different kind, related much more closely to the sentimental recitation pieces than to the character-songs. They make full use of narrative, telling elaborate and detailed stories, often with settings which like those of the character-songs were drawn from the life of the London working classes, but which were very differently viewed and treated. Their prevailing tone was that of the sentimental songs described at the beginning of the chapter, mingled with an exclamatory and sensational appearance of social concern, so that the description of lower-class life was taken over to form the background to more and more sensational stories, which exploit its dramatic and tragic situations for sentimental effect.

The extreme exaggeration of such pieces can be seen as part of their popular nature, for popular art most usually deals in absolutes, in statements of emblematically extreme cases which embody in a large and final form the concerns and pressures from which they spring. The traditional ballads have stories of an extreme, often a violent, kind, figures who are not realistic and endings which are tragically or romantically final and absolute. The early-nineteenth-century popular melodramas worked with similarly extreme statements, so that the good are perfect and the bad epitomise evil, and all the characters go through extremes of trial and distress to reach inevitable happy endings. Realistic compromise and artistic understatement are both equally out of place in works which operate within such frameworks of convention. Similarly the sensational and sentimental ballads of the music halls developed a pattern of conventions of expression and story which were far from realistic, but expressed the lives of their audience in a peculiarly stylised manner.

The earliest examples of these ballads in the music halls are either closely related to the sensational broadsides, the stories of famous murderers and their last dying speeches which continued to find a ready audience and sale when the broadsides were dying out, or to the popular melodrama, or they are derived from the American songs which were made popular in Britain by the vogue for troupes of nigger minstrels. The last was also a link with the sentimentality of the drawing-room, for while broadside goodnights were irredeemably vulgar, and the music halls and cheap theatres were distinctly low, minstrels were acceptable to middle-class audiences who could identify them with a thoroughly respectable feeling of outrage about American slavery, and so feel they were performing a social service in patronising the entertainments and weeping over the sentimental songs of groups of men who were, more often than not, white Americans, or even Englishmen, blacked up.

The minstrels, whose early history is recorded elsewhere,[31] moved between the halls and the concert platform, where middle-class audiences who would not go near a theatre received them with joy; and their songs were eagerly taken up by numerous amateurs, who took the tradition of home entertainment built upon theatrical songs to its logical conclusion by forming themselves into imitations of professional troupes and putting on full-dress minstrel performances. Songs dealing, like theirs, in extremes of sentiment, sensation, and pathos, also moved between various levels of the popular audience in the repertoires of certain other performers who made places for themselves in several kinds of entertainment. Albert Chevalier's acceptability to all classes was a personal matter, but performers like Bransby Williams (whose most famous piece was 'The Green Eye of the Little Yellow God') were acceptable not for their personal gifts or background but because their material was common to all. There was an established style of 'act' for presenting these ballads which could be transposed from music hall to concert room, even to church hall or private house. It was used by professionals, singers like Jenny Hill and reciters like Williams, and by amateurs. The ingredients were a strong voice, and a magic lantern: the performer stood in strong spot-light or in dramatic silhouette, and a series of slides depicting scenes in the ballad were thrown on the wall or screen behind, while the artist delivered the ballad with all the dramatic gesturing and vocal acrobatics at his or her command. The more humble amateur might have to do without the illustrations, in a private performance, but would strive to make up the loss by added colour conned from the many guides to recitation which were available.

The subjects of these recitals and recitations, whether deriving from the English or the American tradition, were extreme examples of the swing of popular taste to sentiment and sensation. The American 'weepie' ballads[32] were perhaps the more extreme, but the difference is of degree rather than of kind. There is perhaps, too, a spectrum of exaggeration within the English songs, the more extreme belonging to the lower end of the popular audience, but the minstrel songs from America which the middle classes loved were as exaggerated as any. They fitted neatly into the established range of sentimental subjects, taking up the early theatrical exploitation of 'Home Sweet Home', and concentrating particularly upon family relationships. No more than in the tragic and often bloody family clashes of the traditional ballads were domestic relationships looked upon as sources of happy security; more often they were seen as actual or potential bereavements. The centre of the home and family is mother, in these songs, and mother is perpetually threatened by the departure of her children, their ungrateful disrespect or disregard, by misfortune, illness, old age, and death. There would almost seem to be more desire to whip up feelings of filial guilt than to sing the mother's praises. The Mohawk Minstrels exhort us, in a song by Harry Hunter, to

> '. . . go, my darling boy,
> Win your fortune and enjoy,
> But remember ev'ry honest man's your brother:
> And never let your pride,
> Push affection on one side,
> *Never be ashamed of your mother.*'[33]

Exhortation has always proved in vain, as far as the heroes of the ballads on this subject are concerned, for when they remember the advice 'Don't leave your mother when her hair turns grey', or, in one case, 'Don't leave your father, boy', an injunction delivered by the mother herself, they hurry home only in time to pluck a violet from the grave. Some, like the travelling actor in 'Your mother, Jack, died here today', are unable even to do that, but must follow their calling with grief in their hearts.

An associated theme, but one which is English as much as American, and springs from an important aspect of working-class life in England, Australia and America, is that of emigration, and the consequent parting of the young and fit from their families and friends. The Victorian working man was continually urged to emigrate, and if he went to the goldfields or to any frontier settlement, he left everyone behind. Songs on this subject, related to the old laments at parting occasioned by the pressgang or by transportation, have often much more of a story than the minstrel 'mammy' ballads, which simply reiterate emotive words, and they frequently show the survival of broadside narrative style in the way they tell it. An example is 'Going Home', written by J. Harrington, composed and sung on the halls by Leo Dryden, whose 'The Miner's Dream of Home' is a more famous working of the same theme. 'Going Home' begins

> In the days of the past I was forced to leave home,
> In the mines of Australia to toil;
> For hard times at home sent me far o'er the sea,
> There was no work for the sons of the soil.[34]

The clumsiness of the last line takes the song straight back to the broadside hack striving to express something of real experience as best he can in terms of the cliché and convention which lies to hand, and marks the song off from the polished banalities of the young Tin Pan Alley with which the minstrels often made do. It goes on to tell of the twelve years the hero has been away, his lucky strike, and his intention of going home; but he is sad because he went with a school friend, who was murdered, and he now has to take the news and a share of their strike back to his bereaved family. He says goodbye to his mates, and

> Then as rough honest hands held my own in their grip
> Somehow the 'good-bye' wouldn't come,
> We knew there was 'one' who'd 'gone home' long before,
> 'Twas my own dear dead school-mate and chum.

It is not far from such sentiments to Tom Brown and the public-school code, yet the theme of emigration and the lumber-camps and gold-fields is essentially lower class: the sentiments, independent of variations in story and in specific attitudes, pervade the whole of popular poetry without distinction and with little change.

The nineteenth century also continued to provide experience which ensured the continuation of the parting lament for soldiers and for sailors, and in these the mingling of all themes into one emotional appeal, which is remarked by Michael Turner in introducing his anthology of parlour song,[35] can be seen. The patriotic hero of soldier songs often, as we noticed when examining him in the last chapter, spares a thought and a tear in the midst of peril for his home, and for his mother; similarly the mother sitting at home sorrowing for her departed son (she largely replaces the mourning sweetheart of earlier folk-song) is proud of his military prowess. The last drop of sentimental appeal is wrung from this situation by means of sensational action and coincidence; in, for instance, the song 'The Shipwrecked Sailor', which goes to the air of 'Don't leave your mother when her hair turns grey',[36] a drowning sailor lad clings to the wreckage of his ship, and before joining his father in a watery grave prays for his aged mother, safe in her 'dear old cottage home':

> Upon the wild wild ocean, far away from home,
> How bitterly the sailor cried, amid the surging foam,
> May God protect my mother she will break her heart for me,
> When she hears that I am sleeping in the deep deep sea.

The other element of the family situation which is used in the ballads of sentiment is the suffering child, and ballads about children in variously dire situations are common on both sides of the Atlantic, at all levels of popular taste, and in combination with most other aspects of the idealisation of everyday life. The heroic child, dying for his country or for some less specific ideal in military action or adventure, has already appeared in the last chapter, and could indeed, in the role of the idealised schoolboy be said to embody the drawing-room ideal of heroism. Lower-class children appear more often in ballads of pathos and sentiment, and are particularly useful as victims. The temperance reform movement, which exploited the popular song for all it was worth by way of emotional appeal, and produced a body of balladry which will be considered in more detail in the next chapter, was particularly fond of the suffering child. The waif, plunged in poverty by drunken parents or by lack of any parents at all, is nevertheless an indigenous inhabitant of the world of music-hall song, where he or she was received with a many-levelled response similar to that which enjoyed tragedy and burlesque at the same time in early songs like 'Villikins' and 'Lord Lovel'.[37] The pathos of 'Th' Little Sawt Lad', a northern music-hall song by Jacob Kershaw, or of Jenny Hill's 'The City Waif' (words by Harrington, the writer of 'Going Home') is unashamed and undiluted:

> Alone, in the streets of London, my papers I sell each day,
> And notice each sight around me, though only a 'waif and stray'.
> I ain't 'ad much eddication – it's wasted on sich as *me* –
> Except what the Ragged School gave me, or else – the reformatry!
> ''Ere you are sir! The *Star* sir? A tanner! Ain't got any change-bank's struck –
> What! Keep it all? Thankee kindly! I'll spit on it, jest for luck.'
> Eh – what cabby? Mind yer 'orse? Yus! My eye, but this 'eres all gay –
> Oh! bother the *Star* and *Ekker* – 'ere's a tanner, and no outlay!
>
> Refrain I'd never no mother nor father to love me, like some I see;
> And what does this big, cold world care for a poor little chap like me?
> Out of my bed in a doorway, Bobbies all hunt me down –
> And no home have I beneath the sky, but the streets of London Town![38]

But the audience's serious response to these, and to such later songs as the American 'Won't you buy my pretty flowers?' was probably enjoyed all the more for its piquancy in the atmosphere of comfort and good fellowship generated by the music hall. A character-song by E. W. Rogers, sung by a coster singer, Alec Hurley, as 'Thick Ear'd Jim', a tough who rose to be chairman of a 'friendly lead' at a singing pub, makes the point succinctly:

> People calls me 'Jim' and I ain't the least put out,
> All their pals they're bringin' here to yer me singing:
> A pafetic song is my 'forty' ne'er a doubt,
> Where little kids git dyin' in the snow.
> When they're six pots strong I can make 'em cry like rain,
> Tears go patter-pitter in their mild-and-bitter –
> They gets thirsty and says, 'Fill them pots again!'[39]

The songs were related to experience, and accepted as conveying certain solemn platitudes about life, but their prime purpose was the pleasure which the audience would feel at the recital of the story and its ideal resolution.

The same pleasure taken in the rehearsal of grotesquely extreme situations of peril and distress, and their resolution in death and destruction, marks the music-hall end of the spectrum of songs based on melodramatic situations which make no pretence of applying, other than romantically, to the lives and experience of the poor. These do sometimes take situations and figures from the streets of the town, but they treat them in exactly the way in which they also handle wildly unlikely disasters which might befall only the wealthier classes. The stress is upon the dramatic and sensationally pathetic or tragic capital which can be made of the situation for the purpose of evoking a pleasurable thrill, or a tear. The connection with the popular melodrama is obvious in these songs, and was often apparent in the elaborately theatrical staging of each as a 'dramatic interlude' or a 'scena'. Their situations and themes are those of the melodrama as described by Michael Booth, with the added compression of the already unlikely plot of such plays occasioned by cramming it into a ballad, often into a single stanza. As in the melodramas, the view of the world presented is recognisably that of folk-art. The typical figures presented are not such as would be part of the audiences', or of anybody's, daily experience, but they nevertheless represent powerful emotional categories. Booth described the melodrama of 1800–70 as 'genuinely *popular* theatre' which was 'a true social reflector of its times . . . portraying industrial unrest as well as urban squalor' and 'the upper classes as heartless oppressors'. Manipulating stock figures, the pathetic old couple, the ruined gentleman, the villainous squire, and, in particular, the innocent child victim and the active, maternal, deeply wronged heroine, 'melodrama appeals directly to the most elemental feelings of the audience . . . it . . . goes straight to its emotional and physical point and never deviates from there.'[40]

These same figures and stories, handled in a very similar way, appear in the melodramatic ballads which flourished after 1870, when the melodrama itself had become a rather more sophisticated entertainment. Their hallmark is extreme and uncompromising action; but in some senses they might be said to differ from the popular melodrama in their social attitudes, which are more traditional, less articulate, than the deliberate championing of the worker which appears in some of the plays. The melodramatic ballads had little to do with the worker: those which are set in lower-class life use only its extreme end, the outcasts of society who were as familiar to, and also as firmly separate from, the ordinary artizan as were the carriage folk. Two similar examples of this kind are 'The Workhouse Door' and 'On the Bridge'. The latter, a very popular piece, is narrated by a man standing on one of the bridges of London, watching the desperate of the city go by, until in the final stanza one of them finally jumps into the river. The same observant but passive narrator seems to be at work in 'The Workhouse Door', where he recounts his experiences on two occasions, separated, presumably as a gesture to credibility, by some weeks. On the first occasion he saw an orphan boy, an aged couple and a 'fallen sister' with a baby, come to the door of the workhouse, and then on another day an old soldier and the exhausted and deserted 'mother of nine sons' in the same sad situation. The list itself is not unlikely, although of course its concentrated presentation is; and the aim of the song seems to be rather to intensify than disperse that unreality, for each stanza concludes with the death of the supplicant described. The old couple are allowed to escape, and so spoil the symmetry, but that is done only in order to stress instead their sad separation when they pass through the door into the House. The song uses phrases suggestive of social concern and even of protest, though their tone is unintentionally comic in its detachment, as though the singer belonged to a social class loftily remote from the situation he is describing: of the orphan he says,

> I saw he was neglected tears stood in his eyes
> The way our poor are treated it fills me with surprise.

About the prostitute and the old soldier his protest is more heartfelt in that it is directed at the callous way in which the doorkeeper in the workhouse rejects their application for admission. This leads him to say,

'It's a disgrace to this country you'll say so I'm sure', and of the soldier, 'He fought and bled for England, and died outside the workhouse door.'[41] This last example sounds more emphatic because it is the last line of a stanza, and the climax of a sensational description, rather than because it expresses any great depth of feeling. The song is not in any way an attack upon the social system which built the workhouses, but rather an invitation to marvel at and enjoy a thrill of indignation about the dreadful things which happen in this world. The more general moralising and head-wagging tone of the last stanza makes this clear:

> The last I saw was worse than all an old woman clothed in rags,
> The mother of nine sons poor soul she was lying on the flags,
> In the streets she said she'd sooner die as on the stones she laid,
> She'd brought up that family but from them had no aid.
> She had to linger day by day in misery sad to say,
> That dear old aged mother in a sad and cruel way,
> Those sons they had no feeling for their mother I am sure,
> They left her to die of hunger outside the workhouse door.

The tut-tutting of old crones enjoying a scandalised gossip is the nearest equivalent. It is, I think, legitimate to notice that given a violent and precarious urban social situation, anything less than these desperate events might well seem tame and even unrealistic. It could be said that the music hall was facing up to the situations it describes with such relish rather more frankly than was the rule in the melodrama. There the same character and situation stereotypes, though they might on occasion be used to make a social or political protest, were almost always given a fairy-tale happy ending. Sensational songs of death and distress are less a protest than an attempt to come to terms with the violence done to human feelings and decency, to push the stresses of everyday life to an extreme in a fantasy situation where they can be resolved, and attitudes for their acceptance tried out. It is also, however, important to keep the human capacity for enjoying horrors and disasters very clearly in mind, and to strike a balance between regarding the songs as mechanisms for protecting the sensitive from a harsh world and acknowledging that they are also expressions of its very hardness and jovial insensitivity.

The relishing of disaster for its own sake is clearly uppermost in those songs which use aristocratic or middle-class settings. Just as the starving orphan, the good old man and good old woman neglected by their children, and the fallen girl with the baby cast out in the snow, are working-class stereotypes taken from the melodrama stock, so the ballads of the music halls took such figures as the once-prosperous drunkard, the penniless gentleman gambler and the prodigal son of an ancient house from the same source. 'The Road to Ruin'[42] exemplifies the type very fully, beginning with a few solemn clichés:

> Life is all a game of chance, some are losers, some are winners,
> Fate and force of circumstance mould us all to saints or sinners.

It goes on to tell a detailed story of the ruin which gambling brings upon a lad who is followed from a card-game in his 'college old and grey' through losses at Ascot, borrowing, squandering of his inheritance, the visit of the cockney bailiffs whom the flunkey cannot turn away, flight with his wife and little children to a foreign hotel where he cannot meet the broken-English demands of the owner, until in the last stanza

> Dawn is stealing chill and grey through an attic window dreary,
> Ushering in a wintry day, and the wind moans wild and eerie,
> All alone within that attic, see a wild despairing man,
> On the floor his work dramatic, failed his last resource and plan.
>
> Refrain Wife and children all – have left him, he will never see them more,
> With a desperate glance around him he secures the chamber door,
> On the table lies a pistol, on the floor a broken toy,
> 'God have mercy and forgive me, bless my wife and baby boy.
> I – I – cannot face the future – see my dear ones starve and die.'
> When they found him he lay silent, face turned to the grey gloomed sky,
> At the end of the Road to Ruin.

This example is comparatively down-to-earth; in for instance 'A Stroke of the Pen', sung by Lottie Eliot, the various situations described in this vein are also wildly unlikely:

> In a dim, yet stately chamber, lies the squire at point of death,
> Listening while his trusted steward reads the will with nervous breath.
> All it now requires is signing, then the shameful deed is done –
> Then the steward will be master, casting out the squire's son.
>
> Refrain 'Now, sir, let me guide your fingers to sign,
> One little effort, sir – here – on this line –
> You promised me the estate should be mine,

I shall be master, and then –'
'Father, forgive me!' they heard a voice call:
The squire holds his hand out – lets the quill fall –
The lad will come into his own after all.
Saved from a stroke of the pen.[43]

The next stanza and chorus tell of a boy forging a cheque in his mother's name, from the consequences of which he is saved by her lying on his behalf, and then, invention flagging, the writer falls back on a story of a last-minute pardon reprieving an officer due to face the firing-squad. The failure to maintain any shadow of originality to the end of a song is very common; each writer sets out with a well-worn saw expressed in proverb and cliché for which he attempts to find new examples, but soon falls back into stories which are as well-worn as the sentiment. In 'Velvet and Rags the World Over', for example, the notion that

Life is full of joys and sorrows,
From the cradle to the grave;
Some have wealth and tire of pleasure,
Others poor, for comforts crave

only inspired Charles Graham to contrast the wealthy landlord and the poor tenant before launching, with the hopeful line 'Still another picture greets us', into the story of the poor girl deserted by her rich seducer. In the last stanza he apparently ran out of appropriate stories completely, and gives a garbled tale of a tramp in Piccadilly being offered a dollar by a small girl in a carriage, and then springing to her aid when her horses bolt, and being killed to save her. The moral of this is apparently that

A tramp may be brave, if there's life to save,
Misfortune p'r'aps stood in his way.[44]

It is on the whole better for such writers to stick to established stories, which have at least the virtue of clarity, and satisfyingly definite endings and messages.

One of the points in the melodrama and in these ballads where the upper and lower classes meet is in the relationship of the seducer, an upper-class reprobate, and the poor girl. Very many of these stories involve the sad end of a heroine who, in the way of the popular tradition, has succumbed to the advances of a lover and so has a child to publish her shame. The range of treatment of this situation is from the feeble contrast between 'velvet and rags' in the last example to the robust and lachrymose stanzas of Billy Bennett's 'She Was Poor but She Was Honest', which has survived in many versions in this century to prove that good music-hall song has a life in oral tradition. There are even some such songs which, justifying themselves by making the union a secret marriage rather than a seduction, let the deserted girl and her baby triumph over the wealthy scoundrel in the end; but clearly the conventional lament over the corpse was at least as satisfactory as such a reversal of fortune. As in 'The Workhouse Door', there seems to be less pleasure for the audience in any protest against social attitudes to women which the songs might contain than in the review and reiteration of accepted notions through well-known stories. The girl always pays – it is a fact of life, and any attempt to deny it or even to blame some specific and mutable social system for it would be to undermine the certainty of things, in which stability resides. The apparently empty, sententious statements with which these songs often begin are completely serious statements of belief. One early singer, Harry Clifton, founded his fame on a series of 'motto songs' made up almost entirely of such banalities as 'paddle your own canoe!', and was regarded as a philosopher. The reactionary fatalism which such an attitude suggests is characteristic of much folk-song; its naiveté is perhaps only the other side of the tendency to idealisation which we have already observed in the music hall's attitude to life in its serious moments.

The melodramatic ballads of 1870–1900, like the earlier descriptive songs about life 'down our street', were an expression of community solidarity: they reiterated old ideas and prejudices by means of stock characters and stories. The audience enjoyed the sharing of familiar responses, being thrilled by the contemplation of horrors and wickedness, comforted by their own comparative safety and virtue, and feeling suitably improved and touched by the sentiments the stories 'proved'. There was, however, an area of ballad-writing in the middle of the century, particularly in the 1860s and 1870s, which might be said to have taken the element of social protest and concern implicit in these situations more seriously. It did not adopt the attitudes of the music hall, ranging from proud description to noisy lamentation of the life of the urban poor; but neither did it adopt the equally fixed pattern of social attitudes enunciated by the drawing-room poets. Willson Disher speaks of the existence of a school of cockney writers seriously attempting to describe and expose the social evils of London, through the music-hall song. The example he gives is the work of J. A. Hardwick, which moves from a wry and surprisingly suggestive song of 1866 called 'Children Objected To', commenting on the need to avoid having children if one is to get lodgings, to a gruesome description of 'A Night in the Workhouse' found in the same songster of 1866:

Bags of hay laid on the floor,
For hunted wretches on to snore,
For one, but holding three or four,
All night in a London workhouse.
In, one by one, the casuals crawled,
In filthy tatters, raiment called,
Like raging fiends they yelled and bawl'd,
While by Daddy overhauled,
Who doled to each a slice of 'toke',
Which eager dirty fingers broke,
No word of thanks for that was spoke,
All night in the London workhouse.

Chorus Swearing, yelling, all the throng,
With jest obscene and ribald song,
Thus passed the weary hours along,
Of a night in a London workhouse.[45]

The example is extreme, both in realism and in bitterness of tone, but others do exist. It is noticeable, however, that there is no presentation of the converse picture of luxury, and no apportioning of blame except, by the suggestion of censure in the mention of the lack of gratitude and the obscene language of the paupers, to the recipients of charity for being where they are. I feel that the extent of the protest this writer is making is strictly limited to fit into the framework of the music-hall sensation ballad, and that in this song the pleasurable contemplation of the evils of others is still as strong as any critical impulse.

To find ballads in which this is not the case, and which are manifestly written as social protest, it is necessary to look at the work of the drawing-room poets. Men like William Cox Bennett and Martin Farquhar Tupper did much of their writing between 1840 and 1870 in the area of ballads about the urban poor, and published in broadside form or in the daily press. They sought to appeal to all levels of the popular audience. The vital distinction between their social protest and that of the music halls is that their view of the question is from outside: the streets they were talking about were not their streets, the povery they described was not waiting outside their doors. The gulf between the working class and the destitute was not a vital distinction on which their self-respect rested; and, partly because their removal from that position was comparatively small – Bennett was the son of a Greenwich watchmaker – they saw very little in any degree of lower-class life in the city which could give pleasure and pride as it did in music-hall song. The inspiration of all such versifiers was reforming zeal, and their model was the epoch-making 'Song of the Shirt', published in *Punch* by Thomas Hood in 1843. In 1844 that had been followed by the scarcely less famous 'The Bridge of Sighs', and Hood had established single-handed the form which Victorian popular poetry dealing with social questions would take. His popularity as a comic writer was long established, and the response to his ballads of protest was enormous. The 'Song of the Shirt' became a by-word, the constant subject of reference both serious and in parody, and it spawned a thousand imitations, as well as a certain amount of practical assistance for the oppressed worker which he had sought to inspire. Snatches of it are still familiar, having become something like proverbial in their own time: 'Oh! God that bread should be so dear, And flesh and blood so cheap!' was one of them, and the whole of the first stanza was almost as universally known:

> With fingers weary and worn,
> With eyelids heavy and red,
> A Woman sat, in unwomanly rags,
> Plying her needle and thread –
> Stitch! stitch! stitch!
> In poverty, hunger, and dirt,
> And still with a voice of dolorous pitch
> She sang the 'Song of the Shirt!'[46]

'The Bridge of Sighs', a lament for a drowned girl and an appeal for charitable judgement of her sins, had a less easily imitated form, and Hood's many earnest but less verbally skilful followers found it easier to stick to simpler ballad forms, like that of the 'Song of the Shirt' and his later protest songs such as 'The Workhouse Clock' and 'The Lay of the Labourer'. Their success can be judged by comparing Bennett's 'The Dressmaker's Thrush', which he published on a single sheet some time in the 1840s, with the 'Song of the Shirt', of which it is an obvious imitation:

> Close is the court and darkened
> On which her bare room looks,
> Whose wealth is its wall's one print,
> And its mantel's few old books,

Her spare cold bed in the corner,
The single worn, worn chair,
And the grate that looks so rusty and dull
As never a fire were there,
And there as she stitches and stitches
She hears her caged thrush sing,
O! would it were never May, green May,
It never were bright, bright Spring.[47]

The obvious resemblance is overridden by the equally glaring failure to write up to the model. Bennett is compromising where Hood is forceful, giving the dressmaker's room picture and books which romanticise her poverty in place of the 'unwomanly rags' which explicitly warn against any such reaction in Hood's poem; he is simply unable to produce the compression and austerity of Hood's effect, needing four more lines to paint a much less clear and striking initial picture. Most damagingly of all, he has not resisted sentimentality, importing not only a sub-Wordsworthian caged thrush but the 'worn, worn chair' which is a standard property of the drawing-room song of sentiment.[48] It would not, however, be fair to leave Bennett represented only by this example, for in some of his single-sheet publications, moved by the same sincere impulse of pity or by the stronger goad of his pet concern, popular education, he hammers out crudely effective verse which combines the lessons of Hood with a vigour reminiscent of older broadsides, in for instance 'Labour's Protest':

Ay, men of trade, we have our rights,
We drudges – we – the poor;
The right to serve, – the right to want,
To work and to endure;
The fireless grate – the freezing bed –
The racking aches that seize
The bones and sinews of the poor,
Ay, we've our right to these.[49]

He can even work up a broadside jingle for ironic comment on current events:

Oh have you heard the news,
High source of gratulation?
It just has been found out
We've lots of education.[50]

The art of Martin Tupper scarcely rises to this level, and though his zeal in the various causes he wrote about is unquestionable, the note of uncompromising social protest grows very faint. The point of view from which he attacked the capitalist exploitation of labour in 1854, in *A Dozen Ballads For the Times About White Slavery*, was one extreme of a view of the world which extended in the other direction to complacent wonder at the miracles of modern science and a comfortable conviction that all was for the best. 'The Factory Slave' from the 1854 volume (p. 10), which includes such stanzas as

> Pale, and shabby, and looking so ill,
> Hungry and cold and wet,
> On a winter's morning going to mill
> The factory-child I met:
>
> All day long among perilous wheels,
> His duty it was to tend
> Spindles and jennies and shuttles and reels,
> A toil without an end,
> For iron never grows weary, nor feels,
> Nor ever made child its friend!

must be set beside 'Rich and Poor (a ballad for union)' from his selected poems of 1874,[51] in which the sixth stanza runs

> Think, justly think, what liberal aids
> Invention gives us all,
> While Truth shines out, and Error fades,
> Alike for great and small;
> How well the rail, the post, the press,
> Help universal Man,
> The highest peer, and hardly less
> The humblest artizan.

This mood of Tupper's, near to the sententious platitudes of his *Proverbial Philosophy* and to the similar solemn enunciation that 'whatever will be, will be' in the serious music-hall song, is found in many drawing-room ballads about the life of the nation, and particularly of the lower classes. The consciousness, indeed the exploitation, of horrific social evils exists in them without any truly radical intention in their exposure; rather the intention is partly the simple popular enjoyment of the description, and partly to express and to substantiate for the audience a particularly middle-class attitude to the social system and to the poor which marks these ballads off decisively from those of the music hall.

As the music-hall songs of the people were calculated to give the audience an ideal picture of themselves which would substantiate their conviction of their own worth and the wisdom and correctness of their moral attitudes, so the songs about working-class life which were intended for a middle-class audience had the same function in respect of their own position. The poets writing for recitation wrote about the working class in a way which would bolster and confirm middle-class attitudes and moral judgements. The oddity of this is of course the choice of working-class settings for this purpose, instead of the straightforward celebration of middle-class heroes. There were ballads of sentiment which did not stress the class of the heroes and heroines, particularly ballads in which the central figure was a lisping child whose golden curls and tiny shoes suggested a home of modest sufficiency; and there were ballads enough in which the heroic deeds of officers and gentlemen were celebrated. But the best-known and most characteristic drawing-room ballads of sentiment and sensation deal with the poor. The way in which they are handled would seem to suggest some of the reasons for this. Victorian literature at every level was of course deeply concerned with social problems and with bringing to light the squalor and poverty of the towns; many novelists made it their business to translate the studies and statistics of governmental and private researchers into a form which would, hopefully, be striking enough to influence public opinion and effect reform. Poets were not committed to the cause in the same way except at the popular level, where Hood's example was eagerly followed; but the emotional engagement of the audience in popular poetry was much more difficult to handle than the response of the novel-reading public. There was an awareness, in the parlours and drawing-rooms, of the plight of the urban poor, an awareness sharpened by the journalists, novelists and reformers; it contained, as they continually pointed out, an element of guilt. In a recited poem, deliberately making a direct and concentrated appeal to an emotional response, such guilt would be unacceptably strong: some reassurance was absolutely necessary to make the verses and their message in any way tolerable. The great unspoken fear which the concept of 'the two nations' fostered was a fear that the poor were not simply deprived, but different: that they were indeed a separate race, with values and judgements and a way of life which were not the same as those of civilised people, and which might at any moment rise up and blot out the Christian society of England. The poor whose lives are so obsessively described and wept over in the drawing-room ballads are, therefore, not only a practical message about the need for reform, but they are also used to confirm and uphold accepted values, and the way of life of the audience. Only when they are seen to be like the audience, to share its view of the world and of their own role, can any sympathy or attention be given to their distressed state. The songs of the music hall which dealt with the working-class way of life and with sentimental idealisations of the soldier or the Londoner made an appeal which invited the audience to identify with and surrender to the warm, easy emotions of family affection or local pride, which said, in effect, 'you can be like the people in my song'. The drawing-room handling of the same subjects makes a less direct appeal, seeking to soothe fears that there existed an easily-swayed, emotionally primitive mass audience, and said instead 'the people in my song can be like you'.

The most famous and the most popular of the balladeers of the deserving poor was George Robert Sims. He and his work are typical of these writers and their ballads, and can be taken as a fair example of the kind in inspiration and achievement. Sims was what he called 'a Bohemian'; his grandfather was a Chartist and his father a factory-owner and businessman, and he divided his time between campaigning for the poor in newspapers, magazines, lucrative melodramas, lurid works of popular sociology, and in his recitation ballads, and living the life of a man-about-town in the clubs and theatres of London. He was a swell, living in Regent's Park and driving about in a carriage attended by dalmatians, and when he descended to the slums to collect his material he laid none of it aside, but, with an instinct for the admiration of the vulgar, swept into hovels smoking fat cigars. He was by no means insincere in his championing of the people, but he nevertheless made a very good thing of it, which of course, since people love success and understood his good wishes, they did not in the least mind.

He did observe what he wrote about at first hand, deliberately seeking confirmation of the living and working conditions which he had heard existed, and getting to know the people who suffered them; his writing has immediacy and authenticity of detail in description and in the recording of speech which shows how accurately he observed his subjects. His ballads were first published in the newspaper *The Referee*, signed with his pseudonym 'Dagonet', and the first series were collected into *The Dagonet Ballads* in 1881. They were written deliberately as material for the reciter, and Sims was more emphatic even than usual among popular poets that he had no desire to be classed as a poet or an airy-fairy artist. The ballads were enormously successful, and were performed by thousands of professional and amateur reciters from Beerbohm Tree downwards. Their success was partly due to the gusto and audacity with which they exploit the stock stories, characters and situations of the melodrama ballad, quite unblushing in their relish of their own sentimental appeal, and partly to Sims's conscious or unconscious success in striking exactly the note of reassurance and comfortable confirmation of their own attitudes while appearing to be treating his audience to a shocking and unpalatable lesson. From his personal experience of the low life of London he draws authentic detail and uncompromising description to substantiate stories which repeat the conventional melodrama patterns. He seems to be out to shock with his realism, setting his stories in the foulest surroundings, alleys which are always described as filthy, airless cellars, empty, freezing rooms, varied only with glaring gin-palaces, the missionary 'midnight meetings' and the inside of police stations and refuges for the fallen and destitute. When he leaves the London streets it is for a story of desperate and heroic action and self-sacrifice on the railways or in the life-boats. The Londoners he describes as realistically as their environment: they are thieves, murderers, wife-beaters and drunks, and the women hags, sluts and prostitutes, the children starving, crippled and forlorn. Even the animals he mentions are ill-treated or decrepit. Each character tells, or has told about him, a story of a characteristic or climatic moment in his life, often in language which is a skilful modulation of colloquial speech, so that the ballad seems to be an artless tale told in the hero's own words.

The dramatic effectiveness of the framework is clear, as is its connection with the music-hall character-song, but the appeal of the cockney or other dialect used here is quite different. While the music-hall dialect convention grew out of the desire to emphasise and symbolise the community of feeling between singer and audience, and their pride in their natural language and way of life, the characters described by Sims do not invite any kind of identification, but rather pity. The silent, or near-silent interlocutor, the observer Sims himself, is the point of identification in the ballad, and the accent of the main speaker serves rather to mark him off as someone of a different class revealing himself, in his pathos and quaintness, to the perceptive and sympathetic listener, his superior. The only ballad in which the main speaker is given the listener's undivided personal identification is 'The Workhouse, Christmas Day', where there is a direct attack upon the condescending gentry in the authorial description of them, and there the pauper who has suffered at the hands of the authorities tells his tale in perfect standard

English. It is pointed out that he was in the past a respectable shopkeeper. The usual pattern uses the authentically observed lower-class speech as a deliberate alienating device. Like the details of the slums and the prostitutes' meetings, it is deliberately meant to be shocking. In 'Told to the Missionary' the old coster who is speaking uses the word 'bitch', most unfamiliar to polite ears; he uses it, however, literally; the shock is of a different order from that of 'Sam Hall' and its curses. The damnation chorus there is the dynamic expression of feeling, not noble or good feeling, but dramatic, and expressed in song to some emotional purpose. The word 'bitch' used by the coster, like the professionally coloured vocabulary and turn of metaphor used by the sailors, railwaymen and actors of the other ballads, is used with an ulterior, and opposite, motive: to show that people even of this class, who use unseemly words and do uncouth jobs, are worthy, religious and even pious beneath it all – a back-handed reassurance and reassertion of the rightness of the accepted middle-class beliefs and values.

These are not people in their own right; each is a skilfully coloured and articulated puppet, and even then not one made to represent an individual, but a type, the faithful, maltreated woman, the broken-hearted clown, the rough coster and his devoted animals, dog, horse, wife, or the suffering innocent child; each type being established so that the thought processes and emotional responses of an entirely alien type, the middle-class Christian moralist, can be 'discovered' in it. Sal Grogan, for instance, whose hideously distorted face is described at length at the beginning of her ballad, is the unwomanly woman of the slums feared by the timidly respectable. She was a beautiful girl, we learn, and took up with a thief, who after their marriage beat her and finally turned her out in favour of another girl, battering her so severely that she was taken to hospital and lost an eye. All this is described in horrifying detail. The conclusion, however, makes all good: in a fire, from which the faithless other woman fled, leaving the thief drunk in bed, Sal risked her life to bring him out, and had her face obliterated in the process by molten lead from the roof. The concluding couplet,

> Oh, who would shudder or sicken, if he knew of the deed of grace
> Enshrined in the ghastly features of poor Sal Grogan's face?[52]

applies not only to her disfigurement, but also to her former life, the marks of which were also obliterated by the falling lead: a woman of the slums, married to a thief, involved in disgusting fighting and deserted by her husband, feels the same selfless devotion and patience and self-sacrifice as the most respectable lady reared on the strictest notions of wifely duty. The same message in a gentler form, together with affirmation that everybody, and not, as they might fear, only those who profit from it, believes in the maintenance of God-given differences of degree, is given in 'The Street Tumblers'. The wife of a poor family of acrobats explains to a passer-by that she and her child are well-off just as they are, in a state of poverty, and that she had Providential confirmation of this fact when she attended the christening of an heir to an earldom, who suddenly died in his nurse's arms. From this random stroke of the fate which threatens every child who ever appears in a parlour ballad she drew the conclusion that

> Street-tumblin' ain't a fortune, but you know how I came to see
> As it's better to rest contented, to be what you've got to be.[53]

In 'Two Women', a much more exciting story, the listener can enjoy a complication of emotional stimuli, all of which go to substantiate his or her own view of the moral world. Sims first describes a midnight meeting held in the slums to convert the prostitutes, shocks with his description of the women, and contrives to criticise the preacher's emotionally loaded sermon while giving enough of it to affect the listener; he concludes with the suicide of one of the women, misguided by the preacher's words, repenting her life but sinning in her death. He then turns his luridly descriptive talents on the vice of the rich, the concubine of a Prince is described in *her* glittering, fashionable 'midnight meeting', and the moral indignation of the listener is given full play over the exotic details of her life and that of her circle, as remote from the audience's experience as were the first set of characters. The final stroke is another of Sims's apparently challenging, shocking attacks upon accepted attitudes, announcing with a pugnacious appearance of moral rectitude,

> But when, at the great uprising, they meet for the Judgement Day,
> I'd rather be that drowned harlot than the beautiful Countess May.[54]

But the tacit assumption which takes the edge off this is, of course, that to be the lady reciter or a comfortable member of her audience is better than either alternative.

Sims's handling of these stereotype situations to give them the appearance of social comment and inject into them reassurance and affirmation of middle-class values is consummately skilful. His chief narrative device for neutralising the pain and injustice he describes is the importation of a directly religious solution: justice and happiness in Heaven are overtly offered as redress for suffering on earth, both in order to calm the conscience, and as a reason the sufferers might be expected to accept for not rising up in their own defence. The angles carrying off the dying waif to a playground in the sky were a sentimentally and socially satisfying solution to a problem which admitted of no easy remedy, and they were even in some sense the gift of the rich to the poor, who would never have heard of them had it not been for charitable ladies and gentlemen and their tracts and Sunday Schools. The vaguely stoic or fatalistic morals and mottoes of the music-hall versions of the stories gave way in all the drawing-room poets to sentimental religiosity, and none use it with greater verve than Sims himself. The crowning example is the favourite ballad of 'Billy's Rose', in which Nelly the orphan runs wildly through the midwinter night looking for a rose for her dying brother, until she stops and prays, when a passing lady in a coach is moved – whether or not by Divine intervention – to cast aside the rose given to her by her lover. Nelly thanks Jesus for his prompt answer to her prayer of the previous stanza, and both children are awarded the happy ending of all their kind:

> Lo that night from out the alley did a child's soul pass away,
> From dirt and sin and misery to where God's children play.
> Lo that night, a wild, fierce snowstorm burst in fury o'er the land,
> And at morn they found Nell frozen, with the red rose in her hand.
>
> Billy's dead and gone to glory – so is Billy's sister Nell;
> Am I bold to say this happened in the land where angels dwell: –
> That the children met in heaven, after all their earthly woes,
> And that Nellie kissed her brother, and said, 'Billy, here's your rose'?[55]

Sim's work very quickly became the standard model for the recitation piece. Metrically its framework is very simple, almost invariably using either four- or eight-line stanzas made up of couplets, the lines having fifteen syllables and six stresses, with a heavy pause in the middle, as in all the examples quoted so far, or an eight-line stanza derived from the double-ballad stanza but shortened to three stresses per line. The difference is largely visual: each line in the long stanza breaks up in recitation into one unrhymed and one rhymed line of a short stanza. The effect is dramatically abrupt and colloquial, particularly since it is coupled with, and often has its formal beat overriden by, Sims's characteristic use of direct speech. His favourite device is to tell the poor man's story in his own words. The advantages of the method are various: it gives an impression of independence to the puppet figure which allays suspicion of the author's manipulation, and makes the sentiments it expresses seem the authentic voice of the people; the uneducated speech can be quaint in itself, a chance for the reciter to display talent, and also excitingly racy; and its way of expressing pious sentiments in a rough, untutored manner can be made pathetic or heart-warming. With Sims's gift of convincing dialect and colloquial writing, the manner of expression can offset the manifest improbability of the stories told; and above all a character whose speech is lower class is instantly furnished with a shorthand signal to a complexity of reactions which the author requires from the audience.

Sims was by no means the first to attempt to write in a variety of English which was not his own in order to create special poetic effects, but his immediate models had not aimed at the same range of assumptions as he, for they were Americans. Col. John Hay, following the tradition of Mark Twain and particularly of Bret Harte, attempted to lay aside his cultured and sophisticated style and write the verse of the people of America. His *Pike County Ballads* appeared in the newspapers and then in a collected form in the United States in 1871; they were a great popular success, and appeared in pirated forms in London very quickly. Sims, just then embarking on his journalistic career, found then a good model. The aspects of Hay's ballads which Sims adopted can be seen in this passage from 'Golyer', the story of a coach driver who had few affections except for a love of orphan children, one of whom was riding beside him when they were attacked by Indians:

> Over hill and holler and ford and creek,
> Jest like the hosses had wings, we tore;
> We got to Looney's, and Ben come in
> And laid down the baby and axed for his gin,
> And dropped in a heap on the floor.
>
> Said he, 'When they fired, I kivered the kid' –
> Although I ain't pretty, I'm middlin' broad;
> And look! he ain't fazed by arrow nor ball –
> Thank God! my own carcase stopped them all.'
> Then we seen his eye glaze, and his lower jaw fall, –
> And he carried his thanks to God.[56]

Much of the Sims appeal is there: the pathos of the innocent orphan child and his ability to touch and improve the heart of a rough, the rough himself who may ask for gin but has finer feelings and is capable of noble self-sacrifice, and the piquant combination of his simple, self-deprecating, heroically restrained description of the event in his own words and the piety which is discovered in them. Hay, however, means nothing more than this. He is only seeking to establish the nobility, piety and sentimental capacity of the type he describes, in order to adorn further an image he and all his nation already admire, almost, indeed, to justify sentiment and piety by associating them with the sterner virtues of the American hero. The frontiersman is the norm, the American ideal man, and the object of writing poetry in his dialect is to fortify and Americanise poetry.

When Sims took up the writing of dialect, however, and used the speech of the working man of England, the inescapable and complex overtones of class changed the effect completely. Poetry was being used to justify, and to humanise, the characters described by their unwonted association with the tenderer emotions, and the piquancy of an inarticulate, incorrect English voice struggling to express fine feelings was quite unlike that of the American ballad. When the struggle is genuine, of course, in the verse of the street and the music halls, this is not the case, but when it is simulated for the gratification of the middle-class members of the popular audience Sims's ulterior motive is obvious, and to the modern reader often becomes offensive.

His skill in creating the natural, colloqial effect is great: he can fit complicated conversational exchanges into his stanza form, and convey the character of each speaker, as in the opening of 'The Lifeboat':

> Been out in the lifeboat often? Ay, ay, sir, oft enough.
> When it's rougher than this? Lor' bless you! This ain't what *we* calls
> rough![57]

The use of a dialect was, however, as widely copied as his other techniques, and was not always as convincing or as well adapted to its purpose, perplexing the reader with complicated phonetic renderings where Sims managed to create an authentic effect very simply. Recitation would of course remove part of the difficulty, but would no doubt create other trials for the audience if the performer were inexpert and found the painstaking transcriptions of the writer less than perfectly evocative of the sounds heard. Other writers simply fail to get any distinctive impression of the speech they imitate, as in Alfred Austin's attempt at a countrywoman's speech in 'Farmhouse Dirge':

'Must you be going? It seems so short. But thank you for thinking to come;
It does me good to talk of it all, and grief feels doubled when dumb.
And the butter's not quite so good this week, if you please, ma'am, you must not mind,
And I'll not forget to send the ducks and all the eggs we can find;
I've scarcely had time to look round me yet, work gets into such arrears,
With only one pair of hands, and those fast wiping away one's tears.'[58]

Frederick Langbridge in *Sent Back by the Angels* makes a great point of defining the dialect he is using as being 'in the main the speech which I heard, five-and-twenty years ago, from the lips of my old nurse, in what was then a pretty rural spot on the Staffordshire fringe of Birmingham', but the result is vague:

'Shake hands, and I ax your pardon –
'Twas chaffing I knowed you were;
But a hint or a slur or a joke upon *her*
Is a thing I can't abear.
And what if she has her fancies?
Why, so has us all, old chap;
Not many's the roof as is reg'lar proof,
If a bit of a whim's a gap.'[59]

Langbridge points out in his introduction, however, the essential feature of this way of writing, and rightly says that it is not really the dialect that is important, but the fact that the speech is colloquial. All the writers do convey the one essential piece of information about the characters who speak, that they are members of a class whose speech is not standard English. His earlier collection, gathered up, from the magazines where they were first published, in 1887, made the point succinctly in the title, *Poor Folks' Lives*.

Only one writer challenges Sims's skill in this area, and his failure to make anything more of the form than Sims did confirms the vitiating artistic falsity of the whole endeavour. In 1880 Tennyson published his collection of *Ballads and other Poems*, and in it the first poem shows clearly the inspiration of the whole:

'Wait a little,' you say, 'you are sure it'll all come right,'
But the boy was born i' trouble, an' looks so wan an' so white:
Wait! an' once I ha' waited – I hadn't to wait for long.
Now I wait, wait, wait for Harry. – No, no, you are doing me wrong!

Harry and I were married: the boy can hold up his head,
The boy was born in wedlock, but after my man was dead;
I ha' worked for him fifteen years, an' I work an' I wait to the end.
I am all alone in the world, an' you are my only friend.[60]

Even in some of his Lincolnshire dialect poems the influence of the Sims ballad makes itself felt, and reduces Tennyson to the level of the middle-class popular poet. 'Owd Roa' is such an exact parallel to Sims's 'Told to the Missionary' that Tennyson's wholehearted sharing of Sims's aims cannot be doubted. Both stories blend pathos and drama, and both are told retrospectively in the words of common men in their old age, speaking to silent sympathisers. Tennyson's old farmer tells the story of a fire in which the old dog Rover, now lying deaf and blind upon the hearthrug, came by those infirmities in saving the life of the son whom he is addressing. The coster's bitch in Sims's story is also old and decrepit, and has had her moment of heroism too, when she saved the coster, who was in the very act of drowning her because he had not the cost of a licence, from dying in the canal himself. Both lay on the tough, outspoken dialect very thickly, and convey through it a defiantly sentimental attitude to the dogs, and affirm the primitive uncouth speakers' hearts of gold: compare Tennyson's

Naäy, noä mander o'use to be callin' 'im Roa, Roä, Roä,
For the dog's stoän-deäf, an' 'e's blind, 'e can neither stan' nor goä.
But I meäns fur to maäke 'is owd aäge as 'appy as iver I can,
For I owäs owd Roäver moor nor I iver owäd mottal man[61]

with Sims's

'She's a rum-looking bitch, that I own to, and there *is* a fierce look in her eyes,
But if any cove sez she's vicious, I sez in his teeth, he lies.
Soh! gently old 'ooman! come here now, and set by my side on the bed;
I wonder who'll have yer, my beauty, when him as you're all to's dead!'[62]

Both ballads use this suggested combination of earthy strength and warm sentimentality to press upon the reader a few home truths about gratitude and self-sacrifice:

'An' 'e sarved me sa well when 'e lived, that, Dick, when 'e cooms to be deäd,
I thinks as I'd like fur to hev soom soort of a sarvice reäd . . .

. . . 'Faäthful an' True' – them words be i' Scriptur – an' Faäthful an' True
Ull be fun' upo' four short legs ten times for one upo' two.'

and

'And it's thinkin' about that story, and all as He did for us,
As makes me so fond o' my dawg, sir, especially now I'm wus;
For a-savin' o' folks who'd kill us is a beautiful act, the which
I never heard tell o' no one, 'cept o' Him, and o' that there bitch.'

The blend of shock and reassurance in the religious reference is identical in each. Tennyson, of course, wrote for another audience as well as the popular, and was not always confined to this level; but when he was catering for it he was no more able than Sims to neglect its conventions of attitude and expression, and found no better way than his of meeting its demands.

It is to be regretted that the drawing-room poets used the characters and stories of the sentimental urban ballad to confirm their own view of the world, since the falsifications to which this gives rise are artistically damaging. But the middle-class audience did enjoy the stories and setting of the melodramatic ballads in other ways, apart from the bias they were given by Sims and his fellows, and in this they shared the reactions of the lower levels of the popular audience. The stock of subjects and stories was common, and the stress fell upon the same emotional and sentimental satisfactions to be found in them. If 'She Was Poor but She Was Honest' was too crudely expressed, and lacked the correct modulation of moral tone for a middle-class audience, the story was perfectly satisfactory, and so the unknown author of 'The Village-born Beauty' made it over for recitation. Most music-hall writers lacked the skill and control of the recitation poets, and relied heavily on performance and on the music to make clear the story, which was often compressed into a single stanza, but the drawing-room poets only elaborated these bare outlines, without adding anything except further emotive words. The song 'The Workhouse Door', for instance, tells in one stanza the story of the old woman deserted by ungrateful children of which Will Carleton the American balladeer made two lengthy parlour poems, 'Over the Hill to the Poor-house' and 'Over the Hill from the Poor-house'. The extreme situations, wild coincidences leading to pathetic, tragic or miraculously happy endings, the concern with strong feeling played out by a narrow range of stock characters against a simplified backdrop of city street, slum, or pastoral cottage, are common to the whole of the popular audience, and express simply and emblematically the concerns and emotions which are common to all mankind.

The typically Victorian preoccupation with death, rather than the other pole of human experience, is found in all the ballads, for being a living form of folk-art they all reflect faithfully the bias of contemporary attitudes to the world. In the parlour ballads death, and children, loom even larger than they do in the music-hall variety, for there the balladeers were even more closely restricted in the handling of sex, and the simple celebration of the joys of life which formed part of the music hall repertoire was a lyric rather than a narrative subject, and belonged in the drawing-room to the writers of songs. The favourite drawing-room ballad character is the innocent, usually suffering child, and the favoured ending is death and translation. The great relevance of the figure to the everyday experience of the Victorian family is obvious, and their lack of inhibition about it probably healthful; but the preoccupation is really rather more than that. The story in which horrific tribulations in the shape of poverty, ill-treatment, disease or neglect afflict an innocent creature, who is finally rescued by the forces of charitable or Divine benevolence, epitomises the various functions of the melodramatic ballad. Action and setting may be exciting and thrillingly sordid; the social conscience can be gratified by giving sympathy and attention to a member of the lower classes who is neither threatening nor ungrateful nor morally suspect, and the solution, whether it is the intervention of the forces of charity or translation to the Heavenly playground, can be more conclusive and optimistic than the cautious and complex social reforms which were necessary to deal with the real problem of poverty as it affected intractable masses of adults whose continuance in their humble station was economically necessary. To the value of the story as entertainment, indulgence of the sentiments of melancholy and exercise of the imagination in dealing with the stresses of probable bereavement, and its function in relation to the social conscience, was added its educative value. Many drawing-room ballads were aimed at certain sections of the community whom it was hoped to affect and reform by touching example, but these were usually specially written, and the children who appear in them will be considered in their place in the next chapter. But the beginning of the recitation ballad was as an adjunct to the schoolroom, an extension of the hearing of a child's lesson learnt by heart; and at the end of the century these stories of suffering children were still most usually written to be party pieces for the more fortunate young. From them the reciters were expected to learn the virtues of endurance, simple piety, faith and love which the little ones displayed in their sufferings, and additionally to understand how well-off they were themselves in comparison with these potential angels of the slums.

In reading the ballads, however, one feels most strongly the unabashed and straightforward enjoyment of the pathetic sentiment evoked. Other impulses, probably more important in establishing the type, are subordinated to the determination to wring every ounce of feeling from it. This can be felt in the work of all the popular writers, from Tennyson downwards. His child example is the dying orphan Emmie, in a children's hospital, who asks her neighbour what she should do, and is advised to pray.

> 'Yes, and I will,' said Emmie, 'but then if I call to the Lord,
> How should he know that it's me? such a lot of beds in the ward!'
> That was a puzzle for Annie. Again she consider'd and said:
> 'Emmie, you put out your arms, and you leave 'em outside on the bed –
> The Lord has so *much* to see to! but, Emmie, you tell it him plain,
> It's the little girl with her arms lying out on the counterpane.'[63]

Sims's range of quaint and pathetic creatures has already been exemplified in Billy's sister Nell; scarcely any of them survive their stories. The determination to get in the death scene sometimes appears quite gratuitously perverse, in ballads such as Langbridge's story of 'Sammy',[64] who sells his little go-cart to buy food for his father, ill from the effects of tippling, who is so touched by the devotion of his son that he gives up his evil ways and is soon able to buy the toy back. This happy conclusion is suddenly crowned, in the last four lines, by the child fading and dying, for no discoverable reason or purpose beyond the balladeer's habit and for the sake of a final emotional pang. Amongst the wilderness of ballads put out on single sheets by aspiring but irredeemably obscure popular poets the subject is easily the favourite; a typical example is a pamphlet, a single folded sheet, by J. J. Pull, entitled 'The Waif', imitating the death of Jo in *Bleak House* reciting the Lord's Prayer. It begins

> The weary feet, in the cold wet street,
> Of a tiny waif were straying;
> 'OUR FATHER,' dear, 'WHICH ART IN HEAVEN'
> The pallid lips were saying

and ends, to the sound of a distant choir, with

Lifeless and beautiful she lay
No mortal could restore her;
For angels on their wings of gold
To a better land had borne her.

Gerald Massey, one of the worthies of Samuel Smiles's *Self-help*, who started work in a silk mill at the age of eight, produced a more vigorously described, but still doomed child called little Willie:

You remember little Willie,
Fair and funny fellow! he
Sprang like a lily
From the dirt of poverty.
Poor little Willie!
Not a friend was nigh,
When from the cold world
He crouch'd down to die.[65]

The fair flower blooming in the mud is a recurrent image in these ballads, and suggests the limitation of the audience to those who would not take the implied criticism of urban squalor too personally. The most universally popular of the dying children was not an orphan or even a city child, but Little Jim, who died in his neat though lowly home with his devoted collier father hurrying to his side just too late, and his mother with him, with the immortal exclamation

'I have no pain, dear mother, now,
But oh! I am so dry;
Just moisten poor Jim's lips again,
And, mother, don't you cry.'[66]

Michael Turner ascribes the ballad to Edward Farmer, but it is virtually traditional, written in an unimproved ballad stanza, and appearing in innumerable variants on broadsides, in reciters, and next to 'We Are Seven' in a school textbook of the 1890s, fulfilling every possible function of the popular sentimental ballad.

Those functions are, as I hope I have indicated, extraordinarily mixed and impure, for they are related to every level of the popular audience and each group required of them a different combination of effects. The sentimental ballad is rooted in theatrical song, broadside, foreign importations and the indigenous folk-song, belonging to the local traditions of writing in dialect on the one hand and to the beginning of the mass culture on the other; and its manifestations are correspondingly diverse. The lower-class hero celebrated by the Lancashire poets and the London music-hall stars is handled in verse and often music which is vigorous and subtle, and in these ballads we have some of the best of the Victorian manifestations of the folk tradition and assumptions; the verse of Sims and his followers is equally subtle in the way in which the attitudes of the audience are directed and substantiated by the story they are told, but here the indirection is insidious, and the vigour of the writing is empty of artistic honesty, and so is undermined. The divisions of the form are manifold, however, and between these extremes artistic success is sporadic and unrelated to the writers' intentions: it is, indeed, most often found in the ballads which have moved out of the hands of the original writer and been reformed by oral tradition, a fate which has only befallen those ballads which express exactly one of the areas of popular interest. Hood's 'Song of the Shirt' was vastly successful in itself because it was published at the moment when the social concerns it embodies had reached the stage of needing popular expression, and it needed no adaptation to pass into popular circulation. On the other hand no amount of earnest social intention expressed in broadside platitudes could rescue later imitations of the Song from oblivion, while music-hall tales which treated poverty and suffering as the common lot, and enjoyed a thrill of horror at the most unlikely extremes of distress, became current. Such songs as 'The Workhouse Door' were initially sung by the singer to whom they were sold, but subsequently printed legally and illegally in varying forms, and presumably sung from memory of performance or of song-book by innumerable amateurs, who would cut ruthlessly to the emotional nub of the matter. The most vigorous, and also those which evolved in such a way that they were no longer printable, like 'She Was Poor but She Was Honest', survived the first few weeks of life and were not replaced by a later hit, passing into the permanent repertoire of singers throughout the country. They were rejected by Cecil Sharp and his fellow revivalists when they made the round of folk singers of the shires as not being authentically 'folk'; but the people clearly thought they were, and they do deal with the ancient themes of the popular culture and maintain popular attitudes. The same can be said of the sensational and melodramatic recitation pieces, when they are not written with some specific design upon the reader which distorts the basic appeal of horror, pathos and sentiment. Such a ballad as 'Little Jim', orally transmitted and printed by every kind of popular publisher, is evidence of the universality of the sentimental ballad in its appeal to a popular audience whose unity of feeling and experience sometimes transcended divisions of class, and represented the changed but unbroken continuation of the folk tradition.

5 *Propaganda*

There remain to be considered, as a pendant to the ballads about the life of the common man, those ballads and songs which were addressed to him with some didactic purpose or palpable design, and made use of the description of his own life, in his own familiar poetic forms, to preach a message or propagate a cause amongst the people. The broadside tradition allowed of certain kinds of ballad with a message. Stories of personal tragedies, and pious retellings of Biblical or allegorical tales with a heavily pointed moral, had long been in use as aids to begging, seeking to move the listener to charity towards the singer which simple appreciation of the ballad sung would not evoke. By the end of the era of the street singer his income must have been at least as much derived from this kind of performance and response as from anyone's real desire to hear and buy the ballads he affected to sell.[1] For begging purposes the songs preferred were moralistic and pious, designed to impress the deserving respectability of the performer upon his benefactors, who were likely to be of all classes but, if they were able to give charity, were most likely 'respectable'. More lively, but still by the nineteenth century declining in vigour and skill, were the ballads which represented the remnants of the political tradition of the broadside, which sought to convert the auditor to the writer's persuasion on some current political concern. The Romantic poets mentioned in Chapter 1 as writing some occasional verse of this kind and publishing it on broadsides were the last broadside-writing contributors to a long tradition which passed in the Victorian period into a different form, and sought its wide audience by publishing in the newspaper and periodical press rather than on the obsolescent broadsides, which no longer interested or penetrated to any but the lowest classes. Some few writers stuck to the form for ideological reasons or because their writing was simply not good enough to be accepted by the papers; their work, honest but generally feeble, remains to be considered here.

There is also a much larger class of writers who published in broadside form, and later in the other forms of popular publication which were developed during the nineteenth century, and whose propagandist intentions were less straightforward, if apparently more altruistic. As the old broadside declined, and its audience became more exclusively limited to the lower classes, there emerged writers who saw the form as a way of influencing not simply public opinion, in the favour of their political cause or the alleviation of their own poverty, but specifically of influencing the poor, for their own good. Battening on the broadside form at first, and then on all kinds of popular poetry and song, these writers produced a species of parasitic verse with the appearance and, they hoped, the appeal, of real popular poetry, but concealing a hidden design to use the story to improve, convert, or enlighten the reader or listener.

The first inventor of the device was Hannah More, and the ballads of the Cheap Repository were actually intended, and carefully got up, as an imposition on their audience: Henry Thornton went to great lengths to print and distribute Mrs More's pious moral tales exactly as if they were ordinary broadsides, and at the same rates. The insistence upon sale rather than allowing missionary ladies bundles to give away was not only to increase the circulation, by using pedlars as distributors, but also was intended to make the recipient value the sermon he bought more highly. The Cheap Repository Tracts, which began to be published in 1795, were a natural consequence of the reviving awareness of ballads and popular literature of all kinds amongst the classes of society which had been cut off from experience of it for a century or more, and now discovered the remnants of the ancient ballad tradition they were beginning to admire still extant in the countryside in what they took to be a very degenerate form. Wordsworth's adoption of it was not only a gesture of revolt against established literary form and of solidarity with the oppressed, but also was intended as a contribution to the replacement of scurrilous and debased popular poems by worthwhile and improving verse. He said in a letter about the ballads he had come across that

> I have so much felt the influence of these straggling papers, that I have many a time wished that I had talents to produce songs, poems and little histories, that might circulate among other good things in this way, supplanting partly the bad; flowers and useful herbs to take [the] place of weeds. Indeed some of the Poems which I have published were composed, not without a hope that at some time or other they might answer this purpose.[2]

Mrs More and her lady assistants were not nearly as hesitant about their own poetic powers as Wordsworth, and turned out a stream of ballads based upon broadside verse forms and story patterns to serve the reformatory purpose, enunciated by Henry Thornton:

> to furnish the People at large with useful Reading, at so low a price as to be within reach of the poorest purchaser. Most of the Tracts are made entertaining, with a view to supplant the corrupt and vicious little books and ballads which have been hung out at windows in the most alluring forms, and hawked through Town and Country, and have been found so highly mischievous to the Community, as to require every attention to counteract them.[3]

Some writers took happily to the sensational and horrific narrative conventions of the broadsides in their decline and produced dreadful tales such as 'The Execution of Wild Robert',[4] in which

> Wild Robert was a graceless youth,
> And bold in every sin;
> In early life with petty thefts
> His course he did begin.

Naturally his course leads him speedily to the gallows, where he makes a last dying speech like any ballad criminal, but in it blames his parents for his downfall:

> 'Blame not the law which dooms your son,
> Compar'd with you 'tis mild;
> 'Tis you have sentenc'd me to death,
> To hell have doom'd your child'

because they did not check his childish faults; his mother is, most dramatically, felled at his feet by his words, 'by conscience struck with death.' The whole production, although it skips very sketchily over the criminal acts which lead to his end in order to get to the message, is lively and sensational enough to satisfy at least some of the expectations its carefully copied broadside appearance, complete with a woodcut, would excite. Mrs More, however, is more unbending towards the vicious little books she imitates, and although she can produce several broadside metres, and indeed fits her ballads to existing tunes, in some cases, she makes little concession to the expectation of stirring action and event, and attempts to substitute the austere excitements of theological debate or rational argument, condescending so far in one or two examples as to use some incident to illustrate the argument which makes up the body of the verse. Her didacticism is directed to two ends: religious and social resignation, and obedience. Her villains are such as Tom, in 'The Riot, or half a loaf is better than no bread',[5] which goes to the tune of 'A Cobbler there was', who begins

> 'Come neighbours, no longer be patient and quiet,
> Come let us go kick up a bit of a riot;
> I am hungry, my lads, but I've little to eat,
> So we'll pull down the mills, and seize all the meat:
> I'll give you good sport, boys, as ever you saw,
> So a fig for the Justice, a fig for the law.
> Derry down.'

Having thus thoroughly undermined his own case in the stating of it, he falls silent for the rest of the ballad, while Jack Anvil patiently points out all the errors carefully set up in his argument, leading him to exclaim, in a final couplet,

> '. . . thou art right. If I rise, I'm a Turk,
> So he threw down his pitchfork, and went to his work.'

Her heroes, on the other hand, are men like Patient Joe the Newcastle collier:[6]

> Have you heard of a collier of honest renown,
> Who dwelt on the borders of Newcastle town?
> His name it was Joseph – you better may know
> If I tell you he always was call'd patient JOE.

This irritating tone of ingratiating familiarity with the reader, who cannot possibly have heard of this paragon, since he is a figment of Mrs More's imagination, is a recurring feature of writing which apes the popular with the intention of 'improving' upon the original: it descends rapidly to the realm of moral writing for children; one feels from these tracts that Mrs More is inclined to regard her popular audience as little more intelligent or sophisticated than a dull child. The story of patient Joe is a case in point: the hero, mocked by unbelievers who disparage his religion and his social attitudes, maintains a patient, resigned, and grateful submission to God and to his employers, regarding every trial and distress as sent for a purpose. The dénouement comes when a dog steals his dinner, to the amusement of Tim Jenkins, who asks if that too is all for the best. Joe remarks stiffly that it probably is, but since it is his duty to eat, he is bound to stop work and chase the animal; off he goes, and the pit collapses upon his tormentor. Her writing all has this heavily pointed moral inevitability, though sometimes it is enunciated with some vigour of language; even her strongest climaxes are clearly the work of a lady attempting to be emphatic, rather than the product of the careless vigour of unimproved popular verse:

> The Drunkard Murders Child and Wife,
> Nor matters it a pin,
> Whether he stabs them with his knife,
> Or starves them with his gin.[7]

The danger of exciting the contempt of foul-mouthed drunks and also of intelligent, atheist plus politically subversive, artizans was a source of anxiety to her later followers and imitators, but the first bold attempts of Mrs More to take over a literature she despised for the edification of a class she looked down upon were uninhibited by any inkling of her potential ridiculousness.

The planners and distributors of the Cheap Repository Tracts were well aware that their wares were suitable for children as well as for the poor, however, and from early in their history provision was made for their purchase by the gentry for distribution in their own households and in boarding schools. Among the first printings in 1795 was a tract containing Dr Watts' Hymns for children; and other philanthropic and even commercial printers followed this example and provided penny sheets and chapbooks of religious and moral verses for distribution to the young. There was a strong connection with the Sunday School movement in this endeavour, thus combining the edification of the child with the appeal to the poor in a form they could afford and would recognise, for the Sunday Schools were at first exclusively a mission to the lowest classes. In the 1820s Thomas Richardson of Derby, for instance, had printed a series of chapbooks including Watt's *Divine Songs*, 6d, *Pious Child's Delight*, 2d, Barbauld's *Hymns*, 2d, and *The Sunday School Scholar's Reward*, 1d, 'As an humble attempt to promote the great cause of Religion in the Sabbath schools' (p. vi). The reward book was a tiny twenty-seven-page volume in a coloured paper jacket, each page containing a heading, a more or less appropriate cut, and a few extracted texts, sometimes supplemented with an original verse or two. Often such publications were capable of being broken down into single folded sheets, for the more economic rewarding of endeavour on the pupils' part. They remained available in this humble form well into the Victorian period: T. Nelson and Sons were still producing four-page

Rewards, with a decorated first page announcing the topic of 'Rudeness', 'Seek Pardon Before you Sleep', 'Obedience', or 'The Little Reprover', followed by a moral tale in prose and a verse tag, in the 1850s and 1860s; and indeed text-cards are still in 1975 printed by the religious publishers, even occasionally still containing original verse. In the mid- and late-Victorian periods, however, earnest lady writers elaborated upon the original idea of the improving ballad tale to a great extent, specifically for this captive child audience, and produced long poems which were published in book form with all the glitter and colour of the Victorian childrens' book.

A typical and very popular example of such writers is Mrs Sewell, whose social interests embraced most of the Causes of her day, and found expression in doggerel ballads. The titles of her work include *The Children of Summerbrook*, 'Scenes of Village Life described in Simple Verse', *The Little Forester*, 'A ballad of Olden Time', and *Davie Blake the Sailor*, which is a compendium of her anxieties, addressed to children but containing impassioned tirades against all threats to the heroic Jack Tar, from drink to overloaded coffin ships. Her best-known ballad was, however, *Mother's Last Words*, which is rather more closely directed at the audience to which it was distributed, and which epitomises the method and message of these pseudo-ballads. It tells of two poor children left alone in the world, who determined to make their own living rather than become a burden on the rates, and so took to sweeping a crossing. The elder was tempted by opportunity and need to steal boots for his dying little brother, but was then moved by the memory of a lady at the church who had been kind to him to return them. The consequence of his sin and repentance was first the death of his brother, presumably to expiate his initial weakness, and then his own rescue:

His friend, the lady at the house,
When little Chris was dead and gone,
Bound John apprentice to a trade,
And so he did not feel alone.[8]

This tale appears in a variety of published forms clearly designed to reach the working class and even the destitute child by as many routes as possible: it was produced at 2d in a plain wrapper, to be paid for out of his own pocket, as he would have bought chapbooks and ballads and music-hall songsters; at 3d in 'stiff enamelled paper' as a gift, perhaps from a parent or slum worker; at 1s with 'Six Full-paged Coloured Pictures, in Kronheim's best style', or at 3s 6d 'Elegantly Bound in Cloth, Gilt

Edges', both versions clearly intended as prize books or rewards for Sunday Schools. The sales figures claimed for such works suggest that this variety of lines of attack worked: in 1875 *Mother's Last Words* was said to be in its 719th thousand.

Its effect upon the recipient is less clear. The elements of the story are in some ways promising, drawing upon the stock formulae evolved from popular sources in the nineteenth century, such as the description of the life of the urban poor and the use of the suffering child as a central figure, to whom the happy ending awarded to their prototypes in melodrama and cut off by Wordsworth for the sake of artistic and psychological truth is now restored by the intervention of Christian philanthropy. The use made of the elements in Mrs Sewell's moral pattern is less satisfactory, however, both artistically and from the point of view of the moral benefit the child reader might hope to gain, for there is a vitiating confusion of intention in the stories which betrays the writer's moral vision, however sincere, as something less than clear sighted and honest. Mrs Sewell tries to speak up for the poor child in his suffering and exploitation, presumably because she would like to see the deliberate drowning of sailor boys and the starvation of crossing sweepers done away with; and at the same time she tries to present the situation to the victims of social injustice as a trial of their self-control against the temptations of drink and of stolen comforts, which they must resist, or they will have only themselves to blame for the consequences. The setting and circumstances present themselves to her as evil social conditions to be denounced, but the characters are presented to the reader as objects of emulation. The poor child who reads the story and identifies with the hero is invited to witness, but not to share, the writer's indignant attack upon those who exploit him, maintaining in himself pious and long-suffering temperance. It seems a great deal to ask of the starving orphan; Wordsworth's numinous vision of the outcast's place in the universe had only required him to be and to suffer.

The sub-Wordsworthian adaptation of the broadside ballad became firmly confined to the Sunday School audience, but Causes and Movement with designs on the working-class adult reader, often seeking to promote some very specific hobby-horse, turned their attention to the direct imitation of more modern popular literature, produced ballads and songs with a message after the fashion of music-hall or recitation pieces, and published them in the same forms as the originals. Topical newspaper verse often took the form of the exhortatory recitation piece, called a ballad though containing little narrative of any kind. The range of talent which was devoted to such writing was enormous, taking in Tennyson's 'National Songs' of 1852[9] and Tupper's 'War Ballads', 'Rifle Ballads', 'Protestant Ballads', all intended to foster Anglo-American friendship and recruitment to the volunteers, which are assembled with many single offerings on even more specific topics in his selected miscellaneous *Poems* of 1874. The most famous writers of the land and earnest unknowns, particularly ladies, were united in the service of their various causes in this manner. The strongest cause (after the national interest, as represented by the ceaseless flow of poeticising upon international news and internal affairs) was probably the Temperance movement, and its supporters borrowed every existing form of popular writing and publication known to them to transmit their message to the people, feeling that in doing so they gave literary endeavour a nobler purpose and elevated the popular forms to a moral status transcending art.

By its use of the motifs of popular writing the Temperance movement soon developed a jargon and a set of images which were peculiarly its own, taken over from music-hall and recitation ballads and crossed with the catch-phrases of popular religion and of other common causes. A persistent example is the use of metaphors drawn from the sea, and particularly from the work of the lifeboat service. Lifeboats were a subject of interest and pride to the nineteenth-century Briton, representing a kind of heroism dear to the national self-image, in that the heroes were not only concerned with the sea, but were ordinary working men who risked their lives for others without payment and without fuss, in boats which were either dangerously old, displaying the daring and skill of the men who sailed them, or were of the new, safe type which was the product of British technology and were moreover paid for by nationwide subscription, not out of the taxes. Parlour poets also seized upon them, and the ballads about them include examples by Clement Scott and Sims; for the temperance writers they had an obvious relevance to the subject in hand, and images of rescue from a wet, though not a watery, grave sprang to mind. A typical product is the 'Temperance Lifeboat Crew's Songster', a collection of temperance songs on this theme which, like many more, was printed and published in imitation of the Songster booklets in which the words of current music-hall hits were issued, at 2d or 4d, for the use of singers or devotees who had learnt the tune from performance on the stage and wanted a note of the text.

Michael Turner[10] records that there was a formally organised offshoot of the movement, 'the Temperance Lifeboat Crews, originating in Staffordshire in 1861, [who] carried the metaphor as far as to dress up as lifeboat men . . . They marched with model boats to protest outside public houses, and the whole business of casting life-lines to drunkards was attended by much procedural mumbo-jumbo in imitation of the freemasons.' He quotes an American version of the metaphor, written and composed by Rev. E. S. Ufford, called 'Throw out the Life-Line!', which begins

> Throw out the Life-Line across the dark wave!
> There is a brother whom someone should save;
> Somebody's brother! oh, who then will dare
> To throw out the Life-Line, his peril to share?
>
> Chorus Throw out the Life-Line!
> Throw out the Life-Line!
> Someone is drifting away:
> Throw out the Life-Line!
> Throw out the Life-Line!
> Someone is sinking today.

This more or less coincidental appropriateness of a subject of popular interest to the pens of the Temperance movement had only a limited possible range of variations, but when they turned to exploiting the subject of the working man's life, home, sufferings, and particularly his family and dependent children, they struck upon a motif of folk poetry capable of almost indefinite variation within the bounds of their theme. They could argue, with some emotional force if with little sociological cogency, that liquor was the root cause and only reason for the poverty about which other ballad writers from the halls to the drawing-rooms were already so much concerned; there were indeed many songs and ballads by writers not directly intending to preach the Temperance cause which dwelt with relish upon the sufferings of the drunkard's children and wife while regarding his state as either fatally inevitable, part of his disastrous downward path, or as a natural manifestation of his class. The temperance writer had only to stress the role of drink in the pathetic scene he took for his dramatic climax, and the pattern was converted to the uses of propaganda. The insistence with which this was done is indicated by the titles offered in *A Temperance Album*, quoted by Maurice Willson Disher[11] as 'Papa Stay Home, I'm Motherless Now', 'I Want to Kiss Papa Goodnight', 'Father Bring Home your Money Tonight', 'Father Won't Drink Any Now', 'Oh Papa Don't Go out Tonight', with only Offenbach's 'Water Bright and Pure as Dew Drops' by way of relief.

The seminal text of this large group of lachrymose ballads is the American song known as 'Little Mary's Song' from its traditional use in W. W. Pratt's melodrama *Ten Nights in a Bar-Room*, first performed in 1858. The song is by Henry Clay Work, and had originally a chorus enjoining us to

> Hear the sweet voice of the child,
> Which the night-winds repeat as they roam!
> Oh! who could resist this most plaintive of pray'rs?
> Please, father, dear father, come home.[12]

Its three stanzas are appeals, with progressively heart-rending urgency, in the voice of the child, asking as the clock strikes one that the father return to the fireless house where his wife watches with the sick brother Benny in her arms; as it strikes two she reports that 'The night has grown colder and Benny is worse', rapidly reinforced with the mother's message, 'Come quickly, or he will be gone.' By three, mother and daughter are weeping over the corpse, whose last words were 'I want to kiss papa goodnight', and father has still not yielded to her appeal. The song called 'I Want to Kiss Papa Goodnight' is clearly a direct offshoot of this, while others take up the story at different points ('Oh papa don't go out tonight') or even add optimistic conclusions to it, moving from death to repentance ('Father has come home'). Others pick up the dramatis personae and plunge them into other situations, introducing other actors ('The day poor Benny died').

The last two are interesting examples of the way in which the specifically Temperance writing and inspiration was sometimes, when it used genuine popular themes, reabsorbed into the mainstream of popular poetry with the propaganda aspects removed or exchanged for more generally applicable pathetic details, and causes of distress. The two songs appear together on a Fortey broadside in the Crampton collection.[13] The first is headed 'Answer to "Come Home, Father"'; its first two stanzas are spoken, largely because of the need to follow the model in stanzaic arrangement, by the father referring to himself in the third person, assuring Mary 'your father's come home,' and going on to describe his reunion with his wife. The only reference to drink is indirect: 'He was deaf to your pleadings, for reason was drown'd', and the husband's repentance is rather for his general neglect of the home and for forfeiting his wife's trust by his absence on that particular occasion, an omission for which he, with popular practicality, tries to make amends – he

> . . . kneels at our little boy's bed,
> He prays for God's help, that he may soon fill,
> The place of the boy that is dead.

In the last stanza his voice is replaced by a narrator describing the wife who flies to 'welcome the wanderer home' and forgive him when he 'promised no more he would roam.' 'The Day Poor Benny Died' shows a further stage in the absorption of the story into the stock of popular tales. It goes to the tune of 'Nothing More', which the stanza form shows to be of the standard long-line ballad kind, and it uses narrative devices rooted in the folk tradition, beginning

> One day as through the streets I rambled, careless on my way
> I saw a little child alone, while others were at play;
> His little cheeks were sunken in, he looked so pale and thin,
> My heart it melted at the sight, and thus I spoke to him:–

This is a (hitherto unmentioned) brother of the family, who tells their tale on the day of Benny's death with certain major changes: Mary, 'my only sister left', is dying of the cold and hunger that despatched Benny, and the mother is ill, but the father is no longer explicitly a drunkard: the family has seen better days and was then wasteful, but their hardship now is attributed to his being out of work, a much more deeply rooted popular affliction than the evils of drink. There are other traditional echoes in the verse – at one point the bereaved child says 'I wish that I was with him now, in the cold grave, by his side,' making very effective indeed the next line, 'It was from cold and hunger that my brother Benny died.' The whole ballad is an interesting mixture of the crude exaggeration of the Victorian themes and solutions, and vigorous touches of the extreme statement which belongs to the genre of the folk-song rather than to any specific period. Its conclusion is the scrambled happy ending of the broadside tale rather than the final tableau of the Temperance reformer's dream:

> Cheer up, my little boy, I said, and dry those falling tears,
> For Him you have been appealing to, I trust, has sent me here
> Relief I gave, his home I saved, found his father work beside,
> And bless the day I passed that way – the day poor Benny died.

If the Temperance ballads merged without a join into the old broadside patterns and the drinking songs of the music halls, at another level they much more self-consciously strove to maintain the distinction between their seriously inspired use of popular forms and the mere entertainment which the unimproved article offered. There could be no possible doubt of the message intended to be conveyed by the Temperance recitation, and some writers waxed fervent in expressing their belief in the importance and the efficacy of the form. A good example is Mrs Clement Nugent Jackson's pseudonymous *Gordon League Ballads* by 'Jim's Wife', which include some dedicated Temperance pieces and some with other moral designs upon the 'Working Men and Women' to whom they are addressed. In her 'Preface to the Reciter'[14] Mrs Jackson makes certain familiar points about recitation pieces: they are not to be regarded as poetry, but as dramatic material, the impact of which depends upon the effective delivery of the reciter, who should be trying to give a realistic impersonation of the supposed speaker, including costume if possible; the stories, however dramatic, are literally true, and the character of Jim's wife is drawn from life; her manner, social standing, and particularly her accent which is lower-class but not cockney, and shows some signs of her country origin, are pointed out as vital details. Mrs Jackson also, however, makes enthusiastic assertions and claims which go beyond anything enunciated by the mainstream of drawing-room ballad writers, and which indicate how seriously she regarded her writing as a social and moral weapon. They deserve to be quoted at length, for they embody the extremes to which reforming zeal could carry optimism about the effects of pseudo-popular poetry.

> In these earnest days of social activity, when the Classes and the Masses approach and meet and mingle with an interchange of benefit undreamed of in more exclusive times, the Reciter plays no unimportant part. He, or she, becomes not merely an instrument of conviviality, an entertainer, but a teacher: a medium through which the dreams, the hopes, the life-struggle, the very heart of one class may reach and inspire the other.

This is the opening paragraph, and it would seem to suggest that the ballads of the humble life that she is introducing are intended primarily to display the working classes to the middle classes, as many other reciters aimed to do, for whatever ends. But Mrs Jackson means more than this, as her next paragraph suggests:

> The man and woman who can confront an assembly of their fellow-creatures, possessed by the consciousness that in the space of a few flying

> minutes they can – through a little rhyme or prose – deliver a message which is worth delivering, send home to the human hearts before them a truth which will enkindle and uplift, have a mission only secondary to that of the Orator and Preacher. To attain this consciousness, to fulfil this mission, should be the aim of all true reciters, whether addressing crowded audiences in a great city, or a few yokels in a village school-house.

The exalted mission to which she feels called had taken her first to the poorer section of the popular audience, and indeed leads her in the preface to cast aspersions upon those writers – clearly meant to indicate Sims and his followers – who concentrate upon the more sensational aspects of the life of the cities for the mere amusement of those less intimately involved in it:

> As the title implies, these ballads were written originally for the Gordon League, the society founded in memory of the great soldier-martyr soon after the tragedy at Khartoum.
>
> They were written for that wonderful audience of rough folk – often a thousand strong – where men form three-fourths of the whole, which has met on Sunday evenings in London for many years past. An audience which in itself is Inspiration to the performer who faces it from the platform.
>
> They were written for the People, for the Poor, by one who knows and loves the Poor, and who wishes to dwell not on the dark and unlovely aspect of their lives, upon the 'fever-den', the 'foul alley', and the 'evil way of life', of which we hear so much, but upon the brighter side, the manly and womanly side, the frequently heroic side. . . . It was . . . to the Totally Unregenerate that Jim's Wife first addressed herself, and on those, in any city, it will yet be found that her words have the most powerful effect.

They are not, however, completely confined to the Totally Unregenerate, and several titles on the contents pages are annotated with specific instructions as to the audiences to which they should be addressed. 'Lissy' is 'A true story. An appeal for the Children's Holiday Fund. Specially adapted to an audience of the cultured and wealthy classes', while 'Harry' is 'A story of the army. Suitable for any audience, but specially for "Smoking Concerts" in Barracks, and at Working Men's Clubs.' Several are labelled as being suitable for Temperance Entertainments, and to one of these, 'Timothy Crab', there is prefixed a detailed description[15] of how it might be performed on such an occasion, so as to form the groundwork of the whole evening. The reciter is encouraged with stirring words: 'The whole ethical power of it will depend upon the earnestness of the Reciter. Mere elocutionary ability will avail little. . . . In proportion to the depth of her personal conviction will be the effect she produces on the audience.' The rest of the parish is mobilised to her assistance, to provide piano accompaniment to the recitation, and also to perform in a series of illustrative 'Living pictures' of scenes from the ballad which will be presented, to the accompaniment of the appropriate lines, after the initial recitation of the story is complete. In these pictures the audience sees the whole career of the drunkard Crab and his unfortunate family, from the point where his daughter dies in their impoverished room while he is too drunk to understand what is happening – a variation upon the father's absence at the pub – to his being persuaded to sign the pledge, and subsequently walking out in his Sunday hat and coat, regenerate, with indeed his costume 'slightly exaggerated for the sake of effect', from his 'polished boots' to his 'huge buttonhole'.

The only flaw in the whole didactic structure of the *Gordon League Ballads* would seem to be the verses themselves: their author makes the conventional disclaimer about their poetic qualities, but some are not even possessed of the energy and skilled effectiveness of the work of professional fabricators like Sims; rather they are barely adequate to convey the stories they tell, prolix and slow, the baldness of their diction uncompensated for by stories which are neither convincing nor particularly gripping or exciting in any way. This is less true of those which are nearest to the popular roots of her form, such as 'The Story of a Crime',[16] a lurid incident 'read by the author in the *Oxford Times*' and resembling quite closely the broadside murder ballads in its story, though even here the inclination to spell out not only the warning against drink which it implies but also a further moral, that the love of drink sprang itself from '*the want of love to God*', which left the murderess in time of trouble with 'Nothing to pull her through', weakens the power of the narrative. Working from her own stories built on hints significant only to a mind looking out for moral exempla, the authoress is often tedious and digressive, as in 'How Harry Won his Wife':

Do I see you looking scared
At the thought that the Lord in Heaven had heard *my* prayer, or cared?
If it wasn't for bits of praying I do about this and that,
I should *die* of work and worry! and that's the truth told flat!
There's a verse in the dear old Bible that's been more help to me
Than all my own relations (and I've had forty-three!)
You'll find it in Philippians – if I trust my memory –
'*In everything, by prayer . . . let your wants be made known to God.*'[17]

The stories she tells are often shapeless and dull. Her intentions are admirable, and she has imitated the popular forms with great care, but one cannot escape the impression that doctrine so obviously allowed to dominate its medium, and looked upon by the writer as the only justification for the use of the medium, can only be convincing to those who share it, while those whose contact with the writer is through familiarity with the forms to which she condescends will be bound to pass an adverse judgement upon the ballads themselves. The final paragraph of her preface, in which she stresses that the verses are 'ethical rather than popular', is true in more ways than she intended. One must add, however, that she must have met with at least some of the success she confidently anticipates in her preface, for further volumes appeared, claiming sales in the thousands, and containing ballads dedicated to ever more specific and important audiences, such as 'A Sad Trade', 'Specially intended for Annual Temperance Festivals, and Large meetings where Members of Parliament and Magistrates are present.'[18] It is probably true, as she and her predecessors in the writing of recitation ballads constantly maintained, that the performance was vital to the effect of the verse, and 'the ballad droops upon the printed page as helplessly as the oarless boat lies by the bank lacking the propelling power that carries it out, and on.'[19] This fact is no excuse for the slackness of very much of such writing, and the absurdities of the stories they told and their conventions of expression were seized upon with delight by parodists of every kind, from the music hall to the pages of *Punch*, whose merciless attacks finally destroyed the grip the recitation piece had upon popular audiences. These parodies are part of the huge proliferation of comic balladry which is the finest artistic success of the Victorian popular tradition, and which is dealt with at length in the next chapters.

In the area of political rather than moral propàganda, too, comic and satirical balladry published in newspapers and the periodical press, and forming the staple of the best music-hall repertoires, was much more important than the directly exhortatory verse which carried on the tradition of the political broadside. The decline of this function of the single-sheet presses was an inevitable result of their readership coming to be confined to the lowest classes, for serious political writers were rarely concerned to influence only the least articulate and influential levels of society, or even to make a special effort to influence them in a uniquely appropriate way while approaching others by other means. Some few were, however, concerned to do exactly this, and so occasional broadsides by Shelley, Byron, and later by Dickens do exist (and were mentioned in Part One) but they represent the tail end of a dying tradition. There were also a few writers who can be regarded more widely and completely as popular poets, working within the popular tradition and writing political ballads and songs in no anachronistic way but with full commitment to speaking to the people through their own forms of verse. The strongest active continuation of this tradition was in the north of England, where the popular writers mentioned in the last chapter, men like Tommy Armstrong, directed their verse towards various ends and regarded it as the voice of the people on all subjects including some which could be regarded as political. There is, for instance, no hard dividing line which can be drawn to separate ballads about pit disasters written for the purposes of begging assistance from those intended primarily as explicit political and social songs of protest, and these motives fluctuate from writer to writer and from decade to decade. The same unselfconscious continuation of the tradition of controversial broadside writing, in this case with an uncompromisingly clear intention of making and exciting social and political protest, can be seen in the work of Ernest Jones, who wrote in support of the Chartist movement, and whose 'Song of the Lower Classes' became very widely known and indeed still lingers in the popular memory in detached phrases:

> We're not too low – the bread to grow,
> But too low the bread to eat.[20]

This is writing for the people by the people, and has genuine vigour in its obvious and direct connection with the folk tradition. There was also, however, another layer of political popular writing which continued in the Victorian period and which resembles the religious and moral propaganda in intention and in its very limited success. In the later years of the century there were men of both political complexions who were concerned to preach their message to the lower classes *de haut en bas*, and who therefore took up popular forms and produced something which is imitation rather than use of those conventions; their predecessor is Mrs More rather than Ernest Jones. Examples on the radical side are the *Chants for Socialists* by William Morris, published in pamphlet form by the Socialist League in the 1880s. They are outstanding as literary rather than as popular ballads, their diction and tone inextricably entwined in literary and idealogical medievalism. The simplest, most straightforward moments they have are like the following section of 'The Day is Coming':

> For then – laugh not, but listen, to this strange tale of mine –
> The folk that are in England shall be better lodged than swine.
>
> Then a man shall work and bethink him, and rejoice in the deeds of his hand,
> Nor yet come home in the even too faint and weary to stand.[21]

It may well be that this tone positively commended itself to the expected audience of the pamphlets, the intelligent working man already full of zeal for progress and self-improvement, for whom rhetorical flourishes and snatches of Latin, which Morris uses as chorus-lines, would represent a literary ideal which was the object of his pursuit; but this kind of success, connected with the whole Victorian movement to improve popular taste by education in the fine arts, is in no way connected with the tradition of popular poetry, and indeed is seeking to supplant and suppress it.

In some ways the efforts of the other political extreme of late Victorian politics, prompted into making a popular appeal by the needs of the moment (election time, for instance) are more closely related to the popular model, although the artistic value of their productions is very low indeed. In 1884, for instance, there appeared *A Pen'oth o' Poetry for the Poor by Peter Primrose*, decked out in a primrose-decorated wrapper and dedicated to 'the Poorer Classes'. It claimed that its intention was 'to show [the poor] that even poverty as compared with wealth is not without some advantages; to satisfy them that the general condition of the poor is at the present time far better than it has been at any other period of our country's existence . . . and generally to cultivate amongst them a spirit of content.' The first ballad in the pamphlet is called 'Let Well Alone'; the objects of attack are numerous, ranging from the 'Rads' and the Communists, Malthus and William Morris, to the sensational 'papers', that is *Punch*, which had attacked slum landowners, and also those subversives who wished to keep the poor man from his 'tonic', beer, which

> . . . brings him force to work right on
> Where else we oft had missed him,
> To all his centres gives a tone,
> And braces up his system.[22]

This kind of doggerel indicates the depths to which the trenchant, witty, and controversial broadsides of the preceding centuries had sunk by the end of their life, largely as the result of their narrowing audience and the consequent neglect of the form by major writers, who left it to the clumsy pens of propagandists for whom the grinding of religious or political axes was the only reason for writing in a form for which they had otherwise no feeling but contempt and condescension. This was not, however, the case with the comic ballads of the halls and the magazines, and indeed these were the fields in which the major talents of Victorian popular poetry worked.

6 *Comic Ballads in the Music Hall*

A number of factors contributed to the supremacy of the comic ballad as the form in which Victorian popular poetry reached the high point of artistic achievement. It can confidently be said that in comedy the popular ballad of the nineteenth century surpassed the achievements of earlier periods; comic ballads were produced at every level of popular writing which display some of the best and most artistically desirable characteristics of the folk tradition, while expressing the particular sensibility of the age in which they were produced, as manifest at the level of the majority of people. In the music halls, on broadsides and in every kind of popular song-book, in magazines and newspapers of every degree of respectability, a comic tradition of verse-writing flourished and grew from the early years of the century, and from it writers and performers emerged whose work in the popular tradition was and still is some of the most enjoyable fruit of Victorian culture.

Some contributory reasons for this can perhaps be suggested at the outset. An important factor was the change in social climate which is usually indicated by phrases such as 'Victorian prudery': the change which inhibited the free discussion and expression of intimate emotions, and particularly of sexual matters, and imposed a much stricter censorship, both direct and through a change in public taste and opinion, upon the use of these areas of experience in art, especially in the theatre. This restriction affected popular comic writing profoundly, and in two main ways, both of them beneficial to its artistic development. Its first effect, gradually coming to influence every level of popular writing down to the least respectable,[1] was to put an end to the threadbare reiteration of the old jokes about sex in the old words and with the same old range of innuendoes and variations, and to force writers, however unskilled, and however undemanding their audiences, to look for new ways of making their point. The sexual jokes of the broadsides had long ceased to have any freshness or interest, their few verbal tricks had been developed to their logical conclusions and no new idea had entered to vary the tired clichés for half a century. The extreme they had reached was one of explicit statement and exaggeration, and so the new climate of opinion eventually suppressed the old ballads more or less completely, and, since their subjects remained the only lasting topics for popular humour, new and often better ways of making the old points were found, and so a new, very lively tradition was established.

There was also a much less obvious, but equally important, effect upon popular taste at a level more profound than that of verbal expression, which served to change the emphasis of ballad humour and provided a new way of making situations comic, for a new emotional purpose. The suppression of the aggressively open treatment of sexual matters in song reflected changing manners and acceptable social behaviour in general; and changing manners and mores bring into prominence feelings which under a different social dispensation are ignored or easily altered. Decorum fosters inhibition; and humour is called upon to help the audience deal with emotions they are too shy to approach in any other way. Serious, tragic self-revelation is found to be embarrassing, but important topics can be dealt with indirectly through irony and humour which protect the participators from self-consciousness. The comic pathos of the songs of Gus Elen and the other cockney singers discussed in Chapter 4 is such a case, and the effect upon the artistic achievement of the writers and singers is clearly far from destructive; similarly there are more directly comic songs which draw their strength from the complex of emotions which surrounds the simple sexual act in an inhibited age, and which obviously helped their audience to recognise and deal with these emotions. Comedy and debunking as a release from high-minded restraint and as an antidote to impossible moral demands existed too in the areas, discussed in the earlier chapters, of heroism and sentiment. Virtually without exception, every important song of heroic action, patriotic militarism or sentimental suffering was accompanied in the music hall, often in the same bill and by the same artist, by an explicit parody, and very many of the drawing-room poems were parodied both in written versions and orally, by the young reciter. In both areas of ballad-writing there was probably as much comic verse produced as serious, and the standard of effectiveness which it has in common with the sentimental ballads is not, in this case, undermined, but is enriched, by the complexity of the attitudes which lie behind its assumptions.

All these related factors in the growth of the Victorian comic ballad tradition are also tied up with another for which it is difficult to account, but which is too obviously a product of the period to admit of any doubt that it is in some way specifically Victorian. This facet of the Victorian consciousness is a consuming fascination, which affected a wide cross-section of educational and social levels, with words, and with the behaviour of language itself. The famous Victorian penchant for bad puns is only part of a taste for verbal humour of every possible kind, from nonsense syllables set to music to the most complicated patter songs and elaborate games with rhyme, alliteration, riddles, plays on words, and the comic use of every real and imaginary dialect and variation upon standard English. One might speculate upon the possible analogy between this acutely word-conscious period, in which the rate of literacy was rapidly rising, and the stage of development in the individual's use of words when the child who can just read is fascinated by the odd ways words behave; but this is probably to over-simplify the situation. Whatever the cause, an interest in verbal humour for its own sake certainly existed throughout the popular audience from the 1830s onwards, and gave extra impetus to the exploration of new ways of making the old jokes of the folk tradition. It also made possible the establishment of what is virtually a new kind of popular humour out of parody and fantastic adaptations of old ballad elements, which was used by the major comic poets of the Victorian popular tradition.

The comic ballad exists as separate kind of popular song from the earliest recorded periods of ballad composition, and from its inception dealt with certain aspects of the popular view of the world in its own way. There is, however, a distinction made by Professor Child between the tragic and romantic ballads in his collection and those which have a comic tone. The latter, such ballads as 'The Knight and the Shepherd's Daughter' (*E.S.P.B.* no. 110), 'Crow and Pie' (*E.S.P.B.* no. 111), 'The Boy and the Mantle' (*E.S.P.B.* no. 29), 'Get up and bar the door' (*E.S.P.B.* no. 275) and many others, are, he says, distinguished from the tragic ballads. They 'are clearly not of the same rise, and not meant for the same ears . . . They would come down by professional rather than by domestic tradition, through minstrels rather than knitters and weavers.'[2] Whether or not one need agree with his perhaps rather censorious judgement that they are the songs of the tavern rather than the cottage, they remained the common staple of professional or semi-professional country singers' repertoires and were the majority of the broadside texts throughout the lifetime of the traditional and broadside ballads. The collectors of rural folk-song, particularly in the nineteenth century, found more of them than of the romantic and tragic ballads and lyrics they preferred. It is now fairly clear that omission, and alteration of texts that were admitted, have altered the balance in collections of rural folk-song, which do not, therefore, reflect the preference of singers and printers for the comic. Nevertheless enough remains of the robust tradition of comic ballads to show wherein its appeal lay, and what happened to it to make not only the scholars and collectors, but the larger part of the popular audience itself, reject it in the end.

The reason for the popularity of comic subjects for broadside ballads is fairly clear, and increasing use was made of them throughout the seventeenth and eighteenth centuries. For the professional, writing for profit, wide and immediate appeal with the minimum of effort was the first consideration. Low humour, such as the discomfiture of a famous man by someone of a lower station – the Robin Hood cycle contains several of this kind – required little from the writer beyond a reshuffling of names and situations, and the archetypal sexual jokes, the seducer outwitted, the jealous husband cuckolded, the metaphorical description of the way of a man with a maid, are perennially attractive. A conventional pattern was established that suited both writers and audience; what distinction remained between good and bad examples of the kind depended on the relative success of each writer in expressing the old jokes in a lively or ingenious way. The jokes themselves can be briefly described, and can be seen recurring in appropriate forms in every period. They reflect the common concerns of their audience as accurately, in their way, as do the serious folk-songs. There is a large group, including, as mentioned above, some Robin Hood ballads, (such as 'Robin Hood and the beggar', *E.S.P.B.* no. 134, 'Robin Hood and the Shepherd', *E.S.P.B.* no. 135, and 'Robin Hood and the Pedlars', *E.S.P.B.* no. 137) as well as later broadsides like 'The Crafty Farmer' (*E.S.P.B.* no. 283), and versions of the riddle song pattern like 'King John and the Bishop (*E.S.P.B.* no. 45), all of which hinge upon the victory of a poor or apparently weak person over a stronger opponent. Sometimes it is a battle of wits which is won, but whether the struggle is physical or mental, the outcome is most often the physical discomfiture and humiliation of the superior. In the ballads mentioned, Robin Hood is subjected not only to defeat in fighting but to beatings, broken heads, and the mocking administration by a jubilant pedlar of a 'balsam' which turns out to be an emetic. The element of wish-fulfilment revenge and victory, elevating the poorest listener to the status of possible hero in struggles with admired, successful figures, is obvious in such stories; but it is clear that the nature of the victory, its expression in crudely basic physical terms, has much to do with the pleasure which is to be gained from it. There is a similar satisfaction in the stories of practical jokes of a physical kind played upon figures of authority and dignity who in reality reduce the self-esteem of the ordinary man by their social and mental superiority. If they are not only outwitted, but outwitted so as to precipitate them into tangible, bodily humiliation, the intangible insults and contempt which they have heaped upon us are the more satisfyingly avenged. A further dimension is added when the trick is worked by playing upon a human, physical weakness which the supposedly superior person has betrayed. Many anti-clerical songs take this form, for instance 'The Friar in the Well' (*E.S.P.B.* no. 276), and 'Friar and Boy' (Percy MS), but it extends to much later ballads and tales, such as Dibdin's 'The Exciseman Outwitted'. The simple contemplation of someone else in physical distress is enough of a joke to form the only point of very many ballads, both early and late; to be fat or thin, naked, drunk or vomiting, frustrated or impotent, or simply to fart, is to be hilariously funny, because it releases the listener from embarrassment of his own, perhaps, and certainly places him in the superior role of one who has at least not lost control of his body. If the physical distress falls upon someone with pretensions to higher things, particularly when he is actively asserting his authority in some way, then the incongruity of his disgrace adds greatly to its piquancy; but the practical joke story is by no means always directed to deflation or debunking, and the victim may be perfectly likeable and innocent and still be seen as comic in his distress. The situation itself contains enough emotional force for the audience to find its exposition, and its happening to somebody else, a release which occasions laughter. The humour is clearly that of the underdog, whose laughter is self-defence.

The main area of subject-matter for the comic ballad was from the first the area of sexual relations. All ballads and folk-songs deal primarily with the personal, private areas of experience, handling even battles and wars as events befalling single individuals whose reactions are more important than the historic outcome of the conflict, and dealing with personal relationships in private lives at least as often as with any other subject. The comic ballad specialises in personal relationships, particularly in marriage, and usually gives its stories the physical, earth-bound emphasis which can be observed in the general comic pattern, and which reflects the needs of the audience for whom it is intended.

The characteristic popular attitude to the woman, already discussed in the heroic and sentimental contexts, is evident in most of the jokes about sex in these ballads, both early and late. The women represented do not by any means confine their interest in sex relations to the stage of courtship, and those ballads which do deal with that stage of the contact between a man and a woman treat it with little reference to courtly convention, and make assumptions which differ from those of the literary tradition even when that is expressed in humorous writing. The high comedy of manners is related to the serious poetic assumptions about the nature of women – their purity, their aloofness, which may lead writers to use comedy for the manipulation of social roles so that a more equal relationship, in which courtship is possible, will be set up, or alternatively will lead to the division of women into the lovable, who can only be treated seriously, and the unlovable, whose various comic, unwomanly characteristics constitute a means of revenge upon the female sex for the indifference to male needs which it is assumed they feel. Popular art approaches courtship quite differently. It does not assume that the woman is bound to react with feigned indifference and reluctance to amorous advances, though such a reaction is a possibility, and is played out with full consciousness of its illusory quality by both parties. Just as frequently, however, the girl is friendly and immediately willing, or will herself initiate the exchange, and the ballad passes on to an exuberant description of the consummation of the courtship with no time lost. A further possibility is genuine reluctance on the girl's part, so that the humour and pleasure of the ballad lies in the ingenuity with which she avoids the man and comes off unharmed; or she may react with an appearance of reluctance and caution in order to test the worthiness of the suitor before making him her choice. These are all reactions which are part of the popular culture's different selection from life; they are also, it would seem, reflections of a culture which is less exclusively the creation of the male mind, in which women have played an active part in shaping the artistic tradition. It is well known that there have always been women folk-singers, and that neither sex has been confined to singing 'appropriate' songs; and most attitudes to the composition of folk-song assign each individual singer some role in the creation of the material he or she performs.

This observation applies with equal or greater force to the large number of comic ballads which deal with marriage, an area of the sexual relationship on which the courtly poetic tradition tends to be silent, but which dominates everyday experience, and is faithfully reflected in a dominating majority of comic songs and tales. The lyrical, serious song on this subject is almost always from the woman's viewpoint, and there are comic songs about the problems of marriage which reflect not merely supposed female attitudes which a man might imagine – such as the many songs in female character which bewail the lack of a man, the pains of virginity or the status of old maid – but also many jokes which are squarely from the woman's point of view, about problems which can reflect no pleasure or credit upon a male listener, but genuinely express and relieve problems of the woman. There is sometimes this emphasis in songs in which the joke is that the man cannot satisfy the woman's desires, however hard he tries and however willing and encouraging she is; texts, sometimes even texts of the same song, may emphasise her superiority, or they may set up the impotent man as a butt for the laughter of frustrated female and superior-feeling male auditors alike. They may also, on the other hand, tend to the fulfilment of male fantasy in stressing the extraordinary lecherousness of the girl, a notion which both entices with the promise of extra pleasures and justifies the timid or weak for his failure by blaming it on the wicked lasciviousness of the female. More clearly and unequivocally women's jokes are those in which the quick-witted girl runs circles round her undesirable husband or lover, masquerades in male roles, and in some way escapes from a fate which the world has sought to impose upon her. The situation of the young girl and the old husband, for instance, may be treated with rueful seriousness as a warning song, possibly incorporating advice about taking a young lover to make up his deficiencies, or it may tell the story of a girl who defies her parents and the old man himself and refuses to marry someone rich but unattractive, in a series of witty and mountingly impudent speeches. The fantasy of the female sailor may well be a masculine idea, but the female highwayman who robs all and sundry in male disguise and is not much disconcerted when discovery leads to a sexual encounter, and the mercenary young lady who contracts for a fee and successfully pursues her claim to it into court, all the while talking in elaborate metaphorical terms, are heroines of their own sex.[3]

Probably the biggest group of marriage ballads are those which deal with cuckoldry, and here there is a general unanimity of male and female attitudes, as the lovers unite to outwit, frustrate, befuddle and humiliate the husband. For the purposes of the song he represents authority, legal claims and opposition to love, and to put him down is at least as pleasurable for the participants and the audience as the act in aid of which he is outwitted. The variations upon this theme are legion in the folk tradition of every nation, and the reference they have to the life of the people is as direct and obvious as that of the equally large group of songs which simply describe a seduction. There are other themes, too, which reflect very clearly the concerns of the ordinary experience of marriage, and which are just as firmly established as these, although with fewer texts. One is the theme of 'maistrie', of the struggle for dominance within a marriage, and particularly the jokes that are made about the fact that the woman sometimes wins. This is clearly a joke for men, asserting their own dominance and deflecting suspicion of weakness, answering female demands by an assertion that the natural order of things is in their favour, and again bolstering the confidence of those whose position in society gives them little chance of a dominant role in any other relationships they have. A man may in reality be in a position of complete dependence, often in fact also dependent upon his wife's earning power, but he can laugh at the unmanly failure of the character in a tale who is subservient to his own wife, or to his helpless uxoriousness or passion for an unkind girl. The reality of the situation adds a layer of sympathy, too, which is also felt in songs which deal with other humiliations the married state may inflict, ranging from a drunken, indecorous wife to the fathering of embarrassing numbers of children. All these more or less intimate hazards of marriage are the facts of life, and jokes about them are the staple of the comic ballad from the earliest times, using laughter to ameliorate and the excuse of a funny story to air and to some extent explain the common problems of humanity. They remained constant in ballads in oral circulation and in print from the earliest known examples until the last days of the broadsides; but the expression of them tended rather to deteriorate than to improve, simply by process of attrition and lack of any impetus to creative change. The high point was reached as early as the seventeenth century, when the metaphorical seduction, for example, was embodied in such inventive and warm sets of verses as 'The Tinker':[4]

There was a Lady in this Land,
That lov'd a Gentleman,
And could not have him secretly
As she would now and then,
Till she divis'd to dress him like
A Tinker in Vocation:
And thus, disguis'd, she bid him say,
He came to clout her Cauldron . . .

I am a Tinker, then quoth he,
That worketh for my Fee,
If you have Vessels for to mend,
Then bring them unto me:
For I have brass within my bag,

And target in my Apron,
And with my skill I can well clout,
And mend a broken Cauldron . . .

Then to the Brew-house hyed they fast
This broken piece to mend,
He said he would no company,
His Craft should not be kend,
But only to your self, he said,
That must pay me my Fee:
I am no common Tinker,
But work most curiously.

And I also have made a Vow
I'll keep it if I may,
There shall no mankind see my work,
That I may stop or stay:
Then barred he the Brew-house door,
The place was very dark,
He cast his Budget from his back,
And frankly fell to work.

And whilst he play'd and made her sport
Their craft the more to hide,
She with his hammer stroke full hard
Against the Cauldron side:
Which made them all to think and say,
The Tinker wrought apace,
And so be sure he did indeed,
But in another place . . .

The Lady to her Coffer went,
And took a Hundred Mark,
And gave the Tinker for his pains,
That did so well his work;
Tinker, said she, take here thy fee,
Sith here you'll not remain,
But I must have my Cauldron now
Once scoured o'er again . . .

Much circumstantial detail is here omitted, and the song ends with the Lady offering him a yearly pension to clout her cauldron quarterly, to which the husband suddenly objects, saying he would rather buy a new, and the singer ends with a threat to any tinker who might think of visiting his own wife. Even more complicated analogies are worked out, and the trades and occupations invoked are many, progressing with changing experience from largely rural metaphors (related to depths of significance lost to the comic versifier, which connected copulation to ploughing and reaping) to the utilisation of highly complex jargon and reference to describe it in terms of machines, from threshers to looms. The variations are not endless, however, and while a song linking human activity to hunting or cultivation is an affirmation of the unity of things, describing sex in terms of machines may be equally comic, but has overtones which are by comparison not only sterile but menacing and ugly, and might well be said to be pornographic. By the turn of the nineteenth century the metaphorical structure of such songs had become perfunctory, in many cases, an excuse for or a means of brutalising the act described, as in 'A new Irish Song, called Young Tedie's Oak Stick', in a garland[5] of the last twenty years of the eighteenth century, which has the chorus

> He hardly waits to lay them down
> But he leathers away with his oak stick

or the nineteenth-century version of 'The Threshing Machine'[6] which goes through the usual analogy and then ends on a grotesque twist, presumably meant to be funny:

> When six months were over, I remember it well,
> Molly's front parlour began for to swell
> And very soon after she had got a wean,
> The fruits of her labour a young threshing machine.

It is clear from such examples that the convention was running out of genuinely comic impetus, and these texts both appear as isolated instances in collections which turn to other forms, which had developed from the theatre or the magazines, for the majority of their comic songs. Writers turned to other forms, whether from artistic dissatisfaction with the old innuendoes or from a sense of their becoming unacceptable to a growing part of their audience; talent shifted to a new area, and adapted to the changed demands and taboos which that involved. The broadside formulae withered, and respectability demanded restraint which closed that avenue, but stimulated, on the other hand, the exploration of others, which did suit modern taste.

The taste of the patrons of the music halls was for a different formulation, a greater range and variety of expression, and for sophistications of diction which had no place in the less polished, professional performance of the street ballad-seller or the amateur rural performer; but it was the taste of the same section of the population which had previously found diversion in the broadsides, and the private and personal preoccupations of the people, and so the jokes they liked, had not undergone any deep change. The same feelings, the same problems, were still to be dealt with and tamed by the comedian, and in addition he had now to take up the slack of situations and feelings which were no longer, because of growing self-consciousness and inhibition, dealt with directly in serious, tragic and lyrical song. To help him in the task of extending the scope and significance of comic song he had a potentially much larger and richer fund of shared experience on which to draw: the life of the city provided the audience with a multitude of impressions, and quickened the responses of those who adapted to it successfully. Expressed, therefore, in different ways, all the themes for humour and kinds of comedy that have been described as belonging to the comic ballad tradition can be found at the basis of the humour of the music halls. This folk tradition is the foundation of the success of the halls, and the best productions of the most talented writers and singers draw their life from the organic relation to the audience which it gives them. The preoccupations and the values of the songs have not changed, contact with the most basic aspects of life shows in them direct and unromanticised, and the context of relationships remains the major interest of the ballad-singer and his audience. Max Beerbohm listed the subjects he found most frequently used in music-hall jokes as 'Mothers-in-law, hen-pecked husbands, twins, old maids, Jews, Germans, Italians, niggers . . .'[7] It is an impressionistic list, which excludes some very obvious subjects, the Irish, for example, and the various appetites, food, drink, sex, all of which are approached in some way in the songs of every comic performer, and includes four separate categories of foreigner largely for effect, since he wished to go on to assert that the public's humour is based upon delight in suffering, and contempt for the unfamiliar. A less biased assessment of the significance of the popularity of such jokes might find them simply the nineteenth-century version of the perennial preoccupations of the majority. Those things which touch everyone most nearly, about which they therefore seek reassurance and confirmation that they are shared by others, are the suffering caused by relationships and the need to feel that these ties are worth while by creating a community of feeling against the unfamiliar and foreign. The popular tradition expresses precisely these concerns at every period, and to attack it on the grounds that it does so is to make a social rather than a literary judgement. As works of art, the ballads of the music hall are strong and lively representatives of the convention to which they belong; their artistic function is performed in relation to an audience whose requirements and assumptions differ radically from those which shape the literary tradition. Judgements which ignore the context so completely are bound to distort and fail to appreciate the rough excellencies of the comic song, its humanity and its odd compassion.

The jokes of the music hall are just as primitive and as physical, as concerned with the body, as were the broadside ballad jests. At the climax of 'The Ratcatcher's Daughter'[8]

> Ven Lily-vite Sand 'e 'eard the news,
> His eyes ran down vith vater,
> Said 'e, 'In love I'll constant prove;
> And – blow me if I'll live long arter.'
> So he cut 'is throat vith a pane of glass,
> And stabb'd 'is donkey arter!

The joke is not only that he waited until he had cut his own throat to see to the donkey, which puts the whole picture into the realm of grotesque fantasy, where the clumsy instrument of death is but an added detail, but that he killed himself at all, an action which all Victorian comic verse finds hilarious. Most of the practical jokes, however, do stop short of decapitation, contenting themselves with the extreme physical discomfiture and humiliation of the protagonist. Sometimes the victim is a figure of authority, or the joke is played by one who at first seemed about to suffer himself but manages to turn the tables. In, for instance, Wilkie Bard's song 'Can't You Go Further Than That?' written by Frank Leo,[9] the singer shows his quick wit and encourages the audience to identify with him in the first stanza:

> Now round our neighbourhood, strange to say, we seldom have any excitement,
> But yesterday morning, I'll have you to know,
> A fellow came there with a travelling show
> And I went and paid tuppence and climbed into a swing –
> As I was trying to touch the sky,
> A pal of mine started to sing:
>
> 'What! Can't you go further than that?
> Can't you go further than that?'
> He called the boss and he paid two D,
> And he took the swing that was next to me;

He went up to a marvellous height,
Said I, 'What the deuce are you at?'
As he fell to the ground with a terrible crash,
I said *'Can't you go further than that?'*

The clever friend who gets his deserts from the singer is often replaced by someone whose discomfiture will give even greater satisfaction because he is in a position of authority, and uses his advantages in life to the annoyance of the average man. He may be a snooty clerk or shop assistant, or a doctor or lawyer who is confounded by homely wisdom or earthy contempt; the favourite figure, however, is the policeman. His position, and the way he is treated in the comic song of the halls, has some points of resemblance to the figure of the friar of older popular tales. He is officially a superior of the ordinary man, given power over him and supposed to be personally free from the vices he has authority to chastise in others; but in the eyes of the people he is not only unfitted for the position he holds by incompetence and addiction to the sins he is meant to suppress, but he is all too likely to pursue his personal desires by abuse of the authority he is given. The friar in 'The Friar in the Well' (*E.S.P.B.* no. 276) for example, uses a typical ruse to get his way:

He came to the maid when she went to bed,
Desiring to have her maidenhead,
But she denyëd his desire,
And told him that she feard hell-fire

'Tush' quoth the fryer, 'thou needest not doubt
If thou wert in hell I could sing thee out.'

The best known song about the police force,[10] 'Ask a Policeman', sung by James Fawn, makes precisely the same point about the coincidence of desire and official duty:

If your wife should want a friend,
Ask a policeman!
Who a watchful eye will lend
Ask a policeman!
Truth and honour you can trace
Written on his manly face;
When you're gone he'll mind your place.
Ask a policeman!

Jokes about the friars and about the police both began as expressions of strong feeling, tinged indeed with bitterness. At first attacks upon friars represented strong anti-clerical feeling; and the early songs about the police made satirical accusations of stupidity or complicity in crime:

> I'm known to all the prigs in town –
> To learned thieves well known my face is;
> The frail ones, too, my favours own,
> And charge me naught for sweet embraces.
> And if they're going a house to rob,
> Don't I watch (as is my duty?)
> But never splits about the job,
> For don't myself get half the booty?

The last line suggests the speaker is Irish, a point often made about the first recruits to the New Police, who were said to have come over without coats to their backs, to be put in a cosy uniform and given authority over their betters. In the same way, friars were scandalously unable to read and write. To mete out condign punishment and humiliation to these upstarts was a fantasy of popular justice which changed little with the change of the authority which issued the uniform to the oppressor. Later in the lives of both stock figures, however, the bitterness ebbed out of the jokes and left only conventional references to the friar as an embodiment of lechery and greed, and to policemen as the devotees of all the cooks whom their profession threw in their way.

The physical comedy of the practical joke is just as frequently, in the music-hall song, turned back upon the persona represented by the singer, and so upon the audience which has identified with him as well as finding him funny. The effect is to create, from a crudely basic joke about physical defects or failures, an atmosphere of friendly understanding and shared laughter which is the reverse of cruel, is rather accepting and assuaging of the humiliations of life. The singer who asks

> Why was I born, I'd like to know, with such a lanky figure?
> Everybody, they pipe me off, because I'm long and thin

is not laughed at as cruelly by the audience as he is in the stories he tells about himself. The stories are not in fact about his being long and thin, rather they are versions of stock situations of embarrassment to which everyone in the audience would have a sympathetically amused response. Often the jokes are completely conventional, intended to evoke recognition which triggers the set response rather than actual amusement: common examples are going swimming and losing one's clothes, or wearing a kilt on a windy day. Some are a little nearer reality:

the corrupt policeman might be viewed from a slightly different angle as the cause of rueful admissions on the part of the singer that he has been worsted in an encounter which he describes for our amusement:

The twinkling stars dispelled the gloom,
The night was calm and clear,
The air was full of sweet perfume,
And I was full of beer.
I swayed about, the bottled stout
Had quite upset my sight;
But a zealous 'slop' soon made me stop –
We were alone that night!

Chorus Only us two, only us two,
Only myself and the joker in blue.
He let go my collar, but kept my 'half dollar';
He smiled when we parted, for I'd 'parted' too![11]

In this song and the last other verses recount a stock comic situation which was very popular with comic broadside writers, that of the lecherous young man who encounters a dishonest girl and is robbed in the course of his attempts at seduction. In broadside versions the point of the ballad was usually either to emphasise the folly of committing oneself to the mercies of loose women who would bring a variety of disasters on the lecherous, or alternatively the situation was reversed at the end to celebrate the clever young man who was up to the dodges that might be pulled, and managed to get away not only with all that he brought with him but often without even paying the lady's fee. In the music hall, however, the singer would represent himself as the victim of the story, either getting himself married when all he had sought was a little harmless fun, or coming off very much the worst from encounters with fast women or prostitutes. The long and thin character quoted above had an embarrassing experience in the West End, accosted by a prostitute whom he could not shake off and being roundly abused by her; the hero of 'Only Us Two' sought the attractions of a lady who took him

Down where the daisies and buttercups grew.
Her love I was seeking, my 'oof' she was sneaking,
She smiled when we parted, for I'd 'parted' too!

T. W. Barrett in the late 1880s had a song by Harrington and Le Brunn on the subject, called 'The Belles of London', recounting his adventures amongst these ladies, which, to judge from the cover of the song, he performed for added piquancy in clerical dress:

Have you heard the London Belles
Singing 'Ding-Dong' to the swells?
Not the bells in the steeples high,
But the ones around the 'Cri'!
You'll find the bells in hundreds there,
Wearing other people's hair:
Once, *I* went, dressed like a Prince –
I've been 'stoney' ever since!

Chorus Oh! The belles of London Town!
Ding-dong! I've been undone!
Clipped and stripped, and dipped, and whipped
By the belles of London!

Maudie was the first, and she
Rang the changes nice on me;
Kissed me twice – then, with a grin,
Said 'Good night', stole my gold pin!
Soon, another petling, Flo',
Said 'Oh! dear, I love you so!'
And this belle, this charming thing,
From my finger wrung my ring!

His misfortunes multiply, to the amusement of the audience but without exciting their censure beyond a knowing conviction that he should have expected such treatment if he let himself in for it. The element of vicarious excitement and identification with his troubles, by young men who shared his desire for bright lights and female company and feared the dangers to which they might be exposed if they ventured into the night life of the West End, would be much the strongest reaction, apart from that of amusement, and it is a sympathetic reaction, with considerable therapeutic value in their social situation. It is an example of the comic song dealing with themes and situations which are peculiar to or whose difficulties are exacerbated by life in the city environment of the nineteenth century under social and moral conditions unlike those of previous generations of the poor. Even for previously unselfconscious social groups, sexuality could no longer be dealt with simply and seriously; but a comic singer had a valuable latitude to discuss both sex itself and the complications with which it was beset in an inhibited age. Representing himself as the victim of his own urges and of the female machinations to which they had committed him, but one who had nevertheless come up smiling, he was inviting the audience to relieve the pressure of their desires and fears by laughing with him.

Similarly, Harry Champion singing 'Right on my Doo-dah', written by Wincott and Leighton, is not presenting himself for the derision of the audience, but sharing with them a comic exaggeration of the situations of daily life in which the unfortunate hero is battered by circumstances and even by his nearest and dearest, but comes through smiling. The tales he tells are again stock ones – the child punished at school, the amateur taking on a professional fighter by mistake, the family hopping party, the house on fire – but each is told with enlivening verve which relates it, preposterously exaggerated as it is, to the kind of cheerfulness which carries the resilient through the real situations of crisis on which it is based. The third stanza, for example, is:

> Talk about the seaside, I have spent
> All my holidays at a game that pays,
> Going out a-hopping with the kids in Kent,
> But I never shall forget –
> Sleeping in the barn one moonlight night,
> Strike a light, straight, it's right!
> There was something buzzing underneath the clothes,
> And soon I felt some Mos-quit-toes –
> Right on me Doo-dah – Right on me Doo-dah-day,
> The wife said, 'Lumme, I have got it Joe!'
> She pick'd up a chopper and she gave one blow,
> 'Oh, lor' a mussy' was all that I could say,
> For it came down smack such a whack, whack, whack,
> Right on me Doo-dah-day.

This material is all thoroughly conventional, whether composed in 1840 or 1914; it is in a literal sense uninspired, the work of professionals moving at ease in a world of formulae separated from the realities which underlie them, putting together songs to a pre-set pattern of expectations. The convention, however, is not a dead one: the incidents are formalised and exaggerated, but they are not fossilised, and have an active relevance to the life of the audience on an emotional level. All popular art works in a similar way, simplifying and paring down experience, rather than exploring it deeply, organised to appeal to and satisfy the emotional rather than the intellectually analytic responses. As such, judged in comparison with earlier popular art, music-hall balladry is not inferior. This last example, a song of the declining years of the music hall and by no means an outstanding one, might well be compared with the famous 'Crabfish' song, a comic ballad in oral tradition from at least 1400 until the present day.[12] The version in the Percy manuscript begins

> Itt was a man of Affrica had a ffaire wiffe,
> Fairest that euer I saw the dayes of my liffe:
> With a ging, boyes, ginge! ginge, boyes, ginge!
> tarradididle, ffarradidle, ging, boyes, ging!
>
> This goodwiffe was bigbellyed, & with a lad,
> & euer shee longed ffor a sea crabbe.

The husband goes and buys one, early in the morning, and then

> The good man went home, & ere he wist,
> & put the Crabb in the Chamber pot where his wiffe pist.
> ging &c.
>
> The good wiffe, she went to doe as shee was wont;
> vp start the Crabfish, & catcht her by the Cunt.
> ging &c.
>
> 'Alas!' quoth the goodwiffe, 'that euer I was borne,
> the devill is in the pispott, & has me on his horne.'
>
> 'If thou be a crabb or crabfish by kind,
> thoule let thy hold goe with a blast of cold wind.'
>
> The good man laid to his mouth, & began to blowe,
> thinkeing therby that they Crab wold lett goe.
>
> 'Alas!' quoth the good man, 'that euer I came hither,
> he has ioyned my wiffes tayle & my nose together!'
>
> They good man called his neigbors in with great wonder,
> to part his wiues tayle & his nose asunder.

The chief difference in the jokes of these two pieces is that the older song is more explicit: ingenuity goes into elaborating the initial comic idea, rather than working the story up in a succession of stanzas to a point at which the substitution of the chorus of nonsense syllables will suggest the unnamed crux of the matter. The chorus-line is needed in both songs, however; and whether its utilisation for the purposes of innuendo is funnier than having it interspersed for the sake of participation into a story that could stand without it is a matter of taste. The music-hall audience laughs at the same thing, but either prefers, or is obliged by the restrictions which can be imposed upon public performance, to exercise its own imagination. A certain minimal development of sophistication is implied, though the printed texts of many music-hall songs are as clearly suggestive as any rural metaphor of courtship in a song, and the element of performance must have supplied the slowest members of the audience with a key. Indeed, the greatest stars of the halls worked often with skeletal material, adding all the real matter of their performance by their presence and by improvisation to suit the particular audience: the example always cited is Marie Lloyd, whose printed songs give one very little idea of her greatness, and particularly of the reason for her scandalous reputation. It has been suggested that this use of innuendo, as opposed to direct statement, implies a degeneration of popular taste connected with corrupting influences of the city: the crabfish song is robust bucolic humour, and 'Doo-dah-day' is smut. Both songs, however, are organised simply and specifically so that the audience may contemplate a crudely physical joke: neither is nearer to reality, each beginning from a real situation, fleas in one case and pregnancy cravings in the other, and taking off in a fantasy of humiliation with sadistic overtones which does not bear logical, or psychological, examination. Whether the object contemplated is given its four-letter name or substituted by a baby-talk synonym does not make very much difference to the effect of the whole; one suspects that the objection raised is simply a reaction of taste trained upon the literary tradition to reject the vulgar, misled into singling out the Victorian comic song because rural and broadside examples have until recently been suppressed or cleaned up, and are in any case given a respectable air by antiquity.

One of the resemblances between 'The Crabfish' and 'Doo-dah-day' is the choice of domestic settings, and the way in which the starting point for the joke is in both one of the trials of family life. A bias towards the events and relationships between the sexes after, rather than before, marriage has already been noticed as one of the facets of the comic ballad. In the music hall the practical joke which is turned against the singer himself is often marriage; his function is partly to be the butt of all the misfortunes consequent upon being a part of the ordinary social organisation of relationships. Thus the bond between the singer and the audience is very close, and they must accept him as typical of themselves even while they laugh at him as a fool and a victim of circumstances and his wife, or else he would seem, in the stories he tells, to be laughing contemptuously at their poverty. They are trapped in the domestic tangles he describes, and need to escape by laughing at them, but also to confirm the value of the way of life to which they are committed by laughing with the man involved in it and at those who are outside.

The domestic situations which are used in this exposition of marriage fall into a few, well-used categories, each reflecting a real concern, and some coinciding with the old-established subjects for popular jokes. The basic difficulty about keeping house for a wife and family is, of course, money – the rich have no need of this kind of domestic comedy. The first result of poverty is insufficient food, and there are innumerable songs about eating, often of a touching simplicity, single-mindedly describing a good meal or a favourite delicacy, the mere contemplation of which is a satisfaction. Providing food for others is funnier, however, and there are songs like Albert Chevalier's 'Blue Ribbon Jane'[13] in which a canny coster looks for a teetotal wife, only to discover that she makes up for it in eating:

She'd a plate o' whelks an' a happle or two,
She'd a hice, 'alf lemon, 'alf cream,
She'd a pound of dates, an' some monkey nuts,
Put chocolate away like steam.
Then she 'over'd round a two-eyed steak
Ate the bloater an' the roe.
When I whispers 'Jane, my own blue ribbon Jane,
'Ave yer finished yet?' she answers 'No!'

Similarly in 'Pennyworth of Winkles' the singer buys himself this treat on the way home from work, puts it on the table, and returns to find his wife and seven kids 'Pickin' all the big ones aht'. More serious financial difficulties lead to non-payment of rent, a constant topic, and the expedient of 'shooting the moon' to avoid payment, as in Marie Lloyd's 'Follow the Van':

We had to move away
'Cos the rent we couldn't pay,
The moving van came round just after dark;
There was me and my old man
Shoving things inside the van
Which we'd often done before, let me remark . . .

A family that does not move quickly enough is embroiled in the next comedy turn, the broker's men, dealt with in Harry Champion's 'We've All Been Having a Go at It':

Talk about a penn'oth of fun,
Yesterday it fair took the bun –
In came the brokers to collar our sticks,
But we were up to all their tricks.

Mother she chased 'em round the room,
Settled their doom with a big broom,
And when father came home at night
And said 'Where's the brokers?' I yelled – 'All right!

We've all been having a go at 'em,
All been having a go at 'em,
One's in the dusthole – *minus pants*,
Another's gone home in an ambulance;
Oh! good gracious didn't we make a show,
Seventeen of us – besides myself – and we've all been having a go!'

The size of this family is typical of the exaggeration of the halls, where, as Beerbohm noticed, the fathering of twins is seen as a comical disaster, and the large family (which was the chief reason for poverty in the eyes of the working man, but at the same time proof of his personal strength and importance) was dealt with in many songs with a mixture of pride and despair. A Tabrar song of 1887 speculates on the joys and sorrows of the popular notion of the Mormon's situation under the title 'Hundreds and Thousands'; in 1882 he wrote a chorus song entitled 'I shouldn't advise you to do it' which included the lines

For when a man's married the trouble begins,
The kids come in couples and add to his sins
If you can't have a wife now without having twins
I shouldn't advise you to do it.

Later another Wincott and Leighton song offers the singer's whole domestic entourage for sale:

Any fellow now who wants to settle down, had better settle up –
Such a bargain you will never have again, as sure as my name's Jupp.
If you buy the missis and my little tribe, to prove that I'm no dodger,
I'll sell you the marriage lines for half of shag, and come and be your young man lodger.

Chorus 1, 2, 3, 4, 5, 6, 7, 8,
Funny little kids at home;
Three tom cats, and a she cat too,
An old Pol parrot, and a Cock-a-doodle-do;
A half-bred dog with his ears cut short,
And a great big fat strong wife.
With a lot like that, I'll eat my hat,
If you can't lead a very merry life.

Gus Elen treats the situation with characteristic humility and resignation, in place of this bravura:

> Before I was married I'd a pocket full o' quids;
> Now I've a pocket full of holes, and seven kids.
> I ought to be the 'appiest individual on the earth,
> But I've been a grumbl-izer since my birth.
> Just because the nippers scream and shout,
> Just because my wife throws plates about,
> Just because she beats me now and then,
> I've come to the conclusion I am not like uvver men.[14]

The whole point is, of course, that he is just like other men; his predicament, and the reaction to it which he is so ashamed of, in the face of the expectation of domestic bliss, are shared by his audience. The situation seen from the woman's angle is just as bleakly funny; expectations of 'our happy little home', in a song of that name by Harry Randall, have given way to the demand for beer money, until credit has run out, the roof is leaking, the stairs have been used for fuel, and 'We haven't paid last quarter, and they're chopping off the water'. The singer, a man appearing as a woman, continues to assert 'I'm just about as happy as they make 'em now-a-days'.

The position of the breadwinner is the most usual source of this kind of humour, however, and responsibility for the home and children can be further aggravated by the imposition of other dependants, particularly the wife's relations; Arthur Lloyd had a famous song with this phrase as its title, and a chorus which enumerated them:

> There's her uncle – and her brother – and her sister – and her mother
> And her auntie – and another –
> Who is cousin to her mother –[15]

in a tone of rising panic. The climax of 'Rose, Rose, Rose' by R. Temple, runs

> But Rose, Rose, Rose,
> I'm not going to marry all those!
> Aunties in dozens, and fat-headed cousins
> In rows, rows, rows!

One of the problems with the mother-in-law is also that 'She'd come on a visit and stop for a year'. These grotesque pictures of domestic life are an exploration of the major problems of everyday existence, couched always in the most concrete, physical terms possible, to cut them down to a manageable size. Squalor, overcrowding and poverty are dealt with by making jokes about fleas.

The worm's eye view, which turns a sardonically earthy glance upon the airy notion of romance and wedded bliss, can be used in the same way to cut down to size other high-flown notions, and once again the deflation works by means of the physical practical joke. It may be directed at revealing the realities behind politics and military heroics, as in the much-quoted, but actually rare, example of topical political satire in the music hall, Macdermott's song about Charles Dilke, M.P., where the impulse was provided by Dilke having committed adultery, and so laid himself open to popular amusement by displaying physical weakness unbefitting his position. Such topically satirical songs are unusual: the music hall prefers its own traditional jokes on its own subjects, and tends to leave the use of its comic ballad-forms for pointed satire to the magazine writers who borrowed them. Sometimes comment on a topical subject might creep in, when that subject fitted into an established pattern, as in the Dilke affair, and then it might well become a staple joke living on when its topicality had long passed; jokes about Bloomers, a short-lived fashion which never seriously caught on in Britain, but which were immortalised in decades of music-hall song, are such an instance. Here the reactionary tendency of the humour of the halls, which served to preserve established social patterns when they fulfilled an emotional purpose for the popular audience, was the reason for the fossilisation of the joke, as part of the attack upon the problem of woman's 'maistrie'. A woman in bloomers was literally, and so presumably metaphorically, wearing the trousers.

Debunking and deflationary attacks upon pretension were more often, in the characteristically popular manner, directed at the upsetting of individual self-aggrandisement than at the government or the Establishment at large. The long and varied tradition of the stage presentation of swells, mashers and knuts, stretching from the Lions Comiques in the 1850s and 1860s to Vesta Tilley's impersonations in the 1890s and 1900s, was in some sense deflationary. It presented these ideals of opulence and pleasure for straightforward admiration, but often at the same time it edged the picture with irony: the individual gentleman depicted was as often as not shown to be overspending his income, or indeed really a poor man having one grand night out, or he was incapably drunk, or fleeced by those he bought his pleasures from, or, very often, seen to be stupid to the point of feeble-mindedness because of his upper-class origins. Vance in 1866 sang about and presumably represented in his appearance the ludicrous exaggeration of male fashion affected by the heavy swell, in a song written by J. B. Geoghegan called 'The Style':

My hair magenta look at that
Of course you'll say its dyed
But no you view its own bright hue
'Tis noticed far and wide
And then my moustachous see the cut
I'm sure so fine a pair
Was never seen
They're ting'd with green
In contrast to my hair.

Chorus This is about the Style Ha! ha!
I think it's just the Style Ha! ha!
My taste excels
The howling swells
By Jove I'm quite the Style ha! ha!

In 1895 Charles Godfrey had a Le Brunn song[16] with the same subject in a more explicitly critical form, called 'Such a Don, Don't you Know!' with stanzas such as this:

He keeps a smart hansom – it hurts him to walk;
He says it's a deuce of a bore to talk;
He can tell champagne by a sniff at the cork –
He's a beastly good judge, don't you know!
Irresistible he is, and none can deny
That ladies turn faint as he passes them by;
With the wickedest wink – and a glass – in his eye –
By God! Don Juan! don't you know!

Similarly the other ranks' view of the army officer was a sardonic perception of the reality behind his pretences to authority and superiority, often good-natured, but firmly putting him in his place by stressing his physical and mental weaknesses as making his self-estimate ludicrous. 'The Galloping Major' and 'Gingah' are both examples of this, while 'On the Staff', in which a newly appointed staff officer is made to boast cheerfully of greater and greater enormities of cowardice, self-indulgence and abuse of his position, is a war-time song, one of many which offset the music-hall cheer leading during the First World War and indeed all previous conflicts. All pretensions to be better than anyone else, and all conventions and ideals to which individual experience did not match up, came under attack, always with the unspoken comment that what really exists, the pleasure that everyone can experience, is preferable to grand abstract notions. In 1898, in the fervour of wars in the Sudan and elsewhere, a singer could raise sympathetic laughter by reporting his conversation with a recruiting sergeant:

'Be a soldier lad' said he,
'Lots of girls and £.s.d.
What say? – Will you join?
You'll mash the girls in jackets red
And live just like a Lord!'
Said I, 'What price the old 'uns
That go in the casual ward?' –

Chorus I'm much better off where I am![17]

The traditional boastfulness of certain young men was treated with amused and knowing tolerance rather than derision, in songs such as 'Dear me! is that possible?' written by Tabrar and sung in the early 1880s by Leybourne, dressed as a sailor. His boasts are a mixture of the topical – surviving a fall from a balloon and a trip down Niagara Falls – and the traditional, including one, the putting out of a house on fire by spitting down the chimney, which has reverberations echoing back into the realm of folk ritual and its talismanic exaggeration. The feats of which he boasts are enjoyed in themselves, and the deflation added by the chorus is of the gentlest kind, as the form of the verse makes clear:

There's a bridge that crosses the river Tyne,
Dear me! is that possible?
I once saw an accident, occurring on the line,
Dear me! is that possible?
Two engines meeting, might and main,
I'd saved lives before, so I did so again,
I put up my arms and stopped the train!
Dear me! is that possible?

The first and second times the refrain occurs it seems gratifyingly appreciative of the wonders narrated, spurring the story-teller on to greater revelations, only to knock the ground from under him, in the most genial possible way, by adding it once again as he gets to the ridiculous climax of his tale.

In almost every case the use of the first person in the music-hall ballad and song has the effect of generalising the faults and weaknesses described, so that they seem to belong to the whole of humanity. The audience are asked to identify with the singer and so accept his experience as a version of their own, rather than to use their laughter as a critical weapon against the faults and follies of others. The comparatively few ballads which use the third person have sometimes a different, and alien, tone of superiority and sophistication. Something of this feeling exists in the critical bite of the Charles Godfrey song, 'Such a Don', already quoted, and it is much more noticeable in some of Vesta Tilley's songs, such as 'That's Pa!' written by E. W. Rogers. The first verse and refrain go through the catalogue of domestic jokes, but with a distinctive and unpleasant edge of contempt for the central figure who is not, in this case, identified with the singer, or identified with by the audience:

> There is a person nicknamed 'Pa' – a perfect howling fraud,
> You'll see his portrait sometimes in a helmet and a sword;
> Strange folks think he's a six-foot Guard, and gaze on him with fear,
> Not knowing he's a dock-clerk and a Peckham Volunteer.
>
> Refrain There's a ginger-whisker'd, five-foot-nothing little bit of man
> That comes running home to tea – that's Pa!
> Who sits mildly eating bread and scrape as gently as can be
> With a baby on each knee – that's Pa!
> Later on he dons an apron, scrubs the floor and shakes the mat,
> While the lodger toddles out with Ma,
> And that baby-minding, kitchen-scrubbing, trod-on little rat –
> That's Pa! that's Pa! that's Pa!!!

There are three more very clever sketches of the lower- and middle-class male, as hypocritical teetotaller sneaking away to the ballet with a lady on each arm, as a fair-weather sailor, and as a gambler, all equally viciously contemptuous, so that one feels that the effect is contrary to the spirit of amelioration, fortitude and cheerfulness which normally pervades even the most crudely grotesque of these songs. Presumably Vesta Tilley's costume for this number suggested that she was a scornful youngster mocking his father, since she usually dressed as an immaculate young man with a real or pretended fashionable life; the character would certainly not take the edge off the song. There is a twist at the end of it, by which the despised father of the verse is transformed in the refrain into a hero, by going to war and winning the Victoria Cross, thus belying his appearance in a different way, but it adds a final touch of sentimentality to the preceding cynicism which makes the whole thing worse; it is too blatantly false to be acceptable as a normal music-hall swing of feeling.

Songs like this, contrary to the whole mood of popular humour, are rare in the music hall, though they do crop up at times throughout its history. Vesta Tilley was a performer of the last decades, but the ugliness of the song, dwelling on deflation and humiliation inflicted for its own sake, can be matched by some of the pieces of Thomas Hudson, one of the earliest singers. 'Cat's Head Apples', a song of the 1830s, is an instance, in which a story is told to explain the name of this fruit, in the manner of a fable. The story itself is gruesome: Widow Tomkins goes away, forgetting her cat, and comes back at last to find that the animal has eaten itself in hunger, until only its head remained, which she buries at the foot of her apple tree, and so affects the fruit. It is told in detail and with much relish, dwelling upon the impossible description with a sly admiration of its own cleverness, and a propensity to asides which are calculated to further the impression of detached superiority:

> This wetted quite his appetite, and tho' the stump was sore,
> The next day he was tempted (sad!) to eat a little more;
> To make his life the longer then, he made his body shorter,
> And one after t'other, 'gad, he eat his hinder quarter.[18]

The explanation of such off-shoots of the popular tradition must be sought by considering the audience for which they are intended, and it will usually be seen to be rather out of the mainstream of lower- and lower-middle-class suburban workers and their wives who formed the staple audience. Thomas Hudson was a performer in the Cyder Cellars, where the entertainment was rather more sophisticated, and certainly less respectable, than that of the later halls. Such a song as this would be sung, probably, late at night, to an audience of Bohemian gentlemen. Its slyness and its condescending attitude to the telling of a story are thus explicable in terms of the audience reaction that it invited: not involvement and identification, but applause for the artist's cleverness and a sense of their own sophistication. Vesta Tilley was in a similar position, in that she was primarily a star of the big West End halls and Palaces of Variety rather than of the homely minor houses; her blasé air, the piquancy of her immaculate drag and the characters she projected and her concealed femininity, are all part of a movement away from popular theatre as represented by the old style of music hall towards the very sophisticated pleasures of the revue and cabaret stage, appealing once again to a select few whose enjoyment of the entertainment depended rather on a sense of its difference from ordinary life than on an easy and comforting identification with one's neighbours. Vesta Tilley herself performed to a large audience, but her kind of entertainment was perhaps not essentially popular.

The difference which manifests itself here is a difference of attitude rather than of the basic ingredients the singers and writers used. Their material was sufficiently like that of the more truly popular singers to be acceptable to the larger audience. Hudson's 'Cat's Head Apples' is quoted here from a broadside printing, and Vesta Tilley did fill the West End halls rather than a revue bar. The quotation from 'That's Pa!' shows her using all the standard jokes, even though in a peculiar way; and 'Cat's Head Apples' is interesting for its relation to the many songs of fantasy and exaggeration which the music hall produced. By puns, plays on words, and particularly by the device of taking literally abstract or metaphorical turns of phrase, the imagination is freed into a world where the fantastic and the physical are comically combined. It is a rather child-like form of humour, delighting in the impossible situation or supposition, escaping from the limitations of the physical laws of the universe by pretending that they do not exist in this case. There is a link, perhaps, with the broadside account of marvels and miraculous happenings, as well as with fairy stories, and the taste for such songs lived as long as the music hall itself, in for example Gracie Fields's 'The Biggest Aspidistra in the World'. Examples occur sporadically from the very earliest days: Leybourne had a song entitled 'I won't believe it', with words by Fred Albert, which began with the line 'O tell me not my love's untrue' and rapidly ran through a series of impossible events which must happen before he would believe she could be. The humour of the song, such as it is, is in this motley list of topical asides – 'When Gladstone and D'Israel fight' – mingled with paradoxes and nonsense:

> When in the ground you plant mutton chops, when out of them grow sheep,
> When babies without feeding bottles at night won't [*sic*; will?] go to sleep,
> When cats won't play on the tiles at night, all concerts they eschew . . .
> No! I won't believe it's true, till carrots they turn blue,
> Till in the gutter you find fresh butter, I won't believe it's true.[19]

A stronger narrative line holds together a later example, Harry Bedford's 'Cooking the Cock o' the North' with words by Harry Wincott:

I went into a raffle once,
And what do you think I got?
Well, a beautiful bird from off McNab,
And the missis went clean off her dot.
We screwed his neck in the wringing machine,
But the cock of the north wouldn't die;
We shoved him into the saucepan then,
But every minute he'd cry –

Chorus 'Cock a doodle, cock a doodle',
That's what he sang in the broth.
We scraped him and faked him,
Boiled him and baked him,
Cooking the cock of the north.

We took him out of the saucepan then,
And covered him over with ice;
We stuck a pin in the parson's nose,
And stuffed him with treacle and rice . .

We stuffed his poverty corner up
With sage and potatoes well,
We fired three shots at his marble arch,
And three at his darby kell.
We shoved him into the oven, and then
We made up the fire nice and high,
But he kick'd the door of the oven right off,
And then again started to cry –

(Chorus)

Finally they are obliged to let him live, tied by the tablecloth to the bedpost, proclaiming his northern origin. Similar fantasies based on colloquial phrases that caught the writer's fancy abound, from early in the history of the halls; there is a song, for instance, called 'Allowed to be Drunk on the Premises', and several different sets of words built on the alleged boarding-house advertisement 'Young Men Taken in and Done For'.[20]

Further examination of this tendency must be reserved for a discussion of the technical aspects of the music-hall ballads, along with their other verbal complexities; there remains to be considered first one remaining area of subject-matter. This is the music-hall treatment of sex, and the preserving there of the popular attitude to the character and treatment of the female which has been described. As was the case in the sentimental songs, women in comic music-hall ballads resemble the women of the rural folk tradition and of the broadsides, in that they are seen in the light of the assumptions peculiar to the popular attitude. They are active rather than passive participants in events of every kind, they have opinions and powers of their own, and are a force to be reckoned with or counted upon rather than a symbol to be admired and revered. It is assumed that they are equal partners in sexual matters and must be expected to be fertile producers of offspring, an activity which also means that they have an aggressive interest in getting married and a role in courtship and after it which is at least as active as that of the man, and moreover is likely to conflict with his interests. The active, vital woman with a life of her own to live is always liable to be in competition with her spouse for mastery of one kind or another, whether simply diverting the whole of the marital budget to her concerns at the expense of his pleasures, wishing to reverse their roles and impose her tasks upon him, or to express herself at the expense of his self-respect and good name, by asserting the sexuality which it is assumed is at least as strong in her as it is in him. This range of assumptions lies behind a variety of kinds of song and story.

The female comic singers of the halls were figures of huge vitality, proclaiming their own sense of life with great verve, using their songs as positive affirmation of the values attached to the female by the popular code. The first wave of cockney coster singers included several women who were of this kind, asserting their independence and strong enjoyment of life. Bessy Bellwood's 'What Cheer, 'Ria', mentioned in Chapter 4, begins:

> I am a girl what's doing wery well in the wegetable line,
> And as I'd saved a bob or two, I thought I'd cut a shine.
> So I goes and buys some toggery, these 'ere wery clothes you see,
> And with the money I had left I thought I'd have a spree.
> So I goes into a music hall where I'd often been afore,
> I don't go in the gallery but on the bottom floor;
> I sits down by the Chairman and calls for a pot of stout,
> My pals in the gallery spotted me and they all commenced to shout.[21]

The story she tells is against herself, in the same way as the men's comic tales of disaster – her adventure is that of a self-sufficient, confident person in no way inhibited by her sex, the very opposite of the Victorian lady, but clearly presented for the affectionate self-identification of the girls of the audience. Similarly Nellie Wallace's song 'Half-past nine on My Wedding Day' displays a most unladylike anticipation of marriage, of which the chorus is

> For next Monday morning is my wedding day;
> When the supper's over if the company wants to stay,
> Me and me Georgie we shall resign,
> We're going to blow the candles out at half-past nine![22]

The survival of the euphemism about blowing out the candles is an indication of the continuity of the sexual attitude from earlier folk-song, such as 'The London Prentice', which is also in the voice of the girl rather than the boy. Marie Lloyd's tremendous projection was clearly also based upon the assumption that she enjoyed the situations at which she hinted quite as much as any man. The sexuality, and therefore the frustration and consequent openness to advances, of the widow, is a popular joke which finds its way into the halls, in such songs as Clifford Gray's 'Widows are Wonderful'. The girl who makes her own way in the world by her wits in broadsides such as 'The Lass of Islington' has many sisters in music-hall song, who have a similar metaphorical way of describing their triumphs:

> Yes, I've learnt to know the bliss
> Of a stolen little kiss,
> When you heave a sigh and softly murmur, 'Pet!'
> As you gaze into his face,
> Wrapt in amorous embrace,
> But I've never lost my last train yet, Oh No!
> I've never lost my last train yet.[23]

This song of Marie Lloyd's, and Alice Lemar's 'And her golden hair was hanging down her back' both also preserve the broadside's contrast between the country girl, expected to be an innocent, and the clever and experienced woman she proves herself to be. The story is a feminine answer to the figure of the smart city man who outwits the yokels, both male and female.

From this assumption of the equally strong sexuality of the female comes also the kind of song often used by the comic whose stage persona was the shy, retiring, put-upon little man, in which his shyness is gloriously overcome by a girl willing and able to take the initiative. The obvious example is 'I'm Shy, Mary Ellen', but there are several more, including Dan Leno's 'I'll marry him!' A prototype of these songs seems to be 'Shy, shy, dreadfully shy', sung by George Leybourne, which begins

I'm nervous, figetty, very reserv'd,
In fact I'm most awfully shy . . .
I can't look a girl in the face, but I blush,
For I feel most awfully shy . . .

Chorus Shy, shy, shy, shy,
Oh! I'm so shy . . . dreadfully shy . . .
Shy, shy, shy, shy,
I can't pass a stay shop because I'm so shy.[24]

He has a last verse which tells an exactly typical story of his falling in love but being too shy to speak, and sitting in silence until the girl is obliged to do the asking; but Leybourne's usual stage persona, of the confident man-about-town always ready with a leer, and the apparent gaps in this song which are clearly to be filled in with material which is for some reason unprintable, suggest that this was delivered very much tongue in cheek, as a skit of those who were shy, or by a knowing card who found it a good line to take with the girls.

Songs by men who apparently enjoyed the domination of independent, self-assertive women, or whose position as hen-pecked husbands was comic and yet not quite without its compensations, also occur from the early days of the halls, like 'The Gymnastic Wife' by G. W. Hunt, in which the husband boasts of and bemoans his athletic wife:

Instead of walking down the stairs
She'll clear the flight at a bound,
Catch hold of me by the tail of my coat,
And swing me round and round.
She throws half-hundred weights about,
And twirls the Indian club;
Or balances two chairs and the cat
On top of the washing tub.[25]

The character impersonated by Vance in the Tabrar song 'Have you seen her?' is more insistent upon his admiration and affection for his formidable and apparently errant sweetheart; the chorus runs:

She's a great big tall girl – on her chin she's got a dimple!
Rare, fair, square girl – on her nose she's got a pimple!
P'rhaps she's gone, this morn, with a Duke or Earl,
But, all I want to know is – have you seen my girl?[26]

The northern singers also had an affection for powerful women, like Cushie Butterfield who was 'a big lass and a bonnie lass and she likes her beer', and whose response to a proposal was to laugh with a roar like a bull; and Nanny, the wife in a song by Tommy Armstrong[27] which recounts an incident in a public house. While waiting for a train to go on a shopping trip to buy clothes for their children, the singer and Nanny drink two gills of beer and nine glasses of gin – all the gin being Nanny's. She discards various parts of her clothes, and launches into song – to his astonishment, since he had never heard her sing – before collapsing spectacularly, smashing four chairs. The last stanza is a nice mixture of feeling, combining embarrassment at her condition, sympathy for her ill-treatment by the landlord, irritation at the inconvenience of it all and his own inability to shift her great bulk, and wondering admiration for her abandonment:

He sez to me, 'Is this yor wife, an' where de ye belang?'
Aa sez, 'It is, an' she's teun a fit wi' tryin' te sing a bit sang.'
He flung his arms around hor waist, an' trailed hor ower the floor,
An' poor aad Nan, like a dorty hoose cat, was hoyed oot side o' the door.
An' there she wes lyin', byeth groanin' and' cryin', te claim hor Aa really thowt shyem;
Aa tried ta lift hor, but Aa cudden't shift hor, an Aa wished Aa had Nanny at hyem.
The papor man said he wad give hor a lift, se we hoisted hor in to the trap:
But Nan was that tight she cuddent sit up, so we fastened her down wiv a strap.
She cuddent sit up an' she waddent lie doon, an' she kicked till she broke the conveyance;
She lost a new basket, hor hat an' hor shaal,
That wummin, wi' lossin' the trains.

These formidable ladies are often viewed as threats to the male domain. The theme of woman's 'maistrie' is very much alive in the music-hall song, as a natural aspect of the whole attitude to women: unhampered by the enforced passivity of the courtly role, the woman has to be kept in her place by some other means, or the male sense of his duty, responsibility and therefore power within the family will be undermined. Some songs, like 'At Trinity Church I met my Doom', treat the situation simply, for comic effect; but in many, as in 'It's a Great Big Shame', discussed in Chapter 4, deeply-felt bitterness and frustration lie behind the comedy.

George Orwell felt that the music-hall songs indicated a reverence for marriage as an institution and a basically moral attitude amongst the people for whom they were written which made it possible to joke about such things without making any serious protest or attempt to undermine existing institutions. Often the ballads of the halls do give the impression of reactionary adherence to established social patterns, but they have room for a larger morality, more variations of the pattern, than such a judgement would imply in the context of Victorian society. Marriage is never seriously attacked and questioned, but neither is its authority accepted in a spirit of solemnity which precludes other attitudes and relationships. Cuckoldry had dropped from its previously paramount position in the comic chapter of relationships, but there was still a cheerful acceptance of songs which used the husband as a figure of authority to be undermined by an alliance of the wife and her 'cousin', or whatever he might be called. The lover had one role which was familiar enough to be used as a passing reference in any song about the trials of marriage, and instances of it have already occurred in several preceding quotations; he was the 'lodger', whose position in the household reflected working-class living conditions, which meant that few families, even those who did rent a house, could afford to live in all of it themselves, and young working people had either to stay in their own crowded homes or lodge elsewhere. It also recalls a story-pattern which goes back to medieval fabliaux, and is used by Chaucer in *The Miller's Tale*. It seems to me that rather than talking of the music-hall songs as upholding or opposing any given social institution, it would be more true to their spirit to describe them as supporting the ancient popular attitudes to life: these had little to do with any deliberate or doctrinaire rebellion against other values, or against social systems regarded as being imposed from above; they rather accepted certain given facts, the laws of nature and the laws of the king, as part of the circumstances of living of which one made what one could.

The translation of the people to an urban life can be argued to have impoverished the tragic and lyric side of their culture, possibly because it removed stability and certainties and the security needed for the free expression of sensibility in this way; but humour, which can be used most effectively in a disturbed and fragmented society to preserve community of feeling by laughing at things together, and to defend individuals against confusion and disintegrating pressures by uniting them with their fellows and attacking outsiders, could and did flourish freely. Popular art is anti-authoritarian in so far as authorities of any kind are anti the individual living his life in his own way and according to the complex primitive patterns of his own community. The comic ballads of the halls are richer and more varied than the comic broadsides partly because much more of the weight of the popular culture falls upon them, in the absence of good serious songs, and partly because their range of reference is as large and varied as their communities. The themes of popular verse are expressed in the comic ballads by means of a set of conventions, as they always are, but their basis is a shared experience so much richer that the conventions themselves are more various, flexible and vivid than those of the old broadsides. The life of the Victorian cities was not only squalid, even for the poorest – it was also exciting and fast-moving, full of novelties and a sense of participation, even if only at a distance or through having to do the dirty work involved, in the nation's progress and expansion. The mindless patriotic song was the expression of a feeling which also issued more fruitfully in thousands of topical comments and jokes, forming a running commentary upon the news of the day, the latest fads, fashions, inventions, not handled satirically but with a sense of enjoyment of being 'up' in what was going on. The life of the city, its transport, its postal services, its new buildings, changing by-laws, advertisements and spectacles formed a rich texture of experience upon which the wit of the city throve, and by means of which the perennial popular concerns could be explored in comic song. What was lost to the serious song in the transition to the cities was in some sense made up by this gain.

The gain in depth and artistry can be seen in every comparison one makes between the old humorous song and the music-hall comic ballad. The slightest representatives of the music-hall tradition, written within its conventions, display at least as much skill and telling understanding of human nature as most of the empty catches and laboured tales which satisfied the pedlar's customers in preceding periods. In for example the use of word-play, the delight in language which the music hall displays so conspicuously, one can see a development of broadside conventions and techniques, but brought to a much higher degree of polish, and moreover made to convey something instead of being mere mouth-music and nonsense. The earlier comparison between 'Doo-dah-day' and 'The Crabfish' in the use each makes of the chorus illustrates this point, but it can be reinforced by reference to the use of dialect in the broadsides and in the music hall. There is a traditional association between the Irish and nonsense humour and the misuse of language, based presumably on the belief that the Irish are stupid and cannot use words properly or tell the truth, and are liable to enmesh themselves in preposterous adventures, real or imaginary. One broadside which bases its humour on this notion is 'The Wonderful Adventures of Mr. O'Flynn, in search of Old Mother Clifton', which begins

> Being told be a friend whom I met t'other day,
> That Mother Clifton's house was blown away,
> Nineteen score miles beyond the moon,
> Think I to myself I'll be after her soon,
> Nine days I was searching in great alarm,
> My shins in my pocket, my head 'neath my arm,
> On the back of a Buck-Flea mounted high;
> O'er buttermilk bog-holes we gaily did fly.

Another early song, printed in *The Vauxhall Comic Song Book* in 1847,[28] shows the use of a nonsense chorus in this context:

> Says I, 'By my shoul, you're monstratiously kind;
> Then you'll sail away, and I'll look mighty queer now,
> When I come up and see myself all left behind.'
> With my tal de ral lal de ral lal de ral la ral la,
> Tal de ral la ral la la ral la la;
> And sing palliluh, whilliluh, pallilih,
> Whack, boderation, and Langlolee.

Neither of these offerings seems comic to the modern ear, and their crude devices of language – exaggeration, impossibility, contradiction – belong to an idea of the humorous which is based upon slow, illiterate responses. The music-hall manipulation of dialect and of language for comic effect is not only more slick and polished, but its aims are higher: the cockney dialect song, and the vernacular writing of northern popular poets like Tommy Armstrong, is intended to provoke complex responses of identification, pleasure and amusement which have already been discussed. Compare these examples with the use of cockney whimsy and fantasy in 'The 'Ouses in Between': in full flood of description of his backyard paradise, Gus Elen says

> There's the bunny shares 'is egg-box wiv the cross-eyed cock and hen,
> Though they 'as got the pip, and 'im the morf;

In a dog's-'ouse on the line-post there was pigeons nine or ten,
Till someone took'd a brick and knocked it off.
The dust-cart, though it seldom comes, is just like 'arvest 'ome,
And we mean to rig a dairy up some'ow;
Put the donkey in the wash-house with some imitation 'orns,
For we're teaching 'im to moo just like a kah [cow].

Chorus Oh! it really is a werry pretty garden,
And 'Endon to the westward could be seen;
And by clinging to the chimbley,
You could see across to Wembley,
If it wasn't for the 'ouses in between.[29]

The statements are no more to be taken for the truth than those of the Irishman in 'Mother Clifton'; but the reason for them is not conventional idiocy, but a comment upon city living, and the triumph of the imagination, with which the listeners can sympathise as they laugh. The use of the dialect is both funny and loving, a characterisation rather than a burlesque, a feature of the best cockney songs which comes out even more clearly in ''E Talks Like a Picture Book', another of Elen's songs. The hero of this story is the 'celebrated working man', the character in every public bar who knows how to run the country better than any M.P., at whose notions the knowing may laugh and at the same time wish they could accept them with the innocence of the solemn little man who sings the song:

Now at the 'Pipe and Pewter' there's a sort o' little club,
And 'Inky' in the chair is just immense;
At argyment, there ain't a cove wot uses that there pub,
Wot can take 'is number down, or talk more sense;
'E sez if all o' England's welf was piled up in ther bank,
So as each man 'ad 'is share, and nuffing more,
There'd be a quid a week for all, no matter what their rank –
Yus; and then he said we shouldn't have no poor.

Chorus Oh! 'e talks just like a picture-book, does 'Inky',
At argyment 'e's quite a forough-bred;
Though 'e deals in coal and coke
'E's an heducated bloke, (*and*)
A man who's got some big fings in 'is 'ed.[30]

This writer (A. R. Marshall) is not as thorough or as phonetic in his cockney as Edgar Bateman in 'The 'Ouses in Between', but he has captured the character's responses perfectly in his language, the modestly proud 'sort 'o little club', the admiring superlative 'just immense' and the trusting solemnity of the last line, with its pause after 'Yus', and the stress laid upon the crowning statement of the pub orator by 'and then he said'. The touching and comic last line of the chorus, the speaker's solemn own opinion, is a triumph of this kind of writing. The skill and dexterity of the writer and the singer are unquestionably far removed from the crude efforts of the broadside writer, and the uses to which they are put are much more subtle. The technical achievement is not, however, a matter of individual genius, but is developed out of the stock of cockney writing which built up in the course of the Victorian period, and the complexity of ideas and emotions expressed is not a matter of individual inspiration and self-expression, but a voice speaking for and about the common man. It is still popular poetry, but of a highly developed kind, reaching its point of ultimate development in the way in which the great tragic ballads did in eighteenth-century hands.

The development of other forms of verbal play and technical skill in the songs of the music halls can also be traced from early, relatively simple or crude examples, through a process of sophistication and growing complexity, as the skill of the writers and the demands of the audience increased. It is difficult for the modern ear to pick up all the puns, allusions and layers of meaning which came to be regularly and as a matter of convention incorporated in songs intended for audiences with little formal education, but with a tradition of humour of this kind on which to found their reactions. In the 1860s the taste for chime and rhyme was satisfied still by songs very little removed from the Irish nonsense ballads which were clearly put together purely to tease the ear, like Arthur Lloyd's 'Tooral-ooral-ooral Lee':

> Oh! I'm a fool as you can see,
> And I've been fool'd as you'll agree;
> When I tell you what occur'd to me,
> And Too-ral-oo-ral-oo-ral Lee;
> When Tooral and me went out to tea
> With Sally Magee, and she sat on my knee,
> And we couldn't agree, 'cos Tooral said he
> Lov'd Sally Magee, and she lov'd he;
> And so all three did disagree
> And Sally Magee upset the tea
> All over me and Too-ral-oo-ral-oo-ral Lee.[31]

Childish fun could be extracted from every aspect of language, as for instance in a song from the same period by Fred Albert about the 'American' practice of the spelling bee, an excuse for comic spellings and giggling about the most harmless slang expressions and vulgar pronunciation:

> They spelt for William – B,I,L, and T,R,O,T, – run,
> Physic – F,I,Z,I,K and P,H,U,N, Fun,
> Geography did confuse them all, tho' one did vainly try,
> With double G, double E, H,O,G,R,A, double F, Y.
> Then Cauliflower a poser proved, they miss'd the mark by far,
> With C,O double L,E, double Y, P,H,L,O,U,R,
> E,C,K,S, with H,A,G, and E,R,A,T,E,
> They thought would spell 'exaggerate' at this famous spelling bee.
> P,I,G, was spelt for pork, and B,U, double L – Beef
> C,H,A,T, was meant for talk, and C,R,Y, for grief;
> L,O,V,E, it stood for nice – all rules they did defy,
> Police – P, double E, L,E,R, and B,O, double B,Y.[32]

Leybourne was not above schoolboy word-play, beginning a song which he claimed to have written himself with a variation on the text-book inscription of name and address:

> In a house, in a square, in a quadrant,
> In a street, in a lane, in a road;
> Turn to the left, on the right hand
> You see there my true love's abode . . .

By the 1880s the skill of writers had developed and songs which seem to show the influence of the comic stage, particularly of W. S. Gilbert, are quite common, and were clearly acceptable to all the popular audience. Patter and pun were universally appreciated, in for instance such a song as 'The girls of today' with words by J. P. Harrington, sung by Bessie Bonehill, which has an ever-changing chorus of word-play:

> She's a real penny novelty girl, a sit in a hovelty girl
> A ladder of ropeity, midnight elopeity girl, like one in the play;
> A sweet 'ladye faire'-ity, don't comb her hairity, *won't* wash her faceity fay;
> A shirkity workity, worse than a Turkity, frivolous girl of the day![33]

Puns had always been a matter of ad-lib interjection by the comic singer as much as a written-in part of the song, and where one finds song-sheets published in the 1880s and 1890s with the patter, or a skeletal version of it, written out, one can get some idea of the basis on which a comic like

Dan Leno, who talked at least as much as he sang, worked. A parody of 'Daddy Wouldn't Buy Me a Bow-wow' called 'Bow-wow on the Brain', with words by Albert Ellis, gives a fair impression of what a determined and self-conscious punster might do. The last spoken interlude begins

> See! Here they come! Pomeranians, Collies, Retrievers, and *Sky-blue* terriers. Why do they *dog* my foot-steps? I hope a coster*monger'll* sneak 'em. *Tyke* 'em away, or I'll drown my miserable self in a *poodle* of water before everybody, so no-one shall know how it oc-*cur*-ed![34]

A writer like J. B. Geoghegan can work this kind of facile stringing together of variations on a theme into a highly-wrought little song, such as 'Oh! Marigold!' The starting point here is flower names, an ancient subject for a love lyric, which he uses conventionally in the chorus:

> Oh! Mari-gold, Mari-gold, Mari-gold,
> Fair as the *Snowdrop*, with eyes like Sloes;
> She's my *Daffodilly*, and my *Lilac* and my *Lily*,
> She's my *Buttercup*, my *Daisy* and my *Wild-white-Rose*.

In the verse, however, he sets off trains of quibbles and metaphors:

> Tho' cold as *Ice-plants* was my *Peach*,
> No *Nettle* stung like she;
> For oh! she kept her *Cuckoo-plant*
> For *Mandrakes* such as me . . .
>
> When I offered her my *Tulips*,
> She became a *Passion-flower*;
> No *Deadly-night-shade* look'd more dark,
> No *Sorrel* half so sour.
>
> She said *Hop* off you *Hellebore*,
> You *Hemlock, Hemp* and *Rue*;
> No *Toadstool* turns *Hyssop*,
> More than *Savin, Sage* or *Yew*.[35]

This set piece belongs to the 1860s; later songs are more fluid, and may be more subtle. Many double meanings are now very difficult to establish: it has been argued, though not conclusively, that 'Daddy Wouldn't Buy me a Bow-wow' is all about a kept woman's dissatisfaction with her 'sugar daddy's' generosity and prowess. Throughout the lifetime of the music halls until their decline began in the twentieth century the use of language at the humdrum level of commonplace comic song was more skilful and lively, and capable of more various effects, that it was in the run-of-the-mill comic broadside of the eighteenth and nineteenth centuries. Where a broadside ballad making use of innuendo would most usually labour one point at length, wringing every last particle of fun out of a correspondence which had been set up or a train of puns which had been laid, music-hall songs of a very ordinary kind often had highly intricate and varied patterns of innuendo playing backwards and forwards across the text, even in printed versions, which would be supplemented a hundredfold by nuance and gesture in a good performance. The broadside ballad 'Wil the Merry Weaver and Charity the Chambermaid' is outstanding enough to be reprinted in *The Common Muse*. After eight stanzas which are mildly erotic and describe the protagonist's lust for the chambermaid, and his creeping to her bedside and contemplating her one night, there is an abrupt shift to a different technique, the exploitation of a metaphor:

This Damozel she was wondrous fair
And her age it was not above fifteen;
And oftentimes complained she,
That she could not learn her A.B.C.

I would some scholler would me show
The Letters of my criss-cross-row;
That my words in order might placed be,
And I might learn my A.B.C.

I wonder young men are such fools,
To keep so long from Venus Schools,
If they did not know so much as me,
They would n'er forget their A.B.C.

I hearing of her thus complain,
Quoth I fair Maid from tears refrain
You need not troubled thus to be,
For learning of your A.B.C.

If you will be (kind sir, she said)
So courteous to a simple Maid,
Most thankful I shall ever be
For learning me my A.B.C.

With that I did myself prepare,
And near I drew to this Maiden fair,

There is some hopes I find, quoth she,
That I shall learn my A.B.C.

I gave her a Fescue in her hand,
And bid her use it at her command;
She said you best know where it should be,
Come put it to my A.B.C.

I found her very ripe of wit,
And for a scholar wondrous fit,
She us'd her art as well as me,
And all to learn her A.B.C.

When I had taught her Lesson plain,
She would repeat it o're again;
Quoth she, this Lesson pleases me,
I like to read my A.B.C.

And now if any Maidens have
A mind to learn this Lesson brave
Though I'm a Weaver of low degree,
Ile teach them to read their A.B.C.[36]

There are flashes of wit in this – the maiden's comment that things are looking up, and she has some hope of learning, and the final jaunty use of the metaphor when the weaver advertises (the 'if any', 'si quis', formula is an early advertising catchphrase) his qualifications as a teacher of the A.B.C., but by and large it is a simple jest rather long drawn-out, with little to sustain the interest except the titillation for which it is designed. The play upon words is a simple substitution of one sense for another in an arbitrary way, comprehensible only because it falls within conventional expectations, not appropriate in any verbal sense and quite unrelated to the narrative situation, which is occupied until this idea is introduced with the description of the girl's appearance as she lay naked in bed. Compared with Vesta Victoria's 'I Want to Play with My Little Dick', or with Marie Lloyd songs such as 'I've Never Lost my Last Train Yet' and 'She Never Had her Ticket Punched Before', where the innuendo leaps and twists round the situation described in a genuinely inventive way, it is a feeble effort, and many forgotten minor texts can easily match it. In for instance 'Hulloa, hulloa, hulloa!' a Marie Lloyd song with words by George Rollit, published in 1899,[37] the tone and attitude is very similar to that of the earlier piece, and the difference lies in the relative complexity of shared experience upon which the writer can draw, and his practised skill in the manipulation of words, trained by the demands of the conventional form of music-hall ballads.

A lot of things we perpetrate are very nice, no doubt,
Until we're, by some blunder, unexpectedly found out.
For instance, take the fellow who at ball or garden fete,
Retires to the conservat'ry to have a tete-a-tete –
With Kate

Chorus For if, by chance, you enter,
You hear a mild report! (Kiss)
You'll say 'I beg you pardon'
(Or something of the sort),
And presently you see them –
Her pretty face aglow –
His coat a mass of powder – Hulloa! Hulloa! Hulloa!!!

A friend of mine took to himself a wife some time ago,
He was commercial traveller with Somebody and Co.
When first they had to part, her flow of tears she could not stem,
But how she smiled when he returned and breathed 'My only gem!'
Ahem! (Bus)

Chorus She took his hat and ulster
And hung them on the rack,
Then got his coat and slippers
And helped him to unpack,
But suddenly extracted
From his portmantio
A dainty pink silk – bootlace – Hulloa! Hulloa! Hulloa!!!

It is a dainty little maid of whom I now would tell,
Her mother's cottage quaintly lies amid a flow'ry dell;
Sweet buttercups and daisies were her pretty soul's delight,
She regularly went to bed at half past eight each night.
Quite right!

Chorus But yesterday I saw her –
A perfect ladidah,
Careering down New Bond Street
In her Victoria;
Rigged out in silk and satin
With diamonds aglow,
And toying with her cheque-book – Hulloa! Hulloa! Hulloa!!!

Whenever at a big hotel down by the sea I stay,
I like to watch the couples who arrive from day to day;
Invariably I scan the book to see what they put down
And I clearly recollect a Mr and Mrs Brown –
From town.

Chorus They make a point of squabbling
In public, it appears,
To give one the impression
That they've been spliced for years.
At breakfast, though, next morning
I heard her ask him 'Joe,
Do you take milk and sugar?' Hulloa! Hulloa! Hulloa!!!

And often at a picnic you'll find a youthful 'he'
Bestowing great attention on a fascinating 'she'
He'll pick her all the dainty bits from out the pigeon-pie,
And when the picnic's over they'll steal off on the sly
(Bus) Bye-bye!

Chorus When time comes for returning,
You'll search for them in vain,
You'll shout out 'Harry! Connie!
Look sharp! We'll lose our train!'
At last you see them coming,
Complacently and slow –
Her hat looks rather rocky. Hulloa! Hulloa! Hulloa!!!

The singer and the audience share an attitude to the stories told which is very close to that of the older song: sexuality is celebrated, we are expected to enjoy the contemplation of it and to find common cause with the experienced in mocking – and initiating – the innocents, who are all eagerness to learn. We enjoy the recollection of such pleasures, and we also enjoy the fact that we are able to recollect them, our knowingness about what the song is getting at is a vital part of our pleasure. There is in this song as in the older one no suggestion of censure in the air of superiority; sex is a conspiracy in which we all join, and if others are less well-versed in it than ourselves then we laugh at them gently and help them on their way. All Marie Lloyd's songs of seduced innocents and hearty young ladies have the same celebratory air, inherited from the bawdy ballads of previous centuries by a direct line through the Lions Comiques and the earlier coster girl singers. This example is not particularly distinguished; verbally it is not as polished as some already quoted, such as 'The Belles of London Town', which has neat phrases in careless abundance, and it lacks the depth of implication inherent in the best cockney songs as well as their subtly dramatic use of words; but it is written within that tradition, and necessarily creates the sense of understanding between singer and audience upon which their success is based.

Behind the song is a body of shared experience common to all the audience, consisting not only of their own lives but also of a complex of myths and conventions about other people and other classes, drawn from the popular tradition and popular art. Just as 'the A.B.C.' was comprehensible in the earlier song because the substitution was conventionally expected, so in a much more complex way this song relies upon the audience's expectations, built up by experience of the convention in other songs, to make its points. In the second verse and chorus the punch-line, feeble in itself, must be built up by expectations set in train at the mention of the words 'commercial traveller'; the whole weight of popular tradition is mobilised by the third stanza as soon as the 'dainty little maid' from the country is mentioned; her fate, never made explicit in the song, is nevertheless quite clear from the start. These conventional motifs are mixed with stories drawn from the kind of life the audience either do lead or are happy to envisage themselves promoted to. It is a lower-middle-class world, of picnics and trips out by train, where glamour and social success are kissing a girl in a conservatory or staying in a big hotel by the sea. The mixture is vividly successful, and the transition from realism to convention, juxtaposing old jokes and new, fills the song with life.

Although the verbal structure is relatively simple, its vivacity does extend to the skilful manipulation of each verse. The singer's attitude to the audience is signalled in the first line by a little, typically Victorian, joke – the use of a long word, 'perpetrate', where a short one would do. The first laugh and catcall would come at this point, and the singer would respond with a look of mock solemnity, burlesquing the air of a serious user of the word, which is usually charged with authoritarian moral indignation. The rest of the stanza and the chorus are fairly straightforward, partly because they are establishing the pattern which is later to be embellished, and until the audience knows what to expect flourishes would be wasted. The extra phrase on the end of the stanza, for instance, is only used at first to impart further information, not as a comment, simply confirming what the listeners had just gathered. In the next stanza, however, it is exploited, to confirm and comment on the ribald reaction to the speech of the commercial traveller to the trusting young wife. If the reaction were not there, of course, the singer would be in trouble: shared, conditioned responses, and a rapport between performer and the listeners as a body is essential, built into the song. The printed version is a very pale reflection of what should be going on by this stage of the song – the laconic note '(Bus)' helps us very little, and the end of this chorus is even less enlightening, supplying the word 'bootlace' after the pregnant pause indicated by the dash, which might or might not be used, but which is no substitute for the by-play, verbal and visual, which clearly surrounded it. After this the audience is in full swing, and their ribald and mocking reactions are obviously intended to counterpoint and be egged on by the saccharine description of the sweet innocent of stanza three. The variety of ways in which the words 'Quite right!' might be delivered, after the audience's response to the news about her bedtime, is food for speculation. The fourth stanza is perhaps the weakest,[38] in that the situation seems to be blurred: two conventional jokes, about the couple who sign the Brighton hotel register in an assumed married name, and the honeymooners who stand out like a beacon in the hotel breakfast-room, have been run together. By this stage, presumably, the audience is not particular, and will respond to the general suggestiveness of the situation without worrying about its exact significance. Part of the effect of the song is to impress each individual with his own deep knowledge of the world and his superiority to the inexperienced or unobservant, and so everyone will go on laughing with only the haziest idea what it is really all implying. The last stanza is firmer and stronger; the business indicated with 'Bye-bye!' epitomises the genial, indulgent, friendly mockery of the whole song, the picture evoked is sharply defined, with its slang and pigeon pie and the appropriate names, and the final stroke is another long word, 'complacently', this time used with underlining precision.

This song is thus a complex of reference, verbal, conventional, and realistic, appealing to a series of responses which the audience is trained and willing to supply and the writer expertly versed in provoking. His outstanding gift is economy – with very few words, because they are precisely the right ones, he can set up a chain of reactions bouncing back and forth between singer and audience and covering a great deal of ground, in the making of his joke. The A.B.C. ballad needed eighteen four-line stanzas to expound one simple situation, while the music-hall song strings together five different stories, in highly structured twelve-line units, upon the pivot of a common refrain.

The complicated stanza and chorus pattern, using widely differing line-lengths, and the comparative economy of the narrative, fragmenting the song into a series of short stories, is characteristic of the music-hall song. It could perhaps be regarded as a logical development of the long, rambling 'vulgar' ballad pattern of the broadsides, which had also a multiplicity of incident, changed by the pressure of the circumstances of theatrical performance. A song for the stage must be simple in outline and strong in impact; it may be long, but not rambling, capable of manipulation to fit the audience, time and mood of the performance, and with a clear division into verse sung by the performer and choruses in which participation was invited. In the early days of the music hall both serious and comic ballads tended to take this form, but the melodramatic and pathetic pieces were not so suited to a style of performance which allowed continual interruption, forcing changes of pace, and they became tales for listening to, in forms which were closer to the old broadside patterns and to recitation pieces. Comic song on the other hand continued to belong to the audience as much as to the performer, and indeed its great pitfall was the tendency to abbreviate the narrative stanzas more and more and allow the participatory chorus to take over completely, as it does in pieces still remembered like 'Down at the Old Bull and Bush' and 'Ta-ra-ra Boom-de-ay'. Wilkie Bard even sang a song about the tyranny of the chorus – 'It gets on your nerves, does the chorus'. Before its degeneration into any sort of nonsense which people could remember and sing, however, the catch-phrase chorus gave limitless scope for the simple enjoyment of language and word-play, and for delight in the number of meanings that could be found for a phrase, and innuendoes it could be given. Such appreciation of verbal wit formed the basis for the controlled subtlety of implication and suggestion which the best songs developed and could use with certainty of the audience's response and understanding. This development of subtlety based upon the common understanding of the idiom was the only significant change in music-hall comic song throughout its successful years, before the twentieth-century decline. The tradition has been handled here as a whole, rather than as a chronological development, for this reason: progression was a matter of accumulation and addition rather than change. The patterns of comic balladry were developed in the early years, out of old theatrical practice and from broadside ballads, and the same techniques and subjects continued in use, varied only by the characteristic contributions of some singers and writers. Any change was slow: an act could easily remain essentially the same for the whole of a career, and only the biggest stars had to seek new material often. The familiar was as welcome as the novel; and in general circulation, that is in the songsters and books published for the amateur who could not afford three or four shillings for the sheet music of a single song, turnover was even less rapid, and a residue of favourite numbers both comic and pathetic built up in the back pages of each publication. Songs which have no discernible extra merit held their places in print for fifty years: a number called 'What Are You Going to Stand?', for example, appears in 1847 in *The Vauxhall Comic Song Book*, and in the 1890s in *The Imperial Songster*. The main features of the music-hall comic convention were already beginning to crystallise in *The Dashing Songster* of 1810, where one can find 'characteristic' and comic ballads using a range of accents and dialects for amusement, and even an example of the catch-phrase chorus, 'all my eye and Betty Martin', by C. F. Barrett. If the phrase is his own, the song is a very early example of the way in which comic song contributed to idiomatic English throughout the century. Even after the performer who popularised a song was dead, and the audiences who heard him had stopped singing it to their children, people still used choruses and odd phrases whose origins were on the music-hall stage, as if they embodied some wisdom or wit above the common.

The role of the audience in creating and transmitting music-hall comic ballads was a vital one, and is both a proof of and a reason for their evolution from the folk roots of popular poetry. These songs took over from the moribund broadside ballad as the expression of the urban people, absorbing the talent in writing and performing which emerged from the mass of the community, and expressing through their art the common concerns of all the undistinguished majority. This art, I hope I have demonstrated, was essentially popular in its forms, material and techniques, and deserves to be regarded as the inheritor of the popular culture of previous ages and as a successor to the rural folk-song, carrying on the life of the folk tradition. It shares the qualities of all comic writing in that it takes as its material the fascinating patterns of social behaviour and everyday life rather than the eternal truths of tragedy; but it is surely possible to appreciate comic as well as tragic genius in the ballad, as one may respond to novels or plays of either kind. If the comic is acceptable beside the tragic ballad, the nineteenth century need not yield to the eighteenth in its contribution to popular art.

7 Comic Ballads in the Drawing-Room

While the songs of the music hall carried on the popular tradition for the audiences which frequented the theatre, several other ways developed for the other portion of the Victorian popular audience, the possessors and creators of the recitation ballads, to share in the flowering of the comic ballad. A strong tradition of comic writing grew up which had several forms, generally based on some kind of parody. It expressed in a different way the Victorian genius for word-play which was influential in the development of the music-hall song; through this propensity for the creation and enjoyment of verbal humour it brought some literary and sophisticated concepts and attitudes into the popular tradition, without losing the vigour and cogency of the folk sources of humour. The interaction of the stage, the growing periodical press and the major Romantic poets which is discussed in Part One made it possible for popular poetry to be thus enriched by kinds of humour not previously found in the folk tradition. Large audiences with little or no knowledge of the literary tradition came to accept and enjoy literary jokes based upon a shared body of knowledge which was drawn from fictional sources and not directly connected with everyday experience.

During the eighteenth century the comic ballad did not share the fashionable eclipse of its more serious counterparts; many poets, including Gay, Pope, Swift and Goldsmith made occasional use of the form for satirical or burlesque writing, and indeed the acceptance of the form of the ballad for this purpose was a factor in the struggle the early ballad scholars had to convince academic and critical audiences that popular poetry was not nugatory and a ludicrous topic for serious scholarly research. The most famous of these ballads, Cowper's 'John Gilpin', was considered so unimportant by the author himself that he did not at first put his name to it. It is, significantly, a parody: unmistakably, although quite good-naturedly, based upon the mockery of broadside ballads and set to the tune of 'Chevy Chase'. The practice of ballad parody was long established before this in broadside writing, where the common folk-song practice of putting sets of new words to old tunes merged, in satirical and controversial writing, into the ridiculing of opponents by constructing versions of well-known songs or of their own propaganda verses in which the force of one's insults was increased by the recollection of the original words. So the comic ballad had, and maintained, a high artistic standard in the area of parody while tragic and romantic ballads, and more straightforward comic writing lost touch with literary taste.

When therefore, the Romantic poets, and particularly the earliest tentative experimenters in literary medievalism, began to model their writings upon what they regarded as ancient popular ballads and romances, they were virtually inviting any sceptic to barb his criticism with the contemporary literary ballad form, the parody. The philistine response of the reactionary reading public to any innovation in poetic form and technique was in this case supplied with a ready-made way of laughing the *avant-garde* to scorn; and long after the small proportion of the public which follows seriously developments in the literary tradition had ceased to laugh at Romantic poetry and its medieval revivals, the popular audience was left with a legacy of comic medievalism, a pool of responses to stock figures which had come into popular consciousness by the devious route of the parodying of the Romantic ballad revival. Ancient ballad heroes, medieval knights and ladies, priests and devils, returned transmogrified to people the world of the Victorian comic ballad and form a set of conventions with a use and meaning for the nineteenth-century middle-class audience very oddly related to their function for the original ballad-makers.

The first mock-medieval ballads were intimately connected with the Romantic movement, and were largely produced by the poets themselves, in moments of frivolity or self-doubt, or else by critics who were opposed to their gathering strength and influence. They were, in other words, strictly within the literary tradition, using popular models, either ancient or modern, in pursuance of an argument about lofty ideals of poetry. This was perhaps least true of Matthew Lewis, author of *The Monk* and compiler and part author of *Tales of Wonder*, who was to some extent a popular writer, concerned with producing successful melodramas and sensational novels. His commitment to the English Romanticism which his translations from the German Romantics helped to establish was wavering and uncertain, and the reservations he had about the seriousness of ballad poetry are expressed in *Tales of Wonder* by an inclination to self-parody. The tone of apparently serious pieces, full of apparitions and horrors, sometimes wavers suddenly and deflatingly into bathos which seems quite deliberate, and there are also included in the book full-scale and avowed parodies of the mode. His own ballad of 'Alonzo the Brave and Fair Imogene' is immediately followed by 'Giles Jollop the Grave and Brown Sally Green', a crude burlesque in which such moments of humour as there are, as 'When a bell – ('twas the dustman's) – toll'd – "one!"' and

> The cats, as they eye'd him, drew back (well they might),
> For his body was pea-green and blue![1]

are taken from an anonymous parody of his original poem which had already appeared.

Jeffrey considered Lewis's style to be a 'mixture of extravagance and jocularity',[2] which would also serve to describe the way in which Robert Southey, although he was apparently more closely connected with the flowering of the Romantic movement, treated the imitation of the ballad with a medieval setting. He too wavered between wholly serious attempts at recapturing the force of ancient popular beliefs, in simple verse, and a frivolous exploitation of the more absurd aspects of pseudo-Gothic horror. His skill with the form is much greater than Lewis's both in his serious adaptations of old stories and ballad diction and in the delighted relish with which he turns his sensitivity to aural impressions to comic effect. When he means to chill the reader he can do so:

> The Raven croak'd as she sate at her meal,
> And the Old Woman knew what he said,
> And she grew pale at the Raven's tale,
> And sicken'd and went to her bed.[3]

He can also parody himself with grim gaiety which was to become a hallmark of the later comic ballad, in verses such as these:

> And they allow'd the Sexton the shroud,
> And they put the coffin back;
> And nose and knees they then did squeeze
> The Surgeon in a sack.
>
> The watchmen as they past along
> Full four yards off could smell,
> And curse bestow'd upon the load
> So disagreeable.[4]

In his best vein it is impossible to say where the line between seriousness and burlesque falls, and the stories are told with dexterity and gusto which is not explicitly comic but which serves to take the edge off their violence while leaving them enough power to thrill. The best example is probably 'God's Judgement on a Wicked Bishop': the rats attack Hatto,

> And in at the windows and in at the door,
> And through the walls helter-skelter they pour,
> And down from the ceiling and up through the floor,
> From the right and the left, from behind and before,
> From within and without, from above and below,
> And all at once to the bishop they go.[5]

In collaboration with Coleridge Southey produced one occasional ballad in this mock-Gothic vein which belongs also to the tradition of polemical broadside writing, 'The Devil's Thoughts', which uses the figure of a horned and tailed Prince of Evil, treated comically, for satirical attacks upon the political and moral state of England. In the history of the ballad revival the devil is more important than the critical message of these verses, for the use of such a figure connects them to the new, nineteenth-century vein of popular poetry, in which comic effect is as strong or stronger than the old broadside function of topical comment. Other Romantic poets made some use of street ballads in their old role of radical commentary and rallying-cry for the people, but such a function was only marginally important in the Victorian upsurge of comic writing. Figures adapted through parody to comic purposes were drawn from Romantic poetry which was never intended to be specifically popular, and these proved the greater Romantic contribution to popular art.

Parody was at first a weapon against the Romantics as well as a means of self-defence resorted to by the less fully committed poets themselves. Peacock, a friend to individual writers but a severe critic of what he conceived to be Romantic excesses and posturings, picked on medievalism and the imitation of popular verse as a weakness of the age, when

> the poet is wallowing in the rubbish of departed ignorance, and raking up the ashes of dead savages to find gewgaws and rattles for the grown babies of the age.[6]

In *Sir Proteus*[7] he launched exact and telling attacks upon most of the writers he considered guilty of this foible, including Southey, Scott, Wordsworth and Coleridge, and later developed a vein of apparently effortless parody for supplying ballads and songs for the characters in his novels to display their silliness upon, such as the Lewis-like story of 'The pool of the Diving Friar',[8] which is written with a delightful deadpan floridity of style which puts Lewis's own efforts to shame:

> The friar haunted ever beside the dark stream;
> The philosopher's stone was his thought and his dream:
> And day after day, ever head under heels
> He dived all the time he could spare from his meals.

Peacock made a major contribution to the establishment of the comic medievalism upon which Victorian popular writers drew, in *Maid Marion*,[9] where the stereotypes of period drama, set in some indeterminate past time when doublet and hose were worn, barons were bold and bad, friars fat and maidens in distress, were firmly spelt out and given an overtone of humour. The novel was made into a successful play, and the popular audience, to whom theatrical events were more significant than orthodox forms of written publication, grasped the comedy of the idea. The parodies of contemporary poetry produced by the brothers Smith, in their *Rejected Addresses*, were also connected with the stage, in that the Address they burlesqued was that given at the reopening of Covent Garden after its rebuilding in 1812, for which a public competition had been held. The offering they attributed to 'M.G.L.', Lewis, is a mock-horrific tale of 'the singe of Miss Drury', carried off by a Lewisian monster called 'the fire king'. The public who went to the theatre were also familiar with Gothic settings through melodrama such as Lewis's 'The Castle Spectre'. The horrific Gothic had a considerable vogue before the reassertion of common-sense and scepticism in the general public confined such absurdities to the comic stage, where, as in the comic ballad, they had an independent life which outlasted their initial burlesque reference.

The interaction of the comic ballad and the stage at the beginning of the century is of some importance in the establishment of a general understanding of the references and comic significance of mock-medievalism. A similar importance rests on the connection between those writers who were parodying romantic stereotypes and the ballad revival, and the growing popular press. Peacock, for example, wrote a topical ballad called 'Rich and Poor' for newspaper publication. A web of interaction between newspapers, periodicals, the musical and music-hall stages, and comic writers who rose from amongst the rank-and-file journalists and hacks serving these organs of popular entertainment, survived and continued to ramify until the end of the nineteenth century. In the periodical press in particular writers were able to develop the style of comic ballad writing which originated in Romantic parody into a genre in its own right, which could be used for a spectrum of comic writing which was topically satirical at one end and, apparently at least, a pure expression of comic exuberance at the other. Reaction against the unrealistic excesses of art led to parody, and parody proved an ideal vehicle for the kind of popular humour based upon the use and abuse of words, so that two impulses fused into a distinctively Victorian comic mode, expressed variously through the popular theatre and the popular press.

Writers like George Sims, Clement Scott and W. S. Gilbert moved at will from the theatres to the press and back again. The interchange of experience was just as important amongst audiences and readers, in that it formed the basis of familiarity and recognition upon which the magazine writers founded their most telling uses of popular ballad. By imitation of popular forms the lost scope of the old broadside ballad, which had reached a wide and varied audience and built new comment and ideas upon established conventions, was in some sort restored. The journalists borrowed the most famous music-hall and broadside songs, or their unmistakable conventions and forms, to serve as vehicles for satire and social comment in middle-class magazines. There was in this practice an additional effectiveness in the tensions set up between the content now poured into the form and what had been allowed to become the simply entertaining, common and vulgar connotations it bore. In the late eighteenth and early nineteenth centuries popular verse had sunk out of sight, and with it the concerns of the people and their often disturbingly different view of the world had been disregarded; the writers of *Punch* redressed this situation by couching their attacks upon social injustice sometimes in parody of traditional ballad, calling romantic sentiment for the ancient poetry of the people to their aid, and sometimes very effectively in versions of current popular ballad forms. Jolly music-hall songs and survivals of country folk-song which everyone knew from convivial singsongs turned up with bitterly serious words to greet injustice and oppression of the poor, whom *Punch* felt were thus aptly represented by their own songs. Favourite choices for adaptation were 'Ye Gentlemen of England' and 'The Lincolnshire Poacher'; during the 1840s and 1850s versions of 'Highland Laddie', 'Yankee Doodle' and 'All round my hat' are repeatedly found. Beside the burgeoning tradition of comic verse enjoyed for its own sake by the middle-class sections of the popular audience, and contributing, in its own way, to their view of the world, there was in the magazines a strong strain of social concern being expressed as fellow-feeling with lower ranks of the people, by the taking up of their songs.

The quality of writing in both these kinds of comic ballad varied greatly, as was to be expected from a convention, the apparent ease of which invited anyone interested to try his hand, and in a publishing situation which demanded ever more contributions to fill increasing numbers of weekly magazines, and favoured topical productions rapidly put together to comment on the passing scene. In the early years from 1840 to the 1860s the refinements of the convention of comic writing had not yet been established in the periodical press, and parody and imitation were often broad and without much point, particularly in lesser magazines such as *Fun*. The first volume of *Fun*, published in 1861, contains a series entitled 'Plebeian Ballads Adapted (for the first time) to Aristocratic Circles'. They include versions of 'Sam Hall', 'Villikins' and others; a typical example is 'Lord Bateman', from the fourth issue:

> Lord Bateman was a noble Lord
> A noble lord of high degree
> A most distinguished member of
> The British aristocracy.
>
> He bought a yacht; he thought it was
> 'The pwoper sort of thing,' said he;
> He called himself the 'Skippa,' and
> He dressed himself like Cooke, T. P.

This series is followed by another, whose purpose is rather more serious social comment, called 'Songs for the Throng or Versification for the Nation', in volumes two and three, not always modelled on music-hall songs. To balance this a purely comic series based on the song 'Billy Barlow' starts on 11 October 1862, using that character as an aspiring contributor to the magazine, on whose doggerel offerings the editor makes scorching comments. The range of reference is small in *Fun*: 'Villikins' and 'The Ratcatcher's Daughter' are used repeatedly, whenever topical satire in verse is needed, 'Villikins' especially becoming in some way identified with lampoons of Bismarck.

Punch, using popular parody, was more adept and at first much more pointed than its later rival; it also, however, ranged more widely over the kinds of popular poetry for its models, taking subjects for imitation and burlesque from drawing-room as well as music hall, sentimental songs and theatrical hits figuring alongside narrative pieces. Mark Lemon, the first editor, had a particularly acid way with a deflating last line used to expose the false sentimentality of songs sung by young ladies with their minds on more material aspects of love and marriage. 'The Ancient Mariner' was from the first a favourite figure of fun, and comic writers discovered the imitable qualities of the *Lays of Ancient Rome* as quickly as more earnest followers of Lord Macaulay. Romantic ballads, particularly 'Lenore' and 'Lochinvar', lent themselves to adaptation, and certain poems proved so irresistibly mockable that not only the pages of *Punch*, but anthologies of recitations printed throughout and beyond the century, teem with the various attempts of more-or-less skilful parodists. 'The Burial of Sir John Moore' is one such favourite, used as a standby for any topical comment that might be called for, as in this from an 1850 number of *Punch* where it is pressed into service for a caustic remark on late-night parliamentary sessions:

> Not a joke was heard, not a troublesome vote,
> As the bills into limbo they hurried;
> Not e'en INGLIS discharged a farewell shot
> O'er the grave where the Jew Bill was buried.

It was equally popular as a subject for simply humorous burlesque, in one version in particular, Barham's story of the bringing home of a drunk, which begins

> Not a *sous* had he got, – not a guinea or note,
> And he look'd confoundedly flurried,
> As he bolted away without paying his shot,
> And the landlady after him hurried.

This became so well known as to be a favourite item of piracy amongst the broadside printers. *The Applause Reciter*, published in 1898, has two versions of 'Excelsior', which was another such favourite. Neither has any satirical point to make by the parody, such humour as they possess arising chiefly from the simple enjoyment of the vagaries of language. The first is 'Paddy's Excelsior' (p. 13), which begins

> 'Twas growing dark so terrible fasht,
> Whin through a town up the mountain there pashed
> A broth of a boy, to his neck in the shnow:
> As he walked, his shillelah he swung to and fro,
> Saying 'It's up to the top I'm bound for to go,
> Be jabbers!'

The other is entitled 'Longfellow's Excelsior (In pigeon English)' (p. 15) and begins

> That nightee teem he come chop-chop
> One young man walkee, no can stop;
> Maskee snow, maskee ice;
> He cally flag with chop so nice –
> Top-side Galah!

The same impulse lay behind some much better parodies and literary burlesques than these, which appeared in the 1840s, and also behind Thackeray's comic ballads which appeared in the next few years. The earlier examples use topical stories, such as that of a young man ruined by railway speculation, which is dressed up as 'A Trew and ryghte Edyfyinge Balladde, Shewing how a seely yonge manne wold sell hys soule to Satan, and what followed therefrom'. It appears in Volume 10 of *Punch*, in 1846 (p. 19), and was written by Percival Leigh, who collaborated with Richard Doyle the illustrator to produce a series of similar pieces. In all of them the humour arises from the juxtaposition of exaggerated Middle English with modern slang terms and the modern situation. The falsity of the Middle English is positively Chattertonian:

> Fulle soone hee stoode within ye roome
> Where ye oulde sage dyd dwelle;
> Strange lynes around and mystic schryppe
> Sette forth a dismalle selle.

'Selle' may be either cell – room, or sell – slang term for hoax, or a pun on the two, but it is certainly not intended to suggest the real Middle English word selle, meaning a saddle. The next verse is a good example of the intended effects:

> What woldst thou here? in awfulle voice
> Thus asked ye manne of synne;
> Ye seedie raskalle wynked hys eye,
> And brefely answered – 'Tinne'.

The series called 'Our Barry-eux Tapestry', a very funny picture strip by Doyle, has a commentary in Leigh's best medieval style:

> And as ye armie past,
> Ye sheep and cows, aghaste,
> Stared over ye embankmente,
> As wondering whatte each ranke meant;
> And ye rusticks, in amazemente,

Looked out from cottage casemente,
Or paused at spade and ploughe,
With a, 'Dang it, what's uppe now?'
Such was ye consternation
Caused by ye French invasion,
Till they reached, with exultation,
Ye London Bridge, its station . . .[10]

This is simple word-play and delight in the materials at hand, with the comic edge supplied automatically by the incongruity of a French invasion in 1848; but there is a strong knowledge of ballad behind the pastiche, clearly visible in 'A Delectable ballad of True Thomas of Scalesbury':

Now where gat you your gold true Thomas,
And where gat you your fee?
I trow it was not from leaf on land,
Nor from ship on the salt, salt sea.[11]

Such distinction is clearly the production of an educated man well versed in the culture of the literary tradition and its revival of interest in the popular ballad, rather than of a poet writing from a popular stance. The use of dialect and of other forms of non-standard English in the magazines also suggest that the writers, although they share the popular fascination for words, and are making the amusement to be drawn from their manipulation the basis of their humour, are aiming at a section of the popular audience to whom the language is not their own. They may read only popular poems, but they find the lower classes and the more uncouth sections of the popular audience comic in a way which distinguishes the cockney and Irish verses written for them from those which were written to amuse the cockney and Irish speakers. They are the same middle-class audience for whom Sims wrote sentimental ballads in the voices of the poor. Such class consciousness can be detected in the faintly patronising overtones of the parodies of 'Excelsior' already quoted. Thackeray's verse in *Punch* is the supreme example of a writer who, himself familiar with both the literary and the popular traditions, is writing popular poetry in a particular way to amuse the middle-class reader. His contributions of verse to *Punch* began with variations on established ballad forms, for example the mock-medieval piece 'Great News', but he developed a personal style of dialect tale based on the music-hall character song, but with a different and distinctive inflection.

He takes topical subjects, but the consistency of the mode itself is its chief attraction and humorous device.

There are two groups of verses clearly written within this style. The earlier is *Lyra Hibernica*, 'The poems of the Molony of Kilballymolony.'[12] The only connection between these and the music-hall ballad is the use of an Irish brogue, and to a certain extent the characteristics of the stage Irishman associated with it: his pugnacity, patriotism and tendency to allow words to run away with him. Thackeray uses the brogue, however, not to make jokes or the verbal humour associated with it on the stage, but to describe current events and spectacles. There are, for instance, Molony's accounts of the Crystal Palace, the Pimlico Pavilion, and a ball given for the Nepalese ambassador. The only connection between the supposed narrator and the events is their very dissociation. While the stage Irishman always tells a story, none of the *Lyra Hibernica* contains more narrative than the descriptions require; the form in which they are cast is not narrative, resembling rather Thackeray's lyrical and sentimental verse, with varying lengths of line, usually very short, and involved rhyme schemes. Occasionally similar forms are found in sentimental music-hall songs. One or two, for example 'The Battle of Limerick', deal with Irish affairs; but in the main the brogue is only used for the sake of the conditioned response of amusement which it had acquired through popular use.

The connection between the language used for *The Ballads of Policeman X*[13] and their subjects is much clearer. The policeman, speaking in cockney, was an established figure in the music hall, like Arthur Lloyd's Policeman 92X, who sings a protracted tale about his wife giving up a soldier to marry him, with the chorus

> I'm the man wot takes to pris'n
> He who steals wot isn't his'n.
> X yer know is my diwision,
> Number ninety-two.[14]

Thackeray's Policeman X tells stories which are both topical and appropriate to the character, almost all being based on legal matters and current cases in the courts. Some, for example 'Damages £200' and 'Jacob Omnium's Hoss', are criticisms of court procedure, others such as 'The Organ Boy's Appeal', of new legislation, and a few deal with other events, like 'Lines on a Late Hospicious Event', 'Three Xmas Waits', 'The Speculators' and 'Protestant Conspiracy'; but the backbone of the series is a group of stories of crimes, and these especially are cast in a spirited pastiche of the broadside and music-hall ballads, reproducing them in style and form. Their titles indicate this, for example 'The Lamentable Ballad of the Foundling of Shoreditch', and 'The Wofle New Ballad of Jane Roney and Mary Brown'. They are set in four-line stanzas that swing along with a pounding directness, cliché-ridden and relishing all the grim details:

> Vile the scoundrle Charley Thompson,
> Lest his wictim should escape,
> Hocust her vith rum and vater,
> Like a fiend in huming shape.

or:

> On account of her conduck so base and so vile,
> That wicked young gurl is committed for trile;
> And if she's transpawted beyond the salt sea,
> It's a proper reward for such willians as she.

Their chief attraction, however, is Thackeray's cockney. One contemporary critic remarked that without it his ballads would not be funny at all. The humorous use of the language is drawn from music-hall song, but there are important differences in the style of writing which are the result of the difference in the writer's attitude and the response he expects from his audience. The cockney song is intended for the ear. The accent is conveyed by the voice of the character-actor who sings it, and the text, whichever writer it is by, contains only those characteristics which need to be written down: the grammar, slang vocabulary, and a few tricks of spelling which are completely conventional indications of the intended effect or occasionally dramatic hints on emphasis to be used in the performance. Similarly the Irish of the music-hall song is a mere indication of the actual sounds, often carefully phrased to enable the singer to use it as fast patter and impose the peculiar intonations and emphasis of the language in performance. The intention is to raise a laugh at the characters portrayed and the stories they tell, but also, especially in the case of the cockney, to aid identification with them. The speech as used by the actor is intended to be realistic, the native language used to voice the philosophy and attitudes of the audience. Thackeray on the other hand writes entirely to be read; his peculiarities are of spelling rather than intonation and vocabulary, and are in no way intended to be realistic or provoke identification. He exaggerates the sounds of both accents into a quaint system of mock phonetics to amuse and puzzle the eye, and suggest the inferior education and lack of refinement of the character. The most extreme example of this is Jeames rather than Policeman X, but it is his constant habit:

> Ah, Judy thru!
> With eyes so blue,
> That you were here to view it!
> And could I screw
> But tu pound tu
> 'Tis I would thrait you to it!

or:

> When they read of this news in the peepers,
> Acrass the Atlantical wave,
> That the last of the Oirish Liftinints
> Of the oisland of Seents has tuck lave.

His cockney is similarly intended to puzzle the eye, for instance by the addition as well as omission of h's, and an almost random transposition of vowels:

> O Signor Broderip you are a wickid ole man
> You wexis us little horgan boys whenever you can,
> How dare you talk of Justice, and go for to seek
> To pussicute us horgin boys, you senguinary Beek?
>
> Though you set in Vestminster surrounded by your crushers
> Harrogint and habsolute like the Hortocrat of hall the Rushers,
> Yet there is a better vurld I'd have you for to know,
> Likewise a place vere the henimies of horgin-boys will go.

Concentration upon making the accent simply ludicrous is successful because his audience, the readers of *Punch*, would not wish for the identification the music-hall audience felt with the cockney singer. The working-class attitudes have indeed been dropped: X is presented as on the right side, the side of authority, even if he is ludicrous; his lower-class scepticism is directed not against law and order in general, but against those abuses of it which trouble the middle class, in the shape of the criminal, and the inefficient processes of the civil courts.

Something of the same air of superiority pervades the work of Thomas Anstey Guthrie, 'F. Anstey', whose talents were a mainstay of the flagging literary side of *Punch* in the 1880s. He produced particularly two series of parodies, later collected as *Burglar Bill* and *Mr Punch's Model Music Hall*,[15] which show an ambivalent attitude to the drawing-room and music-hall ballads which the writer clearly knew very well. All the music-hall songs are written in a villainously distorted spelling to indicate a tortured accent, upon which he adds acid or disingenuous comments. One introduction, for example, notes that 'A phonetic spelling has been adopted where necessary to bring out the rhyme, for the convenience of the reader only, as the singer will instinctively give the vowel-sounds the pronunciation intended by the author'. The song begins

> Oh, I love to sit a-gyzing on the boundless blue horizing,
> When the scorching sun is blyzing down on sands, and ships, and sea![16]

Scorn for the music-hall artist is obvious here, and it is a class dislike of what is felt to be ugly because it is vulgar. However, in the course of the series of imitation music-hall songs he betrays several times his acceptance at an unthinking level of some basic popular attitudes, and, more interestingly still, his middle-class unease at the lengths to which a music-hall artist may go in being critical and cynical in his turn. An illustration of the first is the note to his proffered song for 'the military impersonator', which pours scorn upon the military-patriotic song, hinting that it hardly represents the truth about the regiments whose officers are regularly impersonated, but feels obliged to put in a perfectly serious aside to make clear that this does not apply to 'the last verse [which] illustrates the heroism of our troops in action – a heroism too real and too splendid to be rendered ridiculous.'[17] Guthrie's condescension towards the music hall and its patrons is visibly shaken out of its complacency by several features of music-hall song which he mentions, including the iconoclasm of its parody, which he imitates but feels constrained to treat with jocular deprecation in 'The Duettists'. The style he professes to be parodying, that of the 'knowing' singer who explains to a delighted audience and perhaps a naive partner exactly what makes the world go round, is clearly too cynical and down-beat for his own taste, satirist though he thinks himself. Similarly he is at a loss to explain, although he is well able to imitate, the self-attacking humour he uses in his fifth example, of the style 'The Frankly Canaille'.[18] The introduction begins tongue in cheek, 'Any ditty which accurately reflects the habits and amusements of the people is a valuable human document', and goes on in a tone as much puzzled as mocking to say that the music-hall audiences welcome this style of song, so that it must be a just representation of themselves. The song, entitled 'The Poor Old 'Orse', is so like a comic coster song that it is clear that Guthrie felt additional colouring of his own would be superfluous, and it could easily have been sung by one of the 'ladies adorning the Music-hall stage' whom he mentions. It is a tale of a journey to Kew by hired excursion van, which fails to get to the gardens before closing time; the passengers are arrested for drunkenness on the way home, because, as is explained in the chorus, they

> . . . '*ad* to stop o' course,
> Jest to bait the bloomin' 'orse,
> So we'd pots of ale and porter
> (Or a drop o' something shorter),
> While he drunk his pail o' water,
> He was sech a whale on water!
> That more water than he oughter,
> More water than he oughter,
> 'Ad the poor old 'orse!

The skill of the imitation is remarkable, and suggests a close acquaintance with the material he is supposed to be parodying, but the tone of his note to the song suggests he had not completely understood, because he had not been able to share, the amusement of the people at seeing themselves so unflatteringly represented.

The ballads of *The Young Reciter* are often even better than the model music-hall songs because Guthrie was able to respond fully and seriously, as he said, to the genre. In this area he was himself able to adopt the 'two-faced' attitude of the popular audience – to respond unselfconsciously to serious and pathetic statements of the drawing-room code of values, and to turn them ruthlessly on their heads for fun, secure in convictions which mockery and parody affectionately acknowledged rather than undermined. He prefaces the collection of parodies with a statement of faith in and enjoyment of the reciter's art, the first part of which, at least, is unequivocal:

> The book was not inspired by the least *animus* against Reciters . . . Its writer would have been most ungrateful had it been so, seeing that he owed a debt of intense pleasure to such Masters in the Art as the late Clifford Harrison and others, and had always derived entertainment from the efforts of the most incompetent amateurs . . .[19]

He then proceeds to a ruthless dissection of the incompetent, to show what kind of amusement it was that they afforded him. His parodies cover twelve distinct styles of recitation, each with a characteristic example and a wealth of instructional matter and stage direction in the manner of the popular anthologist and recitation tutor. Sometimes the style of the verse is a specific parody of a favourite recitation poet or piece, as in 'The Wreck of the Steamship Puffin' (which came to grief on the Round Pond in Kensington), sometimes a brilliant evocation of a whole fashion for recitation, as in the vaguely Tennysonian example of the style 'Bucolic Buttonholing', which is 'in the well-known vernacular of Loompshire', as we are informed in a note which is a parody of Frederick Langbridge. The contrast of the 'dialect' of the piece and the directions, suggestive of the reciter's exclusive self-consciousness, is delightful:

(*You should give a brief summary of the situation, thus:*)
'This is supposed to be spoken by a Loompshire cottager to a stranger, who has remarked upon the goodly proportions of the goose in his front garden.'
(*Then start with as broad a drawl as you can assume, remembering always that, in dialect, to be unintelligible is to be effective.*)

'Bewty', I 'ears ya carl her? aye, ya niver spoöke truthfuller wurrëd!
Rammack t' coontry side övver, an' ya weänt see naw foiner burrëd!
Passon, he axed ma to sell her – but a' towld him, 'Beänt o' naw use, –
She's as mooch of a Chris'en as moäst,' I sez, 'if she's nobbut a guse! (*Touch of sarcasm here.*)
Coom then! (*This coaxingly to a hypothetical bird – be careful not to make any invidious distinctions among your audience.*) Naäy but she wunna, – she's gotten a wull of her oän!
Looök at the heye of her – pink an' greëy, loike fire in a hopal stoän.
Howsiver she seems sa hinnercent-loike, she's a follering arl I saäy;
An I boärt 'er at Kettleby Feär, I did, two year coom Cann'lemas Daäy.[20]

The attack here is clearly directed at falsity and superiority of the kind concealed by Sims's pathetic offerings, and which he assails more directly in another piece, 'Positively the last performance', the homely tale of a dying performing canary's spirited last show, rather than at the genuine article in dialect verse. He was by no means above Thackeray's brand of attack upon the stage cockney, as the song quoted earlier demonstrates, but all his parodies of the recitation poems show such unmalicious affection for their objects as to free them from offensive overtones. He is attacking only bad examples, and indifferent performances, of a genre which he obviously enjoys and in some sense respects. With the music-hall songs, his procedure is like Thackeray's, and in both cases it is less benevolent, and artistically far less productive. Both writers took the convention of the cockney and Irish ballads of the halls and adapted it to amuse the middle-class reader, rather than to express the feelings of the working-class audience. As in the case of Sims's ballads of the poor adapted to comfort and bolster the self-confidence of the well-to-do, this treatment of the lower classes as comic serves a psychological and sociological purpose. To laugh at rather than with the coster or the Irish gull is to exclude him from the group to which you belong and to strengthen that group with fellow-feeling. If the outsider is ridiculous, he will seem far less threatening. Other, rather less obvious, overtones of comfort and release from anxiety can also perhaps be found in some later comic verse, for out of this matrix of fluent and fertile, though sometimes mediocre, comic versifying, which was compounded of the various ingredients of easy publication, a vulgar but at least casually literate audience, and a convention and tradition of comic ballad writing which drew upon many literary and popular modes, arose some of the best comic writers of verse in English.

The first of these was Thomas Hood, who invented very many of the characteristics of Victorian humour although his own lifetime fell largely outside the reign of the Queen Empress. His sensibility and his sense of fun were both much more Victorian than anything else, however, though there are traces of rumbustious openness and relish of the irreverent in his work which do serve as a reminder of his Regency youth. How he came to combine the elements of ballad parody, mock-medievalism drawn from Gothic and Romantic poetry, unflagging word-play and an obsession with practical and physical jokes, is partly explained by the way in which his creative life as a writer neatly spans a confused transitional period of the century, and partly in much more personal terms. He was almost always ill, and much of his comic verse was written under both physical and economic stress. His preoccupation with physical disaster and decay as sources of comedy has therefore an obvious personal element, the consciousness of a sick man of his own body and its defects; and his affection for a world in which the physical laws of nature are suspended in favour of ghosts and magic and the trappings of Gothic fantasy could be regarded as simple escapism. Having found that such a combination of opposites, couched in witty doggerel, was to the taste of the general public, its establishment as a convention in his work was a serviceable way of meeting commitments with despatch and a minimum of extra effort.

Very nearly the whole range of ballad poetry up to his own time contributes something to his work. Elements of the kind of poetry he preferred were to be found in several types of ballad. The influence of the bloodthirsty and gloomy tales of murder in the broadside 'Confession' and 'Last Goodnight' can be detected in 'The Dream of Eugene Aram' as well as in his comic verse; but his most characteristic story patterns are drawn from traditional and Gothic ballad, and the assumptions and attitudes built on these are part of the basis of the comic ballad world. Peacock established the knights and ladies and friars of quasi-medieval story as stock figures of this world; Hood's preference was for the supernatural characters, and his use of ghosts and apparitions made them as familiar and acceptable a part of the comic scene. It is interesting that while the supernatural elements of the Gothic ballad must have prepared the ground for comic treatment, and while one can discern the intention to parody Gothic horror in the physical detail of these poems, the apparitions and supernatural characters used by Hood bear a greater resemblance to those of the traditional ballad. A variant of the comic devil who appeared in the work of Coleridge and Southey, and of Shelley, makes an appearance in 'Jack Hall' and 'Death's Ramble', under the name of Death, but he is the only grotesque figure descended from the terrible personages represented in the Gothic ballad. The chief supernatural story-pattern used by Hood is drawn straight from the traditional ballad: the ghost of a dead man appearing to his wife or sweetheart, either to report his own death or to complain of some ill-treatment of his remains or of his memory. Hood has several variations of this story, in each of which the humour is based on some physical oddity of the dead man. In 'Sally Simpkin's Lament' her lover, lost at sea, returns to tell her what has befallen him. He has been bitten in half by a shark, and so only his top half has appeared to her. The shark also appears in 'Bryan and Pereene', a very poor but quite serious eighteenth-century ballad included in the *Reliques*, from which Hood has taken an epigraph for this ballad. The peculiarity of 'Pompey's Ghost', which also appears to tell his beloved of his death, is that unlike other ghosts it is black, because he was a negro. 'Mary's Ghost' is one of a growing number of ballads which base their humour on body-snatching and dissection: Mary appears to complain that her corpse has been stolen and distributed in pieces.

Southey made the same reference in 'The Surgeon's Warning' and Hood repeated it in 'Jack Hall', and later writers made further elaborations on the theme.

It can be seen that Hood's ghosts, far from being disembodied spirits with mysterious or terrible powers, are quite as concerned with the body and its accidents as are his living characters, and that death is presented almost as the ultimate practical joke. The best of the ghost stories, 'The Supper Superstition',[21] is perhaps the most grotesque, combining the appearance of the ghost of a drowned man with derision of superstition, as found in Southey's ballads, and with the suggestion of cannibalism, which is a noticeable trait in some later work, that of W. S. Gilbert, and even of Thackeray. It transcends a dubiously funny theme by the strength of its carefully-handled plot, an hilariously anti-climactic ending, and by the clever way in which Hood uses concrete detail. The ghost is explicit about the shipwreck:

'Just give a look at Norey's chart,
The very place it tells;
I think it says twelve fathom deep,
Clay bottom, mix'd with shells.'

The family is assembled for dinner, cod in oyster and shrimp sauce, at 'Twelve o'clock by Chelsea chimes'; and the test the ghost suggests they should make to see if his warning that the fish now on the table have eaten his dead body is true is eminently practical:

'Don't eat what brutes would never eat,
The brute I used to pat,
They'll know the smell they used to smell,
Just try the dog and cat!'

All these physical, acutely visualised details are set up around the fact of the ghost itself, which we are invited to accept as part of the same, everyday world. The ending is a further complication of fantasy and fact: the family offer the suspected fish to the pets – who eat it, leaving them with the moral 'Put no belief in ghosts' in lieu of their dinner. The humour of the whole ballad rests in incongruity, in the juxtaposition of tragic shipwreck and cod and shrimps, of a sentimental appeal to the loyalty of a pet dog and the unsentimental way it eats the dinner, and above all of the commonplace circumstances of the cosy family meal-time, and the ghost. The first principle in turning the terrible or tragic subjects of the romantic ballad into humour is to set up some such incongruity. Where ghosts and kittens appear in the same world and are accepted with the same literal, matter-of-fact attitude the reader can relish whatever resemblances it may have to the real world as comic, while its unreality preserves him from any involvement in its disasters and pain.

Hood achieves this necessary effect in another group of ballads with similar stories in which a tormented hero, usually rejected by the girl he loves because of some physical defect, ends his life, and the ballad, by committing suicide. The pattern is presumably an indirect and diluted satire of Romantic despair, but its humour is created not by burlesque of Romantic phraseology or posturings, but by jokes about the hero's bodily disadvantages. 'Faithless Sally Brown', one of Hood's most famous ballads, does not fit entirely into this group, since she is unfaithful simply because her lover Ben is absent, but it conforms to the pattern in ending in Ben's suicide. The story is very like a common type of broadside, that in which a man is taken from his sweetheart by the press-gang, and Hood's poem was in fact rapidly pirated by the broadside printers, and became a popular street and tavern song. The grafting of comedy upon the old tragic story is very closely analogous with the early music-hall songs like 'Villikins and Dinah'. 'Faithless Nellie Grey', second to it in popularity, is the prototype of the group: the heroine rejects Ben Battle because he has lost his legs, and he hangs himself. The pattern is closely followed by 'John Day', where a fat coachman, rejected by a barmaid, drowns himself in a water-butt, and in 'John Trot' where the hero is a serving-man who fails to win the love of his mistress because he is so tall, and joins the army, with the result that he is 'cut down to size' by a Frenchman. These stories might seem too grim, or at least too lacking in taste and sensitivity, to be funny, especially when in the case of 'Lieutenant Luff' the hero is driven to suicide not by unrequited love but by the more frightening afflictions of alcoholism and poverty. The modern reader's response of unease is caused not merely by Hood's presentation of physical oddity, in the form of excessive height or weight or even excessive drinking, as amusing. These are still comic subjects, and they are a recognisable variation on the theme of physical discomfiture which is one of the strongest threads in popular humour. Hood's peculiarity is that instead of suppressing or minimising the suffering experienced by the people who are so afflicted, so that the reader may forget the pain and enjoy the joke, he goes to the opposite extreme. He exaggerates the suffering of the characters, and presents it as another odd and laughable peculiarity. In this way he attempts to place his characters once again in a different, though parallel, world; and his creation of it is similar to the procedure of the pseudo-medieval setting. The element of incongruity is still present, in endowing fat coachmen and barmaids with high passion and tragedy, and to this extent there is a suggested parody of the normal world; but the essential difference of the comic world is the literal, matter-of-fact logic of its proceedings, noticed in the supernatural ballads. Not only does the coachman experience Romantic despair and hopeless love because he is fat, but he commits suicide, which is the only strictly logical course to take, and one he shares with counterparts in music-hall song, like Lily-vite Sand and his donkey. Real people, and realistically represented fictional characters, do not take their emotions so literally; or if they do, they do not express them by seeking a watery grave in a brimming barrel. In the comic world water-butts and suicide are no more incongruous than ghosts and baked cod. More perhaps than any other aspect of his work, Hood's comic use of crude physical violence relates his work to older patterns of popular ballad, and through his great popularity this physical freedom found its way into later comic verse. Violent farce was an accepted part of Victorian humour for every level of the popular audience.

Hood's greatest contribution to the comic world was, however, stylistic. His stories form one stage in the progress of a trend, but his versification is the original basis of the Victorian comic ballad in the drawing-room. He makes use of a wide range of verse forms, but imposes upon each of them his peculiar comic emphasis. The poems which he calls 'ballads' are in a regularised version of the common measure, and they are characteristic of the whole of his work. As has already been observed, the humour of the verses depends largely upon the handling, the words used rather than the story itself. Even where some specific joke is the basis of the humour, as in for example the 'ghost' ballads, it is exploited and expanded by verbal and metrical means. The humour is in this sense based upon the sound of the words and the beat of the verse.

The first tool is the metre itself. The ballad stanza is reduced in stature, tamed to exact regularity, and that regularity is mocked and made amusing by exaggerated, jogging emphasis. This is further elaborated by the peculiarity and the deliberate straining of the rhymes, and by internal rhyme, as for example in the stanza

> Of horn and morn, and hark and bark,
> And echo's answering sounds,
> All poet's wit hath ever writ
> In *dog*-rel verse of *hounds*.[22]

As well as playing with metre, Hood plays with words, using multi-syllabic rhymes, as Exhume us/posthumous, conjunction/function, next 'un/sexton, how-d'ye do/crony too, all of which are from the same ballad,[23] and also using alliteration and assonance prompted by mere exuberance, as in the line

> . . . where Bob and Tom,
> In red already ride.[24]

This verbal juggling is the overflow into comedy of the poetic preoccupation with sound and rhythmic structure, forming a kind of joke about poetry. Hood's great weapon, the pun, is for him the ultimate form of this joke. Most of his comic verses, and particularly his ballads, rely on it for their structure. The initial paradox is proposed, for example the fact that Pompey's ghost is black instead of white, and it is then repeated in each stanza in terms of a different pun. Hood possessed an astonishing command of words, and his ability to manipulate them equalled that of his contemporaries in serious verse. He could sustain a narrative almost entirely by means of puns and word-play through, in the case of 'Epping Hunt', 122 stanzas, without his verbal facility and inventiveness flagging for one moment. This poem starts, like his shorter ballads, with a single premise, that the idea of tradesmen turning out to one yearly stag-hunt without the necessary knowledge, equipment or spirit is ludicrous. He elaborates this paradox on every possible level. There are puns based on hunting and hunting terms and on peculiar aspects of this particular hunt, such as the hearse-like cart which was used to bring the 'deer alive' and not the 'dear deceased'. There are puns about the motley appearance and occupations of the hunters, like the

> Butchers on the backs of butcher's hacks
> That shambled to and fro.[25]

There are puns about horses and the various terms for them, and a series of slang and cant words which Hood uses and abuses as a counterpoint between the aristocratic sport and the lower-class language and habits of those pursuing it. This ingenious word-association and juxtaposition naturally leads Hood to a play of concepts and attitudes which is more subtle than the surface word-games, and can be used more seriously, as in 'A Parental Ode', which alternates the two main attitudes of the adult to the small child:

Thou tiny image of myself!
(My love, he's poking peas into his ear!)
. . . Untouch'd by sorrow, and unsoil'd by sin –
(Good heavens! the child is swallowing a pin!)[26]

Both the pun and the further development of it are connected with the comic world, are indeed the ideal expression of the comic world, in that they are based upon a sharp awareness and exploitation of incongruity. The pun must take two quite separate units of meaning and bring them together by the fortuitous resemblance of the sets of sounds we use to express each of them. It must at the same time so arrange their context that the juxtaposition is incongruous but not meaningless, so that the reader observes a new, comic, significance in the units of meaning. A pun thus exploits the logic of language separated from the logic based upon its common significance, as the comic world exploits the logic of objects and emotions separated from the restraints imposed by their common associations; the incongruity of this new order and the natural order is the attraction of the comic world. The strength of this attraction can be seen in the popularity of Hood's work. The music-hall singers and broadside printers pirated it, innumerable writers imitated it, and his methods were absorbed and became the model of comic versification, and the whole nation shared his delight in quibbles and verbal cranks, rhyming intricacy and tumbling metre.

There was no pause in the development of the comic ballad with Hood's defection and death. He was immediately succeeded by three excellent comic balladeers, nurtured upon his example and upon forty years of gradually improving comic journalism. They had several things in common which demonstrate both their inheritance of Hood's mantle and the changing status of their wares as the comic ballad came into its own. In 1840 Barham published the first series of *The Ingoldsby Legends*, under the pseudonym of Thomas Ingoldsby, and in 1845 W. E. Aytoun and Sir Theodore Martin, writing under the joint name of Bon Gaultier, produced *The Book of Ballads*. Book publication was a dignity to which few ballad writers of the past had attained, although like their predecessors these writers had first proved their abilities in magazine writing. Both sets of verses are firmly placed in the nineteenth-century comic tradition of parody, and the extent to which they drew on mock-medievalism as an established comic world is much greater than in previous examples. *The Ingoldsby Legends*, and to a somewhat lesser extent the Bon Gaultier *Ballads*, are books founded upon the parody of medievalism to such a degree that to appreciate them an extensive, if superficial, knowledge of their sources is necessary. Their enormous popularity as well as the elaborate and loving effort which must have gone into them testify to the familiarity and acceptance which comic ballads using the trappings of the traditional ballad and its associations had won with a wide audience. In the widest possible range of applications the word 'ballad' had come to mean 'a comic verse', subsuming all other kinds of ballad and covering most varieties of comedy, with perhaps some closer application to a verse making use of narrative and parodying the style of a serious poet. A natural deduction was that a comic ballad should be a narrative poem in which extravagance, exaggeration and burlesque, of characters, incidents and style, if not of another poet's style, are the sources of humour. Much more particular knowledge of pseudo-medievalism than this also existed in a large number of readers, however; in *The Ingoldsby Legends* in particular, an elaborate and erudite in-joke about the remoter recesses of scholarship can be seen to have found an enthusiastic popular audience.

The acquaintance of the writers with the varieties of ballad which they parody is of course still greater than that of their audiences. Martin was trained by work for *Frazer's Magazine* on topical, literary and political comic writing: an earlier volume of ballads by him called *The Flowers of Hemp, or, The Newgate Garland* was a contribution to the controversy over the allegedly evil influences of criminal romances such as Ainsworth's *Jack Sheppard*, and his work for *Frazer's* was often of this pamphleteering kind. His collaborator in the Bon Gaultier *Ballads* was the same Aytoun who wrote the *Lays of the Scottish Cavaliers*, based upon Macaulay's heroic ballad pattern and upon a lifelong acquaintance with the Scottish traditional ballads which he finally published in a 'definitive' form. Between them these two published a volume of verses with a broad base of specific parody, and containing some examples of the comic medieval ballad which are independent of that inspiration. Martin's contributions are perhaps the more obviously popular of the ballads, and the least distinguished. They include a series of spoofs in which the simple reduction of the poetic model by turning a verse in its style into an advertisement for some banal and unromantic modern commodity is the sole source of humour.[27] There are also, however, several in which one may observe a close union between the popular and the mock-romantic sources of humour, in that they use a surface of medievalism in setting and language to tell stories which are based upon perennial popular jokes. He is as concerned as any music-hall writer with brokers and bailiffs, in for instance 'The Doleful Lay of I. O. Uwins', and with the cuckolding soldier who terrifies the narrator into acquiescence in 'My Wife's Cousin'. In 'The Knight and the Taylzeour's Daughter' he uses the juxtaposition of ancient and modern jargon from which the run-of-the-mill humour in *Punch* ballads of this kind is derived:

> Did you ever hear the story –
> Old the legend is and true –
> How a knyghte of fame and glory
> All aside his armour threw;
> Spouted spear and pawned habergeon,
> Pledged his sword and surcoat gay,
> Sat down cross-legged on the shop-board,
> Sate and stitched the livelong day?[28]

W. E. Aytoun's work is more distinguished, ranging over a great variety of ballad sources and achieving considerably greater comic effect. His fine sense of the ridiculous in the literary and popular heroic ballads of his time is the more remarkable in a writer who undertook serious drawing-room balladry with such success and with, to the modern reader, so insensitive a disregard for the subtleties of the traditional ballad. He was able to show in his comic work both a consciousness of the inadequacy of some varieties of literary ballad and a perception of the real qualities of the folk tradition. His ear for the mockery of literary ballads is as delightful as Peacock's, in verses such as 'The Rhyme of Lancelot Bogle', ascribed to Mrs E[lizabeth] B[arrett] B[rowning]. Here he uses a fanciful post-Romantic stanza form which he can make sound very pretty, in the opening stanzas:

> And there it was I lay, on a beauteous summer's day,
> With the odour of the hay floating by;
> And I heard the blackbirds sing, and the bells demurely ring,
> Chime by chime, ting by ting,
> Droppingly.[29]

After this sly insipidity, however, he launches into a burlesque Scottish moss-trooping tale about 'George of Gorbals', a Glasgow champion, who is met by the stout crusader-cum-Victorian gentleman of the title, described in a series of references and puns which exploit the stanza form with great ingenuity:

To the tower above the moat, like one who heedeth not,
Came the bold Sir Lancelot, half undressed;
On the outer rim he stood, and peered into the wood,
With his arms across him glued
On his breast.[30]

Aytoun's humour is altogether more subtle and precise than Martin's, and indeed more so than Hood's, in many cases. His knowledge of the traditional ballad itself surpasses theirs and enables him to make comic capital out of the peculiarities of the original rather than only of bad Romantic and early Victorian imitations. 'The Massacre of Macpherson' is a parody of the Scottish pipe-tune which closely resembles Peacock's 'War Song of Dinas Vawr'. The latter begins

The mountain sheep are sweeter,
But the valley sheep are fatter;
We therefore deemed it meeter
To carry off the latter.
We made an expedition;
We met a host, and quelled it
We forced a strong position,
And killed the men who held it.[31]

Aytoun has

Fhairson swore a feud
Against the clan M'Tavish;
Marched into their land,
To murder and to rafish;
For he did resolve
To extirpate the vipers,
With four-and-twenty men
And five-and-thirty pipers.[32]

In both cases the national characteristics of the celts – the thieving Welsh and the belligerent Scots – are expressed in a parody of their own justifications phrased as a parody of their own songs, with the delights of verbal ingenuity in the manipulation of their accents added to the amusement of the violent stories which are so calmly told. Aytoun can turn a similar dexterity to making a comic ballad out of a trivial contemporary event by uniting it incongruously with authentic-sounding ballad diction. In a prose piece called 'How I stood for the Dreepdaily Burghs' which appeared in *Blackwoods* in September 1847, there are several perversions of Scottish ballads supposedly sung by a young lady with a political turn of mind, which substitute the vicissitudes of the stock market and the hustings for the more usual triumphs and tragedies of the ballad hero, in for example

> O whaur hae ye been, Augustus, my son?
> O whaur hae ye been, my winsome young man?
> I hae been to the voters – Mither mak my bed soon
> For I'm weary wi' canvassing, and fain wad lay me down.[33]

'The Queen in France',[34] a lengthy topical ballad describing Victoria's visit to France in 1843 which appears in the Bon Gaultier volume, pokes fun at her insular tastes, and more aggressively at Albert's lack of any English qualities, good or bad (this was a common popular complaint). It is remarkable for the way in which it relies for its sustained humour upon its accurate imitation of traditional ballad; it begins, for example,

> It fell upon the August month,
> When landsmen bide at hame,
> That our gude Queen went out to sail
> Upon the saut-sea faem.

In the midst of this accuracy Aytoun descends suddenly into anti-heroic modernity, making full use of the contrast by maintaining the archaism and Scotticism for the jokes, so that they seem to fit in quite normally until the meaning of the phrase rather than its sound comes home, for example

> O weel, weel may the waters rise,
> In welcome o' their Queen;
> What gars ye look sae white, Albert,
> What makes your e'e sae green?

and

> She gied the King the Cheshire cheese,
> But and the porter fine;
> And he gied her the puddock-pies
> But and the blude-red wine.

The Bon Gaultier ballads are based upon this clever but straightforward, relatively simple source of humour, the parody of ballad styles and the incongruity of the stories and the style, which is a development of the mock-medievalism of *Punch. The Ingoldsby Legends* use the same kind of humour for similar effects, but show the technique in a much more advanced and complicated form, in which the original impetus of parody has given way to a less pointed use of the conventions and stock figures of mock-medievalism as an established pool of comic reference. Barham is clearly basing his comic verse on that of Hood and his successors, but he has taken a further step away from the Romantic ballads and also from the use of the form for topical commentary. *The Ingoldsby Legends* merge all popular and literary sources of humour into a rich and distinctive comic mode. Their descent from previous comic ballads is clear from their first appearance in various magazines, particularly *Bentley's Miscellany*, where they included more topical pieces than were collected into three series published in 1840, 1842 and 1847. The selection forms the three series into a coherent whole which displays the mature comic pattern which emerged from previous experiments as typical Victorian humour.

The topical verses which were allowed to remain in the selected volumes are good examples of the kinds of topical magazine verse already discussed: there is, for example, 'Mr Barney Maguire's Account of the Coronation', which is a close counterpart of Thackeray's *Punch* pieces in which solemn events are narrated in mock-Irish for the sake of mildly humorous incongruities and the pleasure of laughing at and patronising the accent imitated. Similar amusement is drawn from the use of popular catch-phrases and criminal cant in 'Misadventures at Margate', with the important difference that the joke is directed against the gentleman who narrates the story, who has been robbed and 'done brown', because he cannot understand what sailors, policemen and vulgar little boys are saying to him. These modern stories link Barham closely with his contemporaries in that he clearly finds inspiration, as they do, in all kinds of verbal play and manipulation. His chief field, however, is the mock-medieval world which developed out of the Romantic revival, and the framework of *The Ingoldsby Legends* is calculated to suit these stories. All the pieces are supposed to be documents from the Ingoldsby family papers, and stories told to Thomas Ingoldsby when he was a child by family friends and retainers. The commentary on these 'reliques' is continuously and ingeniously reminiscent of Scott and of all the collectors of ballads who allowed personal reminiscence, family and national pride, bigoted antiquarianism, and idle speculation to embroider the texts they printed. The stories are legends and pseudo-legends, and they are cumulative in their comic effect, with the linking matter of provenance, genealogies, textual criticism, historical conjecture and spurious scholarship all included in a pattern of reconstruction, the very complexity and improbability of which is a strong part of its appeal. The atmosphere of old documents and recondite information, often sounding very learned and occasionally lapsing into open nonsense, carries the whole series as one long, ingenious joke. Within this framework, the themes and methods of the *Legends* can be seen to combine those of Barham's predecessors, particularly Southey, in his use of medieval legends, and Hood, in his development of comic versification, with an emphasis and tone which is distinctly popular. Sir Leslie Stephen considered Southey's comic ballads superior to Barham's for the interesting reason that they were less vulgar; and indeed for all the erudition of Barham's spoof framework, his treatment of the stories he tells and his whole appeal is popular rather than literary, is even anti-literary, and is founded upon jokes as basic as those of the music-hall comedian. The colouring of romance and literary allusion has passed completely into popular circulation, its parody function becoming secondary to its independent existence as a comic world.

The Ingoldsby Legends are the most complex and fully-developed presentation of this world, both in the stock characters used and in the manner in which they and their environment are made to operate. The characters are those already familiar from earlier ballads: abbots who eat and drink too well, friars with always an eye to profit, lords who are profligate, powerful and often stupid, or old and fussy, together with the supernatural beings with equally well-defined characters and quirks. The Devil frequently appears as a low fellow with a nose for a bargain, be it a free meal or a human soul, and his usual antagonist is a stern, schoolmasterly saint cunning enough to outwit all claims the Devil makes beyond his proper due. He cannot be put off even by murder and dismemberment, but will rise in ghostly pieces to perform miracles until the Devil is defeated. This world is controlled by the laws not of nature but of verbal logic, which obliterates discrepancies between the physical and spiritual personages as it did in the work of Hood. A curse, invoking the Devil, will undoubtedly cause him to appear; the precise wording of the imprecation gives him licence to do what is there requested of him. Since he is evilly rapacious, a saint, who can be summoned just as easily by a prayer, may have to be called in to prevent him from doing more. No one, however, can prevent him from carrying off whatever was named as his: words are the whole law, and anything which can be said can, and must, be done. Saints and Devils have names, and therefore have just as much existence as human characters.

Throughout the book there is an unflagging zest in the colouring and language of a non-existent, book-inspired historical setting of feudal society, and in the vocabulary of the romances, often authentic in its parts, but comic in effect:

> One tale I remember of mickle dread –
> Now lithe and listen, my little boy Ned![35]

The language of the legends, like the pseudo-scholarly framework, owes a great deal to Scott, both to his novels for general colour and to *The Minstrelsy* and his popularisation of ballads and romances for the language and framing. Without the widespread knowledge of and sympathy for ballads and Romances inspired by Scott's work no one, however scholarly, could have made popular such an erudite joke as *The Ingoldsby Legends*. The fashion in its serious manifestation was now over, and the Gothic ballads had also destroyed their own impact by straining credibility too far. The period of direct parody of the Gothic ballad by exaggeration had followed immediately, with *Tales of Terror* [36] and such parodies as the Smiths', and by this date it also had lost its impetus. The parodies prevented the form from being taken seriously again, and therefore ceased to be funny themselves, and the events and trappings of Gothic horror passed into the realm of comic effects evoking an amused response for themselves alone, incorporated as an element in the larger comedy of *The Ingoldsby Legends*.

In the *Legends* then we have a body of material whose common characteristics and assumptions form a separate world, not identical with the real world or with the basic premises of other literary composition. This was the case with the traditional ballad, and it is interesting to note the wide discrepancies between the original and the mid-nineteenth-century descendant. The ballad is tragic, *The Ingoldsby Legends* are comic; but more than that the world of the *Legends* is not even an attempt to mirror or in any way relate to the real world, far less to epitomise and express the most deeply felt relationships, but draws its characters, events and settings almost entirely from literature rather than life. On the other hand it is also true that the *Legends* are not part of the pattern of assumptions made in literature by the Romance and its descendants: within the unreal pattern the physical, literal implications of words and actions are insisted upon, as they are in the traditional ballad. The humour of the whole creation is a mutation of popular attitudes, taking up literary material to work on and bringing it back to the popular sphere.

The vehicle of comic verse which carries the *Legends* is partly the contribution of Hood. They include several echoes and imitations of Hood's verse, for example 'Aunt Fanny' and 'Nursery Reminiscences', both of which are modern in setting, and therefore closer to the Hood ballads. Hood's ghosts are also present, in for instance 'The Dead Drummer', and his particular form of grotesqueries, the references to body-snatching, suicide and coroners, appears as part of the fabric, but its crudity is mellowed and distanced by the medieval setting. The most usual verse-form is a descendant of his, with fewer puns, but a more highly developed metrical and rhyming intricacy. Barham is if possible more fluent, and spreads his tumbling metre over long lines and complicated systems of half-rhymes and caesuras to make patterned stanzas turning and turning again on double and triple rhymes. To achieve this every kind of vocabulary is used, ranging from polysyllabic words and snatches of French and Latin to lower-class cant and aristocratic slang and contractions. In a single tale, for example 'The Witches' Frolic', all these are used, and a thin layer of Middle English phrases such as 'Though thy mother thine idlesse blames', 'a daintie quean', 'She laugh'd with glee loud laughters three' is imposed upon such rhymes as malignity/Dignity, never ate/asserverate, with a strict eye/*corpus delicti*, decorum/jorum/Quorum/before 'em/Cockalorum. Barham can handle metres without any apparent effort, so much the master of his form that he can introduce a totally different style and tone in the middle of a poem, for instance in 'The Old Woman Clothed in Grey' and in 'The Dead Drummer', and then return at will to the humour and continue as before. He had an ear for speech patterns, as Southey had, and used it to comic effect by mixing incongruous characters and ideolects, making a saint or an abbot relapse into low slang, or a fifteenth-century pope speak to us in a mixture of 'appropriate' dog-latin and the oaths of a Victorian book-maker:

> 'Now Thunder and turf!' Pope Gregory said,
> And his hair raised his triple crown right off his head –
> 'Now Thunder and turf! and out and alas!
> A horrible thing has come to pass!
> What! – cut off the head of a reverend Prior,
> And say he was *only*(!!!) a barefoot Friar! –
> What Baron or Squire,
> Or Knight of the shire
> Is half so good as a holy Friar?
> *O, turpissime!*
> *Vir nequissime!*
> *Sceleratissime! – quissime! – issime!*!'[37]

The mixture of vocabulary, and the familiarity of most of it, is the main method of robbing the antique, other-worldly setting of its remoteness and strangeness, fostered for various purposes by Romantic ballad writers, so that its mere peculiarity and instability are exposed and can be laughed at. This is the reverse of the practice of Aytoun, whose best ballads were strictly confined to an authentic sound, while the sense debunked the heroic tone in which it was conveyed. The incongruity, whichever way it is presented, is the means by which the ballad tradition and the literary ballad were channelled into comic verse. Beginning as parody, the contrast became less provoking as the practice continued, and the framework of stanzaic narrative and word-play was developed for its own sake and turned to other uses, with the addition of other elements of popular humour. A brief consideration of the whole of one of Barham's verse tales, for example 'The Auto-da-fe',[38] will show the confluence of various techniques and influences in popular comic verse. This lengthy tale is introduced as having been brought back from Madrid soon after the Peace of Ryswick by Sir Peregrine Ingoldsby. We are given several preliminary historical notes about him, including the suggestion that he was in some way involved in some unspecified political mission, to which veiled allusion can be found in his letters – and so on, in the familiar vein of an historian dealing with an uninteresting figure about whom he knows nothing worth mentioning. The introduction passes on to speculation about the antiquity of the story itself, and launches eventually into pure fantasy:

> That a splendid specimen of the *genus Homo, species Monk,* flourished in the earlier moiety of the 15th century, under the appellation of Torquemada, is notorious, – and this fact might seem to establish the era of the story; but then *his* name was John – not Dominic – though he was a *Dominican*, and hence the mistake, if any, may perhaps have originated – but then again the Spanish Queen to whom he was Confessor was called Isabella, and not Blanche – it is a puzzling affair altogether . . .

The main source of humour in the verse itself is the intermingling of ancient and modern elements: attitudes expressed, phrases used, descriptions and details are a medley of the quasi-historical and the colloquially modern. The King of Spain speaks to his court in the tones of an elderly Victorian gentleman:

> Now I want to ask you,
> Cavaliers true,
> And Councillors sage – what the deuce shall I do? –
> The State – don't you see? – hey? – an heir to the throne –

> Every monarch – you know – should have one of his own –
> Disputed succession – hey? – terrible Go! –
> Hum! – hey? – Old fellows! – you see! – don't you know? –

The mystification of the Hidalgoes and Grandees at this is compared at length to other situations of puzzlement and chagrin, such as an Alderman finding there is no turtle soup left for him and a sailor coming home to find his wife has run off with a tradesman. They grasp the hilts of their swords and turn away,

> This twirling his mustache, that fingering his ruff,
> Like a blue-bottle fly on a rather large scale,
> With a rather large corking-pin stuck through his tail.

The king refuses to walk to Compostella with peas in his shoes as a penance, and his privy purse will not hear of his riding there, since he could not do it, post, at under two shillings a mile. The conclusion eventually reached is that he should show his devotion by 'burning a Jew or two'. The Auto-da-fe itself brings the popular aspect of the *Legends* into prominence: the huge joke of frizzling beards and poking firebrands like 'posies/Of lilies and roses,/Up to the noses/Of Lazarus Levi, and Money Ben Moses' is thoroughly in the vein of popular violence. Barham takes the opportunity to deplore the habit of religious persecution (expressed as popping ladies who held individual opinions about the supremacy of the Pope into ovens and baking them), but the vigour of the violent joke is also fully exploited. He ends upon another thoroughly popular motif: the result of the king's sacrifice and the queen's prayers for offspring is the embarrassment of twins. Without the poor man's financial difficulties over multiple births the point of this is missing, so Barham makes the prayed-for heirs both girls.

Throughout the story at least as much of the reader's amusement comes from incidental verbal humour as from the telling of the comic tale. Barham revels in the opportunity for strange sounds and rhymes afforded by bits of Spanish appropriate to the story, reeling off line upon line of Spanish names and titles made comic only by the very English emphasis the metre forces upon them, rhyming 'Holy *Hermandad*' with 'grave as a grand-dad', even 'Iñeses' and 'Guiness's', and stopping now and again to point out his own ingenuity or comment on the language he is abusing. In the middle of what is already a confidential aside about the court guards not really being 'beefeaters', as he has just called them, he wanders off into general comments on Spanish cooking, which all his friends tell him is bad,

And no one I'm sure will deny it who's tried a
Vile compound they have that's called *Olla podrida*.
(This, by the bye,
's a mere rhyme to the eye,
For in Spanish the *i* is pronounced like an *e*,
And they've not quite our mode of pronouncing the *d*.
In Castille, for instance, it's giv'n through the teeth,
And what we call *Madrid* they sound more like Mad*reeth*,)

after which he wanders back to the guards and bids us call them 'Walloons', or anything we find appropriate. The manipulation of words is highly sophisticated and skilled, but the impulses behind it and the sources of humour are basically popular; feelings about foreigners and about language, differences of rank and of attitudes now and in the past, all reduced to expose the common humanity of all experience and its essentially ludicrous side.

By the middle of the century the comic ballad world was thus established as the domain of the writers who served the middle-class end of the popular audience, and it was adaptable to cater for their tastes and needs in a variety of ways. Two writers then emerged as supreme in whose work, in very different ways, this promise was fulfilled. There was on the one hand Lewis Carroll, who published his first book of comic verse *Phantasmagoria* in 1869 and *The Hunting of the Snark* in 1876, whose work took the comic ballad into the realm of fantasy and escapism, developing it into an art as abstract and devoid of direct relevance as it could well be; and on the other W. S. Gilbert, who collected the *Bab Ballads* into volume form in 1867, and who fulfilled a function parallel to that of Sims in affirming the social and personal identity and solidarity of a class aware of social threats and problems which gave an edge of horror to his comic flirtation with harsh realities.

Dodgson, in his first volume of verse published under the name of Lewis Carroll, approached the comic ballad along conventional paths. In the *Phantasmagoria* volume is a variety of unexceptional comic ballads and songs which includes some conventional popular jokes and subjects, such as the misery of being a fat man with a thin friend and rival (in 'Size and Tears') and the horrors of the seaside, including a conventionally indirect reference to fleas (in 'Sea Dirge'). Besides the popular conventionality of the jokes, the forms used in the telling of them are derived from the expected source of comic verse, the parody: Tennyson (in 'Echoes'), Longfellow (in 'Hiawatha's Photographing'), and Swinburne (in 'Atlanta in Camden Town') are the most obvious contributors. The mock-Scottish ballad tale of 'The Lang Coortin''[39] is no more distinguished than these, and is less vividly effective than the traditional ballad parody of some of his predecessors, such as W. E. Aytoun. It has felicitous touches of humour based upon incongruous juxtaposition of ancient form and modern meaning, and of romanticism and practicality:

> 'And didna ye get the letter, Ladye,
> Tied wi' a silken string,
> Whilk I sent to thee frae the far countrie,
> A message of love to bring?'
>
> 'It cam' to me frae the far countrie
> Wi' its silken string and a';
> But it wasna pre-paid,' said that high-born maid,
> 'Sae I gar'd them tak' it awa''.

The joke, however, is scarcely strong enough to sustain its thirty-seven stanzas, and the incidental humour arising from the ballad commonplaces used of a modern domestic situation is scattered rather than cumulative in its effect. In the title poem of the volume,[40] however, the elements of parody, incongruity, and the figures of the comic ballad world are worked together into a coherent whole which takes off spectacularly into Carroll's peculiarly potent fantasy world.

The poem is divided into seven cantos, titled medievally from 'The Trysting' to 'Sad Souvenaunce', and represents the apotheosis of comic medievalism. It takes the domestication of the other-worldly to such an extreme that it becomes once more potent and strange, and the domestic is felt to share the qualities of the supernatural, instead of the other way round. It displays a self-sufficiency and completeness within its own assumptions which renders the ghostly once more extraordinary. The domestic setting is tangibly realistic, beginning with comfortable matter-of-factness in the first stanza:

> One wintry night, at half-past nine,
> Cold, tired, and cross, and muddy,
> I had come home, too late to dine,
> And supper, with cigars and wine,
> Was waiting in the study.

The cosiness of this picture is later qualified by incidental revelations that the domestic situation described is actually less than perfect: the Villa he calls home is rather small, his study is not as opulent as he tries to suggest –

'Your room's an inconvenient size;
It's neither snug nor spacious.

'That narrow window, I expect,
Serves but to let the dusk in –'
I cried, 'But please to recollect
'Twas fashion'd by an architect
Who pinned his faith on Ruskin!'

It is moreover afflicted with loose doors and draughty wainscotting; while his supper is prepared by a cook who uses old peas and sends the toasted cheese up cold; the cigars and wine are indifferent. Into this picture of ordinariness, and indeed so thoroughly involved with it as to be the voice which utters the criticisms just quoted, comes a Thing, soon particularised as a Phantom; and the inversion of the natural order begins. To start with, the Thing, rather than the human narrator, is afraid; and their relationship, developed in the course of conversation to something like affection, consistently flouts every expectation. The Phantom's attitude changes from the timid to the self-justifying, and then to the informative:

Through driving mists I seemed to see
A form of sheet and bone –
And found that he was telling me
The whole of his biography
In a familiar tone.

He becomes critical, and his human host retreats from curiosity to attempting to score debating points and catch him out; they bicker, and conduct a meaningless argument about punning,

Commencing every single phrase
With 'therefore' or 'because'
I blindly reeled, a hundred ways,
About the syllogistic maze,
Unconscious where I was.

Finally they discover that the Phantom is in the wrong house anyway, and he leaves, with a casual farewell which haunts the narrator for a year:

Yet still they echo in my head,
Those parting words, so kindly said,
'Old Turnip-top, good-night!'

The effect of this reversal of expectations, the narrator's calm acceptance of the ghost and his human relationship with him, is less to tame and make acceptable the ghost as a funny idea than to undermine the reader's convictions about the difference between reality and fantasy. If this very ordinary man, bad at arguments and living in a poky new house with a presumptuous cook and cheap cigars, finds absolutely nothing extraordinary about the visit of a Phantom, perhaps one's own dismissive, amused attitude to the idea is in some way mistaken. The ghost's speeches, which make up the main body of the verse, are both funny and as disturbing as the setting. They take to its final extreme the *Ingoldsby Legends* technique of using strict adherence to verbal logic to set up a parallel world inhabited by supernatural beings subject to a parody of natural law. Carroll reveals the spirit world as a version of the ordinary one, with all its conventional attributes linked with or explained in human terms. The Phantom reveals to the startled narrator that he is as dependent on material considerations as the least spiritual human being, and indeed his self-pitying narrative suggests that his lot is most uncomfortable. Not only is he as liable to physical discomfort and as often hungry and thirsty as Barham's devils, but he is also enmeshed in a restrictive class system, looked down on by Spectres, deprived of preferment by intimidation at elections, and rejected by the snobbish Haunted-House Committee; he is even kept from what a mortal might have thought of as his natural rights by lack of capital. He cannot afford to fly; and when he first set up in business, he says, he

. . . often spent ten pounds on stuff,
In dressing as a Double,
But, though it answers as a puff,
It never has effect enough
To make it worth the trouble.

Long bills soon quenched the little thirst
I had for being funny –
The setting-up is always worst:
Such heaps of things you want at first,
One must be made of money!

For instance, take a haunted tower,
With skull, cross-bones, and sheet;

Blue lights to burn (say) two an hour,
Condensing lens of extra power,
And set of chains, complete . . .

And then, for all you have to do,
One pound a week they offer you,
And find yourself in Bogies!

The humour of this fantasy arises partly from its unexpectedness, the sense of a completely new way of looking at things which is not without consistency and logic, indeed is strictly rational in appearance, but presents notions previously completely unimaginable as if they were prosaic realities. The use of factual reference, which is so disturbingly realistic, to the real world, does not actually mean that the ballad is related to reality at all. As in the case of its predecessors, its relation is to words, concepts and literature detached from the relevance they originally had to fact and physical existence. Carroll creates an imaginary world out of pieces detached from reality by means of the abuse of verbal and conceptual patterns normally used to order and discuss it.

Exactly the same procedure is used in *The Hunting of the Snark*. Out of fragments of factual reality, and by means of literary reference and the manipulation of words freed from their meanings in the ordinary world, Carroll created a dream world ordered by its own purely verbal logic. The detachment of that world from all others is illustrated by the difficulties Henry Holiday, the original illustrator, had with the pictures for it. One, his drawing of the Snark, was rejected by Carroll because 'All his descriptions of the Boojum were quite unimaginable'[41] – they were only verbal, and not even intended to convey a picture to the imagination. They were indeed quite detached from anything but the words they were expressed in, as can be perceived from the synaesthetic statement of the first of the 'Five unmistakable marks' of the snark. It is quite impossible to translate the stanza from words to impressions:

Let us take them in order. The first is the taste,
Which is meagre and hollow, but crisp:
Like a coat that is rather too tight in the waist,
With a flavour of Will-o'-the-wisp.[42]

The picturing of such a creature is clearly not to be done, and most of the important descriptions and events of the poem have the same quality. Holiday's other problem, however, highlights a quality of the whole which would not appear very readily compatible with this singularity:

he said that 'In our correspondence about the illustrations, the coherence and consistency of the nonsense on its own nonsensical understanding often became prominent.'[43] This consistency of the poem is often, as in all Carroll's fantasy writing, called 'dream logic', things having the kind of connections which they have in the suggestive, symbolic, loosely articulated flow of a dream. It is, I feel, better to think of it as something which is much more artistically and consciously created, a logic of verbal connection and suggestion disciplined by reference to the organisational principles and conventions of the ballad tradition. It is as if elements thrown up by free association, and by verbal games (like the party game in which each player in turn has to produce a word connected by some chosen principle, such as its first letter or occurance in a literary quotation, to the last) were organised into a story by literary principles used without reference to likelihood, relevance or possibility, but quite logical and viable in themselves. In such a process of composition a gap yawns between the poem and reality across which are verbal connections which only serve to mislead. W. S. Gilbert's fantasy ballads rely completely upon the connection they have with reality for their humour and their point; but Carroll has taken off into a purely cerebral game of words and literary associations. The poem is not about anything at all, beyond the words of which it is made up.

His reliance upon quite ordinary literary processes of organisation to provide the basis for the fantasy, giving an identifiable and acceptable groundwork for the reader's grasp of the ballad, is the most easily demonstrated aspect of this. He is using a ballad stanza common to many comic verses and versifiers from Hood onwards, a regular four-line stanza enlivened with occasional internal rhymes and double or triple rhyming words, extended lines and frequent use of extra, unstressed syllables to give a conversational, colloquial flow. The language is calculated to provide a deliberately casual, prosaic background against which the nonsense words and ideas will show up the more incongruously and appear the more mind-bendingly peculiar. The urbane relaxation of Carroll's use of words gives the surface a polish which is often itself highly amusing, and might perhaps be said to be descended from the Byronic style:

> The loss of his clothes hardly mattered, because
> He had seven coats on when he came,
> With three pair of boots – but the worst of it was,
> He had wholly forgotten his name . . .

But the valley grew narrow and narrower still,
And the evening got darker and colder,
Till (merely from nervousness, not from goodwill)
They marched along shoulder to shoulder.[44]

The donnish dryness of 'hardly' and 'wholly', the neatness of the parenthesis, and the easy manipulation of the rhyme, are all delightful.

On a larger scale, the continuity of the story, such as it is, depends on a version of ballad technique. The title is of course suggested by 'The Hunting of the Cheviot', and the poem is divided, somewhat arbitrarily, into fits (with a pun upon the word – it is 'an agony in eight fits'). More than this, the only continuity throughout is the use of a kind of ballad repetition: the story leaps from incident to incident, but all is held together by a recurring stanza. It is introduced to recall the minds of readers, and, one feels, participants, to the fact that they are nominally hunting the Snark, and coming in abruptly in a variety of contexts it is just as well that it is, like some ballad refrains, quite devoid of sensible meaning, although redolent of poetic suggestiveness:

They sought it with thimbles, they sought it with care;
They pursued it with forks and hope;
They threatened its life with a railway share;
They charmed it with smiles and soap.

The repetition within the stanza is also of course a common ballad construction, which occurs again, parodying the commonplace which runs

They had not sailed a week, a week,
A week but barely ane [or 'A week but two or three']

in the Bellman's speech in the second fit:

We have sailed many months, we have sailed many weeks
(Four weeks to the month you may mark),
But never as yet ('tis your Captain who speaks)
Have we caught the least glimpse of a Snark!

We have sailed many weeks, we have sailed many days
(Seven days to the week I allow)
But a Snark, on the which we might lovingly gaze,
We have never beheld till now![45]

A reference to this emphatic repetition is surely also behind the same character's opening words, and his statement that 'What I tell you three times is true.'

Within the framework established by these ballad techniques there is a huge amount of echoing and verbal reference, not only to literature, but to all the set phrases and composite units of meaning which make up ordinary conversation. Common verbal intercourse is not actually a matter of pronouncing and attending to each individual word as it is freshly related to each other word, but rather the emission and reception of expected, pre-set patterns of meaning which approximate to the new, or the old idea we wish to communicate. Carroll's technique is partly the breaking up of these units by totally unexpected juxtapositions –

> There was also a beaver, who paced on the deck,
> Or would sit making lace in the bow:[46]

and also partly, because he was so aware of them, a utilisation of the set phrases and verbal patterns in odd contexts so that the reader is pleased and amused by his own recognition of them. The technique was used much more crudely in the punning and parodying of the minor pieces in *Phantasmagoria*, and appears throughout *The Hunting of the Snark*. One of the more obvious examples is the Baker's life-story in the third fit, which he attempts to tell as a popular tale of tragedy, beginning 'My father and mother were honest, though poor –' which the Bellman will not tolerate. Another phrase from popular use is allowed to pass without comment in the first fit, when the Baker is described as having been 'engaged at enormous expense'.

Even the nonsense words, coinages and transpositions of meaning, are made intelligible – or partly so – if a reader recognises their source and the reference involved. 'Uffish', 'beamish', 'galumphing' and 'outgrabe', all of which occur at some point in the history of the Snark, are taken from Carroll's own work, appearing in 'Jabberwocky' in the first chapter of *Through the Looking Glass*, and they are in some cases explained there: Humpty Dumpty defined 'outgribing' as 'something between bellowing and whistling', while 'galumphing' is a portmanteau word from 'triumphant' and 'galloping'. The point and effect of all this is not, however, to convey in a veiled and indirect way some sensible everyday meaning, and recognition of references is pleasing for its own sake without adding anything to the objective comprehension of the context in which they occur. Objective sense is not the intention in the employment of these or any of the words of the piece; they are all employed as units of speech detached from their usual meanings and used to make up a new language in a new world, where different rules apply. What is said is intelligible to us because those rules are a version of the patterns of literature, particularly popular literature.

A good example of the detachment of words from their usual sense is the naming of the crew. Carroll would seem to have begun with the captain, the Bellman. The office of bellman was not simply, as Martin Gardner suggests in *The Annotated Snark*, 'another word for a town crier';[47] in Scotland the 'skellat bellman' of Glasgow, for example, was certainly appointed as town crier, but he had other functions which were a residue of the role of the minstrel or poet of the community. One particularly famous holder of the office, of whom Carroll may well have known, was Dougal Graham, born in 1724, writer and publisher of a series of chapbooks of Scottish tales and jokes. In London, on the other hand, the bellman was rather a night watchman, whose office survived from the fifteenth century until the improvement of the police force in the early nineteenth century, and who traditionally had printed and sold at Christmas a broadside sheet of verses addressed to the householders of his round soliciting their future support and present payment of a seasonal bonus.[48] Carroll was clearly thinking of a ballad story-teller when he used the name, and Holiday would seem to have been thinking of one particular public poet, Alfred Tennyson, when he drew the pictures. The reference is complex – but probably irrelevant. The bellman in the poem, although he makes speeches and is sensitive to the use of literary clichés by others, is a sea captain and a hunter; his literary qualifications do perhaps serve to suggest the verbal, rather than actual, field through which the hunt is conducted.

Having therefore begun with a captain who is a bellman, Carroll proceeded to name the rest of the crew on a purely phonetic principle, with a series of professions beginning with the letter B. Only one, the Butcher (who is not really a butcher, and has moreover forgotten his own name), shows much interest in or preoccupation with his trade. All the others are simply interesting and sonorously appropriate words. The use of the name 'Baker', for instance, adds an extra dimension to the character's actions and fate, but the changing of it, say to 'Boxer' or 'Bagman', or even the substitution of a nonsense word, would not destroy other aspects of the character and its humour. Thus Carroll can make use of words quite arbitrarily selected, and indeed can occasionally change the meaning of a word to suit himself, not only cutting off its old sense but forcing us to assign it another, as in 'in an antediluvian tone' to heighten and intensify the humour of his other world. Gilbert was tied to the contrast with reality for his meaning, and so had to maintain a superficial semblance of possibility and precise meaning for his effects. *The Snark* floats free of relevance and reference. Its connection with reality, if it has one at all, is perhaps philosophic, and many critics have earnestly sought its transcendental meaning, the most recent being Martin Gardner, whose theory is that 'The *Snark* is a poem about being and non-being, an existential poem, a poem of existential agony.'[49] Without agreeing or disagreeing with this sombre pronouncement, one might see in it a possible link between Carroll and Gilbert, for Gilbert is concerned with the 'dimension of anxiety', 'the agony of anticipating one's loss of being', in a much more concrete, and I would suggest conscious, way, in the context of his own class in Victorian society.

Like G. R. Sims, Gilbert is concerned, one feels, with the anxiety of the 'respectable' classes about the precariousness of their way of life in the face of the 'dangerous' classes. He tackles the problem less specifically, but his comic writing reflects unease as strongly as Sims's social whitewashing. The characters and stories of the *Bab Ballads* are grotesque, a violent fantasy whose tone of whimsy is quite at odds with the bloody events related. They are the ultimate development of Hood's comic world; they seem to reflect the fantasies and anxieties of men who live close to a miserable and violent environment, the mid-Victorian slum, but are strictly shielded from it in their own persons and restricted within a very different code of values and range of personal action. Gilbert takes middle-class society, its customs and expressions (of which his observation is as acute as that of Sims in his lower-class sketches) and injects fantastic, grotesquely unsuitable action and ideas. There is for instance the sudden wickedness of a curate, when

> The Tempter said his say,
> Which pierced him like a needle –
> He summoned straight away
> His sexton and his beadle.
>
> (These men were men who could
> Hold liberal opinions:
> On Sundays they were good –
> On weekdays they were minions.)[50]

'Minion' is an expression taken straight from a melodrama, where such men loom darkly behind robber barons in Gothic Italian castles. Similarly there is Mr Brown, who

> . . . traced that gallant sorter to a still suburban square;
> He watched his opportunity and seized him unaware;

He took a life-preserver and he hit him on the head,
And Mrs. Brown dissected him before she went to bed.[51]

'Before she went to bed' is the effective phrase here, suggesting early hours and wholesome suppers.

In the first volume of the collected *Bab Ballads* alone, six of the stories hinge more or less upon slaughter or flogging, besides two concerning Pentonville prison and another on a man who grew too fat to walk. The dark and violent side of Victorian life occupied both the humorous writers concerned with pricking the conscience of the complacent reader, as *Punch* balladeers did in satirical verse upon such things as cholera and penal legislation, and men like Gilbert whose verses satisfied a peculiar relish and craving for the ugly and grotesque that was perhaps a different aspect of the same consciousness. Dickens used the gusty vulgarity of Hood and the early part of the century, in for instance *The Pickwick Papers*, and also the later exaggerated and very physical vision of people, serving a more subtle purpose combining horror, fear and revulsion with fascinated amusement, in such figures as Quilp and the Smallweed family. Gilbert's strongest comic characters have something of the same ambiguity, like the elderly naval man whose

. . . hair was weedy, his beard was long,
And long and weedy was he

who recites 'In a singular minor key' the comic story of how he came to eat the entire crew of his ship;[52] or Effendi Bachsheesh Pasha Allah Achmet, who one day had a pain in his tum which he found very embarrassing to mention, but on discovering that his doctor was his rival in love became very decided and fearless, and

. . . drove right through the Doctor's chest
The sabre and the hand that held it.[53]

There are also the parents of Lenore, the beloved of Guy the Crusader, whose

. . . father incessantly lashed her,
On water and bread
She was grudgingly fed;
Whenever her father he thrashed her
Her mother sat down on her head.[54]

Other fantasies are indulged, less sadistic but equally odd, releasing the most respectable members of society from all proper inhibitions: like

Captain Reece, who danced to his crew to amuse them, and the curate who gave up worsted work and flutes and lambkins in favour of curling his hair and winking at the girls, and the Bishop of Rum-ti-fu, who also took up acrobatic dancing for the diversion of his flock, but suddenly and arbitrarily drew the line:

> But if they saw their Bishop land,
> His leg supported in his hand
> The joke they wouldn't understand –
> 'Twould pain them very much![55]

Another is Baines Carew, a lawyer so tenderhearted that Captain Bagg (wanting a divorce because his wife insists he is a canary) is obliged to take his case elsewhere:

> . . . Baines lay flat upon the floor,
> Convulsed with sympathetic sob –
> The Captain toddled off next door,
> And gave the case to Mr Cobb.[56]

The exaggeration of this vision grows out of Hood's simply comic world, where even death is funny, as does the sheer nonsense of Carroll. The difference between the two descendants lies in the fact that whereas Carroll took the concept of the comic world to its logical conclusion, and created in both 'Phantasmagoria' and *The Hunting of the Snark* a self-consistent structure whose only norm is its own peculiarity, Gilbert made use of the same comic world for the satire he could create out of its relation to reality. Their motives for writing are clearly involved in this divergence. Gilbert was essentially concerned with communication, and his use of the popular ballad for social comment is paralleled by other journalists' use of the form. Carroll was more or less completely detached from the complex of literary and journalistic activity, and was able to develop the simply playful aspect of Hood's work, unhampered by the demands or the restrictions of writing humorous pieces for a living. In the *Bab Ballads* the normal world is the frame of reference which makes the departures from it funny: when a bishop dances or a lawyer weeps the normal behaviour of bishop and lawyer are what make it remarkable. For this reason Carroll can make use of coined words to great effect, while Gilbert must rely for the floating, verbal comedy of his ballads on proper names and incidentals such as rhyme and patter: the content has to have precise meaning on a superfical level for the nonsense to be effective, and so the language has to be sufficiently restrained and normal to convey this.

The language of the *Bab Ballads* is therefore lucid, colloquial English, enlivened with a little slang and laced with fantastic names; it is very carefully drilled to achieve the maximum of humorous effect in sound with ordinary words, by means of rhythm and rhyme, while the intrinsic absurdity of what is said makes its own impact through the factual simplicity of presentation. This ballad style is perhaps the direct descendant of the peculiar stories told in a straight-faced manner by Southey, combined, especially in Gilbert's later and more highly developed works, with the verbal expertise drawn from Hood and the magazine writers who were his immediate successors. A single and straight-forward narrative is essential, as in most popular ballads, but in Gilbert's work the story is enriched and made complex by his observation and use of the fine detail of social convention and habit. Carroll's concern was to use and so show up the oddity of verbal and literary convention; Gilbert does the same for social convention and habit. A good example of Gilbertian humour in its highly-developed verbal and social detail is the ballad 'Etiquette'.[57] The joke here is a twist on his usual pattern of characters released from normal social inhibitions: the two heroes are bound by convention in a situation where no normal person would continue to be so:

> These passengers, by reason of their clinging to a mast,
> Upon a desert island were eventually cast.
> They hunted for their meals, as ALEXANDER SELKIRK used,
> But they couldn't chat together – they had not been introduced.

The joke is improved by the means they find to introduce themselves: one overhears the other mention 'Robinson', whom of all the Robinsons in existence he immediately and correctly takes to be the one with whom he was 'chummies at the Charterhouse'. The description of an embarrassed gentleman introducing himself is acutely observed:

> He walked straight up to Somers, then he turned extremely red,
> Hesitated, hummed and hawed a bit, then cleared his throat, and said:
>
> 'I beg your pardon – pray forgive me if I seem too bold,
> But you have breathed a name I knew familiarly of old.
> You spoke aloud of Robinson – I happened to be by –
> You know him?' 'Yes, extremely well.' 'Allow me – so do I!'

The final twist, their social discomfiture at finding Robinson has been convicted of misappropriating stock, is vividly decribed:

At first they didn't quarrel very openly, I've heard;
They nodded when they met, and now and then exchanged a word:
The word grew rare, and rarer still the nodding of the head,
And when they meet each other now, they cut each other dead.

The details given of their past lives and present behaviour, all totally useless and inappropriate on a desert island, decorate and flavour the narrative:

Young PETER GRAY, who tasted teas for BAKER, CROOP, & Co.,
And SOMERS, who from Eastern shores imported indigo.

This is also the function of the whimsically exaggerated account of the friendship that developed between them after they consented to know each other:

They soon became like brothers from community of wrongs:
They wrote each other little odes and sang each other songs;
They told each other anecdotes disparaging their wives;
On several occasions, too, they saved each other's lives.

The crowning joke is their tastes in food:

On Peter's portion oysters grew – a delicacy rare,
But oysters were a delicacy Peter couldn't bear.
On Somers' side was turtle, on the shingle lying thick,
Which Somers couldn't eat, because it always made him sick.

Gray gnashed his teeth with envy as he saw a mighty store
Of turtle unmolested on his fellow-creature's shore:
The oysters at his feet aside impatiently he shoved,
For turtle and his mother were the only things he loved.

The verbal texture is rich and intricately constructed, for example the stanza:

And Somers sighed in sorrow as he settled in the south,
For the thought of Peter's oysters brought the water to his mouth.
He longed to lay him down upon the shelly bed, and stuff:
He had often eaten oysters, but had never had enough.

The metre is the familiar polysyllabic tumble of four-stress lines rhyming in emphatic couplets, but the effectiveness of Gilbert's patter lies in the enormous and apparently effortless skill with which he makes patterns of sounds within the lines. In this stanza the first line alliterates on 's', six of them, possibly to suggest a sigh, or quite probably only because it sounds funny. The second line has an internal rhyme, thought/brought, assonance or half-rhyme between thought/brought/oysters/water, and the repetition of 'er' in Peter/oysters/water; the third line alliterates on 'l', with a suggestion of rhyme between longed and upon, and the fourth plays with repetition and contrast of vowels and syllables, tempting the reader to tongue-twisting speed. This is the quintessence of comic verse, word-play so entirely for its own sake and independent of, without dictating, the sense, that it resembles a musical joke. Gilbert rarely uses a pun, or any form of language which is 'funny' or departs from ordinary and precise modern English. He relies entirely on the oddity of sound and of speech itself for the texture of his verse, as he draws upon the suppressed peculiarity of human nature for the frame of it, an austerity which creates rich individuality and strange insights, not totally without resemblance to the pattern and effect of the ballad of tradition.

The difference of Gilbert's writing from the work of Sims is suggested by the possibility of such a comparison. Sims used the motifs and techniques of the popular ballad as it developed during the nineteenth century to misrepresent one part of the popular audience to another, and his recitation ballads are spurious; but Gilbert's art is employed with unimpeachable validity upon refining and perfecting the comic ballad which belonged to, was developed by, and spoke to the feelings of the middle-class popular audience. The anxieties and tensions involved are the same, but Gilbert is using a popular art legitimately in their expression, where Sims perverted his in their misrepresentation. Free of such restricting and vitiating distortions, the Victorian comic ballad was developed to its full potential in the drawing-rooms and in the magazines, as well as in the music hall, adding to itself the skills and talents of great writers without losing its popular roots and appeal.

Conclusion

The student of ballads more ancient than these may well feel that I have missed a great opportunity offered by one aspect of the material of this study. Much critical and scholarly effort has gone into the struggle to date ballad texts, and to establish some conjectures about the time of their first appearances. It has often seemed that the study of the traditional ballad has been greatly hampered by lack of any clear literary history, because of these difficulties. Yet the ballads I have dealt with almost all have a clear date, and could have been considered in chronological order, according to when their authors wrote and published them: and I have chosen, on the whole, to ignore the fact. Such apparent perversity perhaps needs justification. It might indeed have added another element to our comprehension of the complexity of the cultures of nineteenth-century Britain had I been at pains to point out that the broadside 'Teddies Oak Stick' and the first Repository Tracts were available at the same time, that *Punch* first appeared in 1841 and the *Lays of Ancient Rome* were published in 1842, that the second half of the 1870s saw *The Hunting of the Snark*, Macdermott's 'War Song', 'The Revenge', and the *Dagonet Ballads*, while the last three years of the century produced 'Vitai Lampada', the *Gordon League Ballads* and 'Hulloa, Hulloa, Hulloa!'; but it would not in fact have added a great deal to our knowledge of the parts these all played in the popular tradition. The measure of a popular ballad's success is its length of life. It may burst upon the public as a blazing success and never be forgotten, like Hood's 'Song of a Shirt', written in 1843 and still quoted, or it might slide unnoticed into the popular memory as a song sung to children, when its origins are generally forgotten, like 'Daddy Wouldn't Buy me a Bow-wow'. Its beginning is not as important as its continuance. If a song fits, catches the right mood, it is born and continues to live and to grow, it is still heard and its influence continues to be felt, to inspire and shape new songs. The 'Song of the Shirt' was as important to the propaganda balladeers of the 1890s as it was fifty years before. To confine the examination of songs to comparison with others in their year or decade of birth would be to distort their significance, therefore, and also to undermine the basic contention upon which serious consideration of them is based: the contention that individual writers within the popular tradition were less important than their songs, which together made up a living tradition of popular balladry and inherited the audiences and the qualities of the dateless, anonymous folksong of earlier times. I hope that by examining the ballads according to their tone and subject-matter, I have indicated the wide emotional range, and something of the depth, which the nineteenth-century ballad possessed.

It only remains to give some indication of what happened next. In tracing the popular tradition I have left aside poets like William Barnes, Thomas Hardy and John Davidson, who belong to the main literary stream but whose work was influenced by folk poetry in some way. Their part in the next development of poetry on both the literary and the popular levels was considerable. So too was the influence of folk-song which was transmitted through the revival of interest in traditional ballad and song brought about by Cecil Sharp and his followers, taking a line which excluded the nineteenth-century popular tradition from consideration as genuine folk-art. Poets and folklorists co-operated in one of the cyclically-recurring attempts to return to simplicity in poetry. On this occasion a new dimension was added to the idea of the appeal to folk-art as basic and uncorrupted: the poetry of the people, of the working classes, came to be regarded by some writers as having not only artistic but also moral superiority to the products of an effete bourgeois culture. The folk-art singled out for praise and imitation, therefore, strictly excluded the 'bourgeois' aspects of the tradition in the last hundred years, and nineteenth-century popular poetry was either rejected in favour of the wholly safe 'peasant' rural songs of earlier generations, or fragmented into the 'real' urban worker's songs and those contaminated with 'phoney' emotions such as sentimentality, and later patriotism. W. B. Yeats appealed to the Irish tradition of popular song as preserving real poetry, and wrote much verse according to its models; but later English writers, such as W. H. Auden, William Plomer, and Lawrence Durrell, approached their national tradition less positively. They chose ballad forms as vehicles for attack upon aspects of their society and its culture, which is a traditional use for the broadside ballad. But the forms they used are not exempt from the contempt they expressed, nor do they present an alternative to the values they deride;

rather the feeling was that the subject was so base that only base and ugly words and structures were suitable to it. The brash doggerel of the modern popular song was chosen as the fitting expression of the distorted soul of the age.

These were activities upon the literary level which made use of and commented upon popular art; they are relevant to the further development of popular song itself because the division between the two kinds of culture has progressively broken down, or at least become more difficult to define, in this century. The placing of modern poets like Charles Causley or Roger McGough on one side of a line dividing popular and literary writing is practically impossible, and dubiously valuable. Their use of popular models is richer, though less precise, than that of their immediate predecessors; the routes by which elements of ballad came into their work, or that of more distinctly popular writers like Bob Dylan and Leonard Cohen, are too many to be traced, and include one which deters me from even entering upon the attempt. Cecil Sharp's dogmatic rejection of the nineteenth-century popular tradition was based upon an element of the material he revived which was quite clearly not shared by what came after it: the folk tradition of English music. The richness and beauty of folk music before 1800 was rediscovered at the beginning of the twentieth century, and its impact was very closely comparable to the impact of the ballad text revival a hundred years before. The revival and development of folk music dominates the forms and patterns of popular poetry in the twentieth century, and has led many to ballads and lyrics who would not have found them through the literary tradition. The complexity of this pattern is one I cannot undertake to trace; but before it is complete the critical history of popular poetry in the twentieth century must take account of the traditions we have inherited from the ballads of the Victorian period.

Notes

Place of publication is London, unless otherwise stated.

Introduction

1 *Edinburgh Review*, vol. VII (Oct 1805–Jan 1806) no. XIV, article VI, pp. 387–413; the work reviewed was *Ancient Engleish Metrical Romanceës*, 3 vols (1802).
2 F. J. Child, *The English and Scottish Popular Ballads*, 5 vols (Boston 1882–98) referred to hereafter as *E.S.P.B.*
3 Robert Graves, *The English Ballad, a short critical survey* (1927) p. 8.
4 *The Ballads* (1950) p. 12.
5 Ibid., p. 45.
6 *A Literary History of the Popular Ballad* (Durham, N.C., 1968).
7 (1957) p. 12.
8 *A Social History of Traditional Song* (1969) p. 181.
9 *The Ballads*, p. 13.
10 (University of Chicago Press, 1961).
11 *The Literary Ballad* (1966).
12 *The Broadside Ballad* (1962) p. 38.
13 *English Folk Song: Some Conclusions*, 1907 (4th ed. repr. 1972) pp. 150–1.
14 It has recently been remarked, however, by R. Pearsall, *Victorian Popular Music* (1973) pp. 205–18, that much nineteenth-century comment on the paucity and inferiority of contemporary folk-song is rather prudery than scholarship.
15 See Florence Emily Hardy, *The Early Life of Thomas Hardy 1840–1891* (1928) pp. 25–6.
16 See G. Grigson, Introduction to the *Faber Book of Popular Verse* (1971) p. 9, where he defines popular verse and points out that 'there have always been different layers, different circles of popularity, separate or overlapping.' In the Victorian period many layers merged together to form a spectrum rich in variety, but clearly continuous.
17 Hodgart, *The Ballads*, pp. 10–11.
18 See V. de Sola Pinto and A. E. Rodway, *The Common Muse* (1957) p. 8.

19 (Oxford, 1932) pp. 36–66, and *passim*.

20 Edward Lee, *Music of the People* (1970) p. 119.

21 This is perhaps the point to recognise a limitation I share with many of the illustrious commentators upon ballad poetry whom I have mentioned here. I am not equipped, and accordingly shall not attempt, to discuss the musical aspect of the ballad tradition. While such a disability is now rightly regarded as rendering the valuable discussion of the ancient ballads impossible, it is not so important a failure with regard to the ballads of the nineteenth century. The tradition I hope to trace was not primarily a musical tradition. The tunes of the music-hall songs do in some cases bear a distant relation to older popular music, but much more frequently they do not; and beyond the halls the ballads passed into an entirely unmusical, though still an oral, phase of existence. The loss of the support and shaping effect of music had effects upon the ballad texts which I shall attempt to explore in their place; but the difficult and largely separate analysis of the relation of folk-music to Victorian composition I must leave to others.

Chapter 1

1 See his letter to Francis Wrangham, *Letters of William and Dorothy Wordsworth, the middle years*, 1806–20, ed. E. de Selincourt, 2 vols (Oxford, 1937) vol. 1, letter 338, p. 222; and also *The Prelude*, ed. E. de Selincourt (Oxford, 1926) text of 1805–6, ll. 202–16, pp. 144, 146. Wordsworth's debt to Bishop Percy's *Reliques of Ancient Poetry*, 3 vols (1765) was also considerable, though a matter of inspiration rather than imitation.

2 The 'Come-all-ye' ballad stanza is described by A. L. Lloyd, *Folk Song in England* (1967) p. 355, as having 'four-lined strophes of 14 (8+6) syllables, its tunes often in 6/8 time, its structure as likely as not an inexorable ABBA pattern . . ., with the outer cadences on the tonic and the inner ones on the dominant or subdominant, mainly of mixolydian or dorian cast when not on the conventional major. Probably of urban origin (from Dublin?)'.

3 *The Ballad Revival* (University of Chicago Press, 1961) p. 269ff.

4 See Scott's own Introduction and notes to the *Minstrelsy of the Scottish Border*, 3 vols (1802–3) the 'Introductory Remarks on Popular Poetry' and 'Essay on Imitations of the Ancient Ballad' appended to the 1830 edition, and also the comments of T. F. Henderson in his edition of the *Minstrelsy*, 4 vols (1902).

5 See for instance his *Tales of Wonder*, 2 vols (1801).

6 Surviving fragments of his projected edition were published by W. A. MacInnes as *Ballads of the English Border* (1925).

7 'Poems of D. G. Rossetti', *Essays and Studies* (1875) pp. 85–6, q.v. for an accurate and interesting account of what a ballad should be, oddly misapplied to praise poems which manifestly fail to fulfil its prescriptions.

Chapter 2

1 Henry Mayhew, *London Labour and the London Poor*, 3 vols (1851); see P. Quennell (ed.), *Mayhew's London* (1969) p. 144.

2 See Leslie Shepard, *John Pitts, Ballad Printer of Seven Dials* (1969) for a full account of this printer's activities.
3 J. W. Sharp, *The Vauxhall Comic Song Book*, ser. 1 (1847) p. 27.
4 From a broadside preserved in the Bodleian Library, press mark 2806 c 13.
5 See Ada Reeve, *Take it for a Fact* [1954] p. 22.
6 'Marie Lloyd', 1923, in *Selected Essays*, 3rd ed. (1951) p. 458.
7 M. H. Spielmann, *The History of Punch* (1895) p. 128.
8 *Poems from Punch 1841–1884* (1908) Introduction, pp. 17–18.
9 *Punch*, vol. 16 (1849) p. 114.

Chapter 3

1 Quoted by Michael Turner, Introduction to *Parlour Poetry* (1967) p. 11.
2 Text from a 2d Fortey publication, *The Aquarium Songster*, a copy of which may be found at British Library, press mark 11602 ee 27 (2).
3 First printed in *Macmillan's Magazine*; text from *The Return of the Guards and other poems* (1866) pp. 105–7.
4 'Hearts of Oak' beaten on the drum became the naval call to quarters, and it was regarded as the naval anthem.
5 *Victorian Song* (1955) p. 51.
6 Text from Frederick Langbridge (ed.), *Ballads of the Brave*, 3rd ed. (1907) p. 292.
7 Text ibid., p. 293.
8 *The Imperial Songster*, copy at the Bodleian Library, press mark 2806 e 56/2.
9 Text from W. E. Henley, *Lyra Heroica* (1892) p. 92. A broadside copy printed by H. P. Such occurs in the *Collection of Broadsides printed in London, collected by T. Crampton*, 7 vols [1860?–70?] preserved in the British Library, vol. 5, p. 166.
10 Copy at British Library, press mark 11621 c 14 (15).
11 *The Broadside Ballad* (1962) p. 149.
12 Text from sheet music published by Goulding, D'Almaine, Potter and Co. (1811). See Lloyd, *Folk Song in England*, pp. 264–86 for an extended consideration of nineteenth-century and earlier songs of the sea, the heroic sailor, and the hated press. Edward Lee, *The Music of the People* (1970) pp. 70–1, makes the point that heroic sailor ballads did not penetrate rural areas or become popular in the ports (presumably excluding the Port of London), where shanties were preferred. Shanties were work songs, belonging strictly to their working context, separate even from the forebitters or ballads sung in leisure time aboard ship, and certainly having no effect upon the entertainment sought by the sailor ashore. They had no more influence than one would expect upon the mainstream of folk-song, which came to belong to the towns. Lee offers little justification for his assumption that this change to urban song was the death of 'folk song proper'.

13 *Peeping Tom*, no. 5 (1859).
14 See Dudley Barker, *G. K. Chesterton* (1973) p. 19.
15 T. B. Macaulay, *Lays of Ancient Rome* (1842) p. 26.
16 Text from 1870 ed., p. 123.
17 Doyle, in the preface to the volume of verse which secured his election to the Professorship of Poetry, *The Return of the Guards* (1866), confessed his philistinism quite openly. See p. ix.
18 *The Poets and Poetry of the Century*, 10 vols (1891–7) vol. 5, pp. 37–8.
19 First published 1829; text from Turner, *Parlour Poetry*, p. 140.
20 Text ibid., p. 58.
21 Text from Alfred H. Miles, *Ballads of Brave Women* [?1908] pp. 91–2.
22 Text from Langbridge, *Ballads of the Brave*, p. 351.
23 *The Power of Red Michael* (1909) p. 19.
24 Text from *Ballads of the Brave*, p. 408.
25 Text ibid., pp. 355–6.
26 Quoted in Charles Tennyson, *Alfred Tennyson* (1949) p. 320.
27 First published in the *Examiner*, 1854; text from *Poems*, ed. Ricks (1969) pp. 1035–6. Doyle also had a version of this episode, entitled 'Balaclava': see *Return of the Guards*, p. 239.
28 First published 1878; text from *Poems*, ed. Ricks, pp. 1244–5.
29 Text from *Ballads of the Brave*, pp. 432–4. Doyle was so moved by this event that he published a black-bordered pamphlet 'To the Memory of General Gordon', containing his poem on the subject, headed 'January 27th, 1885'.
30 Text from J. K. Tomalin, *The World Wide Reciter* (n.d.) p. 98. Such stoicism was moreover not only found in fiction: in Exeter Cathedral there is a memorial plaque which reads

> To the Memory of Arthur Corfe Angel Eldest son of Alfred Angel organist of this Cathedral and his wife Anne born August 1845 He was an officer of the steamship 'London' which foundered in the Bay of Biscay January 11th 1866 on her voyage to Melbourne in one of the most fatal gales on record when only 19 out of 263 souls were saved. A truehearted and dauntless sailor counting duty more precious than life he remained at his post to the last and was seen by survivors with his hand still upon the engine of which he was in charge calmly awaiting death when the waters closed over the ship. In testimony of his worth and in token of sympathy with his bereaved parents this tablet simple as becomes the rare simplicity of his character is placed here by the Dean and Chapter.

31 Quoted by Turner, *Parlour Poetry*, p. 115.
32 Text from *World Wide Reciter*, p. 88.
33 H. Newbolt, *Admirals All* (1897) p. 21.
34 *Admirals All*, 5th ed. (1898) p. 30.
35 'How he saved St. Michael's', text from *Ballads of the Brave*, p. 377.
36 Ibid., p. 349.

37 'The Saving of the Colours', text from ibid., p. 430.
38 p. 262. Doyle attempted this subject too: see *The Return of the Guards*, p. 274.
39 Text from *Ballads of the Brave*, pp. 315–16.
40 First appeared in 'Victoria Regia'. Text from *The Return of the Guards*, pp. 99–104.
41 Broadside printed by Jennings, copy at Bodleian Library, press mark 2806 c 19.
42 Text from *The Definitive Edition of Rudyard Kipling's Verse* (1940) p. 459.
43 In an essay on Kipling in *A Choice of Kipling's Verse* (1941) p. 6.
44 'Rudyard Kipling', 1942, *Collected Essays*, ed. S. Orwell and I. Angus, 4 vols (1968) vol. II, p. 194.
45 *The Complete Barrack-Room Ballads of Rudyard Kipling* (1973).
46 *The Working Classes in Victorian Fiction* (1971) pp. 161–6.
47 *Barrack-Room Ballads and other verses* (1892) p. 112.
48 Quoted from *Definitive Edition*, p. 661; first published in *Rewards and Fairies* (1910).
49 'Romulus and Remus', ibid., p. 641; first published in *Letters to the Family* (1908).
50 Ibid., p. 669; first published in *Rewards and Fairies*.
51 *Something of Myself*, Bombay Edition of the *Works of Rudyard Kipling*, 31 vols (1913–38) vol. XXXI, pp. 95–6.
52 *Barrack-Room Ballads*, p. 55.
53 Ibid., pp. 14–15.
54 Ibid., pp. 57, 59.
55 Ibid., p. 60.
56 Ibid., p. 4.
57 Ibid., pp. 48–9.

Chapter 4

1 For the influence of education in 'classical' music upon popular taste see R Nettel, *A Social History of Traditional Song* (1969) pp. 237–8; and Pearsall, *Victorian Popular Music* (1973) *passim*.
2 Sheet music published by Goulding, D'Almaine, Potter and Co. (n.d.).
3 *Seven Centuries of Popular Song* (1956) p. 199.
4 *A Social History of English Music* (1964) p. 143.
5 *Folk Song in England* (1967) pp. 330–75.
6 *Victorian Song* (1955) p. 223.
7 *The Faber Book of Ballads* (1965) p. 12.
8 *Folk Song in England*, ch. v, pp. 316–411.
9 In a broadside version of *c.*1850, printed by E. Hodges of Seven Dials, copy at British Library, press mark 11621 k 5 358.
10 Examples of Armstrong's music-hall songs (he also wrote in older folk

modes, and in a self-consciously literary manner when he felt the occasion called for it) are given in Peter Davidson, *Songs of the British Music Hall* (New York, 1971) as are 'Keep your Feet Still Geordie Hinny' by Joe Wilson, and 'Cushie Butterfield', a song to the tune of 'Polly Perkins' written by George Ridley, who also wrote 'Bladon Races'.

11 *Folk Song in England*, pp. 388–91.

12 Printed on broadside; quoted here from John Harland, *Lancashire Lyrics: Modern Songs and Ballads of the County Palatine* (1866) pp. 251–4.

13 Text from Crampton, *Collection of Broadsides*, vol. 1, p. 42.

14 Text from a Sam Cowell songbook published by Davidson, reprinted in *Folk Scene*, no. 11 (Sep 1965) p. 4.

15 Harold Scott, *The Early Doors* (1946) p. 242. See also the rather confused note on the continuity of the folk tradition in Disher, *Victorian Song*, p. 129, where he talks about 'Lord Lovel'.

16 'Popular Broadside Ballads', *Folk Scene*, no. 11, p. 3.

17 Text from Lee, *Music of the People* (1970) p. 102. It is copied from Disher, *Victorian Song*, p. 126. Following Disher, Lee also perpetuates a hybrid of two song titles, 'The Ratcatcher's Daughter of Islington', found in Disher, p. 131, where 'The Ratcatcher's Daughter' is quoted without the first verse, which states that she lived in Westminster. Lee picks up the title (p. 103) to make a curious point about burlesque.

18 p. 24.

19 For broadside outlaw heroes, see Lloyd, *Folk Song in England*, pp. 220, 259.

20 'Sam Hall' has attracted much critical and nostalgic commentary over the years; see for instance Thackeray, *Pendennis* (1848–50); A. L. Hayward, *The Days of Dickens* (1925) p. 116; and *Green Room Recollections*, quoted by Harold Scott, *The Early Doors*, p. 238; see also Davidson, *Songs of the British Music Hall*, p. 14. The version quoted here is taken from *The Days of Dickens*.

21 Quoted from Davidson, *Songs of the British Music Hall*, p. 185.

22 Beerbohm, 'The Blight on the Music Halls', in *More* (1899) p. 121.

23 *Sweet Saturday Night* (1967) pp. 130–1.

24 Quoted from ibid., pp. 129–30.

25 *Victorian Song*, p. 224.

26 See Davidson, *Songs of the British Music Hall*, p. 200, for an analysis of ''Arf a Pint of Ale' on these lines.

27 Published by Francis, Day and Hunter (1896).

28 See Davidson, *Songs of the British Music Hall*, pp. 38–9.

29 See Pulling, *They Were Singing*, p. 69.

30 *Songs of the British Music Hall*, pp. 99–101.

31 See Hans Nathan, *Dan Emmett and the Rise of Early Negro Minstrelsy* (University of Oklahoma Press, 1962).

32 See S. Spaeth, *Read 'em and Weep* (New York, 1926).

33 Text from *Mohawk Minstrel's Magazine*, no. 77, vol. 26, published by Francis,

Day and Hunter (n.d.) p. 48. Harry Hunter's songs are a case of the home-grown imitation outdoing the original model, for he and his troupe were English; he started life in the City, became an Interlocutor and a manager of minstrels, and helped to found the publishing company who printed most of the music-hall songs at the end of the century.

34 Text from *The Imperial Songster*, published by W. S. Fortey (n.d. [1894]).

35 Michael Turner and Anthony Miall, *The Parlour Song Book, a Casquet of Vocal Gems* (1972) p. 19.

36 Written by Joseph Tabrar, 1882. The re-use of good tunes for various related or unrelated songs is a common characteristic of older folk-music. Text from a Fortey songster (n.d.).

37 See Davidson, *Songs of the British Music Hall*, pp. 52–3.

38 Composed by G. Le Brunn, published by Francis Bros and Day (n.d. [1889]).

39 For the source of this text see note 9, p. 262.

40 Michael Booth, *English Melodrama* (1965) pp. 56, 136, 123, 38.

41 Text from the same Fortey songster as 'The Ship Wrecked Sailor', above. The air for this song is given as 'Miss them when they're dead'. Colin MacInnes, in *Sweet Saturday Night* (1967) p. 76, says that Charles Godfrey's song 'On Guard', discussed in the last chapter, was presented in a scene set at a workhouse door, where the old soldier of Balaclava is refused entrance and told he is 'not wanted', and sings the song about the occasion on which he was.

42 Sheet music published by Francis Bros and Day; text from *The Aquarium Songster*.

43 Sheet music published by Chas Sheard and Co., written by Charles Osborne. Text from a Fortey songster, copy at Bodleian Library, press mark 2806 d 5(9).

44 Sheet music published by Chas Sheard and Co., text from *The Imperial Songster*.

45 *Victorian Songs*, p. 133.

46 Text from *Poetical Works*, ed. Walter Jerrold (Oxford, 1911) p. 625.

47 Text from *A collection of Poems printed on single sheets* (n.d. [1840–50]).

48 A writer at the other end of the social scale, the Hon. Roden Noel, son of the Earl of Gainsborough, can be cited as another example of a parlour poet who took up the challenge of Hood's song earnestly but with little skill, in an angry, verbose effusion entitled 'Poor People's Christmas' [1890], in which he adds a disabled, suicidal husband and dying children to the seamstress's burden.

49 Text from the collection cited above, n. 47 (no pagination).

50 'A song of triumph for Edward Baines's great discovery of the people having plenty of Education', ibid.

51 *Select Miscellaneous Poems* (1874) p. 127.

52 Text from *The Dagonet Reciter* (n.d. [1909]) p. 17.
53 Ibid., p. 125.
54 Ibid., p. 31.
55 Ibid., pp. 22–3.
56 First published in *New York Tribune*, 1870; *Pike County Ballads*, ed. Henry Morley (1903) pp. 24–5.
57 Sims, *The Dagonet Reciter*, p. 100. It is interesting to observe the strong Sims ballad stanza, as exemplified here, being absorbed into general popular use. In 1899 the Black Watch regiment was badly cut up at the battle of Magersfontein, and a private was inspired to verse by his experience, beginning

'Tell you the tale of the battle, well there's not much to tell;
Nine hundred men went to the slaughter, and nigh four hundred fell.'

The long lines are hard for an amateur, or his verses have been mutilated in transmission, for the metre immediately begins to break down:

'Wire and Mauser rifle, thirst and a burning sun,
Knocked down by hundreds ere the day was done.'

Quoted by Byron Farwell, *Queen Victoria's Little Wars* (1973) p. 344.
58 *Narrative Poems* (1891) pp. 52–3.
59 (1889) pp. viii, 30.
60 pp. 1–2.
61 *The Poems of Tennyson*, ed. Christopher Ricks (1969) p. 1379.
62 *The Dagonet Reciter*, p. 1.
63 *Ballads and other Poems* (1880) pp. 93–4.
64 *Sent Back by the Angels* (1889) pp. 1–10.
65 Michael Turner, *Parlour Poetry* (1965) p. 26.
66 Ibid., p. 21.

Chapter 5

1 This was already the case in Wordsworth's time; see the letter to Francis Wrangham already quoted, ch. 1, p. 13, n. 1. p. 23.
2 Ibid., p. 224.
3 *Cheap Repository Tracts*, vol. 1 (1795) general declaration, bound at the end.
4 Ibid., (The tracts are all separately paginated, so no page reference can be given.).
5 Ibid.
6 Ibid.
7 Ibid.
8 1876 ed., p. 40.
9 See *Poems*, ed. Ricks, p. 997.
10 *Parlour Song Book* (1972) p. 260.
11 *Victorian Song* (1955) pp. 186–7.
12 Quoted from Turner, *Parlour Song Book*, p. 250; the song exists in many versions, like the majority of the most popular ballads. Another is given by

Disher, *Victorian Song*, p. 187.
13 Vol. 7, p. 131.
14 (1897) pp. ix–xvi.
15 Ibid., pp. 43–50.
16 Ibid., pp. 117–27.
17 Ibid., p. 155.
18 *Gordon League Ballads*, 2nd ser. (n.d.) p. viii.
19 Ibid., p. xi. The reviews quoted at the end of this volume all make the same point.
20 Pinto and Rodway, *The Common Muse*, p. 125.
21 William Morris, *Chants for Socialists, No. 1 The Day is Coming* (1885) p. [3].
22 p. 90.

Chapter 6

1 Down to, but not including; the lowest theatrical level, that of the penny gaff, carried on energetically for some decades the most scurrilous and the most pornographic presentations of songs and humour. Mayhew records (in *London Labour and the London Poor*, 3 vols (1851) vol. 1, pp. 40–2) a performance he attended where the features of the show were a song constructed to stress four-letter words at the ends of the stanzas, and an obscene dance and dialogue between two characters, one dressed as a country bumpkin and one in drag.
2 Introduction, *E.S.P.B.* no. 29.
3 It is interesting that Ken Stubbs, collecting songs in the Home Counties in the 1960s, found one cheerful song of female rebellion, in which the girl runs away to become an army drummer, 'like any other private man', was a favourite of women singers, but unknown to men. (Ken Stubbs, *The Life of a Man* (1970) p. 35).
4 Reprinted in *The Common Muse*, pp. 406–10, from *Merry Drollery Collected by W.N., C.B. & J.G.* (1661) p. 134.
5 *The Sailor's Return, a New Garland*, pp. 6–8; copy at British Library, press mark 11621 b 14(2).
6 Copy at Bodleian Library, press mark Firth b 27.
7 'The Humour of the Public', *Yet Again* (1909) pp. 247–61.
8 Text from *120 Popular Comic Songs*, vol. 1 of *D'Alcorn's Musical Miracles* (n.d.).
9 The texts of this song, of 'Daddy Long Legs' (p. 168), 'Doo-dah-day' (p. 171), 'We've All Been Having a Go at it' (p. 175), '1, 2, 3, 4, 5, 6, 7, 8, Funny Little Kids' (p. 175), 'Rose, Rose, Rose' (p. 176), 'That's Pa!' (p. 180) and 'Cooking the Cock o' the North' (p. 183) are all taken from a songster in the possession of the author, lacking covers and identifying marks but apparently printed in 1918 by the firm of Feldman.
10 For an extended description of the songs about the police force, from which these examples are taken, see Pulling, *They Were Singing*, ch. VII.

11 'Only Us Two', burlesque ballad by A. R. Marshall, composed by E. J. Symons, sung by Fred French, published by Francis, Day and Hunter [1891].

12 Lloyd, *Folk Song in England*, pp. 61, 204; text from *Bishop Percy's Folio Manuscript: Loose and Humorous Songs*, ed. F. J. Furnivall (1868) p. 99.

13 Words by Chevalier, music by Charles Ingle, published by Reynolds and Co. (n.d. [1894]).

14 'I'm Very Unkind to my Wife'; text from Pulling, *They were Singing*, pp. 70–1, where it is attributed to Gus Elen; it is however cited by R. Pearsall, *Victorian Popular Music* (1973) p. 54, as a Lion Comique song. The style is characteristically Elen's.

15 *D'Alcorn's Musical Miracles*, no. 15 (n.d.) p. 11.

16 Published by Francis, Day and Hunter.

17 Written by A. J. Mills, composed by Frank Leo, sung by Dan Crawley, published by Francis, Day and Hunter.

18 Broadside version printed by Disley; copy in Crampton Collection, vol. 1, p. 32.

19 *D'Alcorn's Musical Miracles*, no. 14, p. 1.

20 The best known set of verses under this title was performed by Dan Leno, but in *The Imperial Songster* 'Taken in and Done For' is a much wittier song about an ailing rich relation; Leno's was about being captivated by his landlady's daughter. Similarly 'You never can tell where he's been' inspired more than one set of verses. 'Cooking the Cock o' the North' was more than a random variation on a phrase already in use: at the time of its composition, in the first decades of the twentieth century, Piper Findlater, V.C., honourably retired from the Gordon Highlanders, was touring the halls playing the tune 'Cock o' the North', as he had done on the day when he earned his medal, charging the Dargai Heights on the North-West Frontier under withering fire, and continuing to play, propped against a rock, when he was shot through both legs. The cock's refusal to die has therefore an added mock-heroic significance. (See Byron Farwell, *Queen Victoria's Little Wars*, p. 323).

21 Words by Will Herbert; quoted from Davidson, *Songs of the British Music Hall*, p. 34.

22 Written and composed by Charles Collins; ibid., p. 220.

23 Written by George Rollit, composed by George Le Brunn, ibid., p. 106.

24 *D'Alcorn's Musical Miracles*, no. 14, p. 5.

25 Ibid., p. 13.

26 (Hopwood and Crew, n.d. [1887]).

27 'Wor Nanny's a Mazer', Davidson, *Songs of the British Music Hall*, p. 41.

28 Text from *D'Alcorn's Musical Miracles*, no. 1, p. 62. The volume is a collection of comic songs said to be sung by Sam Cowell, and includes two more sets of words, 'Murphey Delaney' and 'Larry O'Lash'em' to the same air and with the same nonsense chorus.

29 Written by Edgar Bateman, composed by George Le Brunn, published by Francis, Day and Hunter (1894).
30 Composed by George Le Brunn, published by Francis, Day and Hunter (1893).
31 *D'Alcorn's Musical Miracles*, no. 4, p. 6.
32 Ibid., no. 19, p. 23.
33 Composed by George Le Brunn, published by Francis Bros and Day (n.d. [1888]).
34 Composed by J. Tabrar, 1893. He also wrote a 'sequel' to the original song, called 'My Daddy's Bought me a Bow-wow', in the same year.
35 *D'Alcorn's Musical Miracles*, no. 4, p. 18.
36 Pinto and Rodway, *The Common Muse*, pp. 399–401, reprinted from Rawlinson Collection of original broadsides, Bodleian Library, press mark 566.50.
37 This is one of the several Marie Lloyd numbers which were singled out as being particularly 'naughty'; see Naomi Jacob, *Our Marie* (1936) p. 81.
38 It is, however, the one singled out as indicative of the power of the song by Naomi Jacob in the passage cited above; she describes it thus: '"Do you take milk and sugar, dear," asks the lady breakfasting at the metropole or some other famous hostelry, of the gentleman who is escorting her for the week-end, and then came Marie's stupendous bit of acting, of wonderful inflection, when she ejaculated: "Hello, hello, HELLO!"'

Chapter 7

1 M. G. Lewis, *Tales of Wonder*, 2 vols (1801) vol. I, p. 26.
2 From a notice of *Rejected Addresses* by the Brothers Smith (1812, repr. in the 20th ed., 1841) p. 100.
3 *Poetical Works of Robert Southey*, 10 vols (1837–8) vol. VI, p. 176.
4 Ibid., p. 184.
5 Ibid., p. 56.
6 *The Four Ages of Poetry*, 1820; *Works*, ed. Brett-Smith and Jones (1934) vol. VIII, p. 19.
7 1814; ibid. (1927) vol. VI, p. 281.
8 From *Crotchet Castle*, 1831; ibid., (1924) vol. IV, p. 172 (second pagination).
9 (1822).
10 *Punch*, vol. 14 (1848) pp. 33–8.
11 Ibid., vol. 13 (1847) p. 107.
12 Ibid., 9 Aug 1845 – 22 Nov 1851.
13 Ibid., 25 Nov 1848 – 1 Oct 1853.
14 Quoted in Pulling, *They Were Singing*, p. 92.
15 First collected in two volumes, 1888 and 1890; quotations from the revised one-volume edition *The Young Reciter and Model Music-hall* (1931).
16 Ibid., p. 193.
17 Ibid., p. 139.

18 Ibid., p. 159. The closeness of this song to its model is further emphasised by the fact that a real music-hall song with the same title passed into oral tradition, and is still sung. The version heard by the author is associated with canal boatmen.
19 Ibid., p. xix.
20 Ibid., pp. 69–70.
21 *Hood's Own*, 1839; *The Poetical Works of Thomas Hood*, ed. W. Jerrold (Oxford, 1911) p. 285.
22 'Epping Hunt', 1829; ibid., p. 198.
23 'Jack Hall', *Whims and Oddities*, 2nd ser. (1827); ibid., p. 98.
24 'Epping Hunt', ibid., p. 200.
25 Ibid., p. 200.
26 Ibid., p. 483.
27 Advertising practice of the day did in fact include such adaptations of poetic effusions to other ends; Warren's blacking was puffed on handbills using Shakespeare in this way.
28 *The Book of Ballads edited by Bon Gaultier* (1845) p. 7.
29 Not included in the first edition; quoted from 10th ed. (1868) p. 180.
30 Ibid., p. 182.
31 Peacock, *The Misfortunes of Elphin* (1829) *ed. cit.*, vol. IV, p. 89.
32 *Bon Gaultier*, p. 134.
33 Reprinted in *Stories and Verse of W. E. Aytoun* (Edinburgh, 1964) p. 78.
34 *Bon Gaultier*, p. 137.
35 'The Witches' Frolic', *Ingoldsby Legends*, 1st ser. (1840) pp. 161–80.
36 Anon. (1801). These parodies of *Tales of Wonder* are variously attributed to an unknown detractor and to Lewis himself; see E. Church, 'A Bibliographical Myth', *M.P.* XIX (1922) pp. 307–14.
37 'The Ingoldsby Penance', *Ingoldsby Legends*, 2nd ser. (1842) pp. 91–109.
38 Ibid., pp. 61–87.
39 *Phantasmagoria* (1869) pp. 77–86.
40 Ibid., pp. 3–57.
41 Quoted in *The Annotated Snark*, ed. Martin Gardner (Penguin ed., 1962) Introduction, p. 18.
42 Ibid., p. 59.
43 Ibid., p. 18.
44 Ibid., pp. 48, 75.
45 Ibid., p. 59.
46 Ibid., p. 48.
47 Ibid., p. 45, n. 5.
48 See L. Shepard, *The History of Street Literature* (1973) pp. 91, 118–20.
49 *The Annotated Snark*, p. 28.
50 'The Rival Curates', *Bab Ballads*, collected ed. (1869) p. 18.
51 'Gentle Alice Brown', ibid., p. 217.

52 'The Yarn of the Nancy Bell', ibid., p. 85.
53 'Ben Allah Achmet', ibid., p. 198.
54 'Sir Guy the Crusader' ibid., p. 36.
55 'The Bishop of Rum-ti-foo', ibid., p. 90.
56 'Baines Carew, Gentleman', ibid., p. 103.
57 First printed in the *Graphic*; quoted from *The Bab Ballads, with which are included Songs of a Savoyard* (1898) pp. 541–6.

Bibliography

This list is intended to indicate the main sources only of the material used in this book, and to suggest possible sources of further information on some subjects touched upon here. Editions given are those used in the text; place of publication is London, unless otherwise stated.

I. THE BALLADS

F. Anstey. *The Young Reciter and Model Music Hall*, rev. ed., 1931.

A. Austin. *Narrative Poems*, 1891.

W. E. Aytoun. *Lays of the Scottish Cavaliers* (1849) 1870.

——. *Stories and Verse*, with an introduction by W. L. Renwick, Edinburgh, 1964.

W. E. Aytoun and Sir Theodore Martin. *The Ballad Book edited by Bon Gaultier*, 1845.

R. H. Barham. *Ingoldsby Legends*, ser. I, II and III, 1840, 1842, 1846.

W. C. Bennett. A collection of poems printed on single sheets [1840–50].

Broadsides, sheet music and songsters preserved in the collections of the British and Bodleian libraries, under various press marks cited in references.

F. C. Burnand (ed.). *Poems from Punch 1841–1884*, 1908.

L. Carroll. *Phantasmagoria*, 1869.

——. *The Hunting of the Snark* (1876) annotated edition, ed. M. Gardner, 1962.

F. J. Child (ed.). *The English and Scottish Popular Ballads*, 5 vols, Boston, 1882–98.

T. Crampton (ed.). *Collection of Broadsides printed in London, collected by T. Crampton*, 7 vols [1860?–70?].

P. Davidson (ed.). *Songs of the British Music Hall*, New York, 1971.

V. De Sola Pinto and A. E. Rodway (ed.). *The Common Muse*, 1957.

Sir Francis Hastings Doyle. *The Return of the Guards and other Poems*, 1866.

A. H. Ehrenpreis (ed.). *The Literary Ballad*, 1966.

W. S. Gilbert. *The Bab Ballads*, collected edition, 1869.

——. *The Bab Ballads and Songs of a Savoyard*, 1898.

J. Harland (ed.). *Lancashire Lyrics: Modern Songs and Ballads of the County Palatine*, 1866.

Col. John Hay. *Pike County Ballads* (1871) ed. H. Morley, 1903.

W. E. Henley (ed.). *Lyra Heroica*, 1892.
T. Hood. *Whims and Oddities*, ser. I and II, 1826, 1827.
——. *Hood's Own*, 1839.
——. *Poetical Works of Thomas Hood*, ed. W. Jerrold, Oxford, 1911.
S. Hugill (ed.). *Shanties and Sailor's Songs*, 1969.
Mrs C. N. Jackson. *Gordon League Ballads*, 1st ser. 1897, 2nd ser. n.d.
R. Kipling. *Barrack-room Ballads and other Verses*, 1892.
——. *The Works of Rudyard Kipling*, Bombay Edition, 31 vols, 1913–38.
F. Langbridge. *Poor Folks' Lives*, 1887.
——. *Sent Back by the Angels*, 1889.
——. *The Power of Red Michael*, 1909.
——(ed.). *Ballads of the Brave* (1889) 3rd ed., 1907.
——(ed.). *Poets at Play: a Handbook of Humorous Recitations*, n.d.
M. G. Lewis (ed.). *Tales of Wonder*, 2 vols, 1801.
Lord Macaulay. *Lays of Ancient Rome*, 1842.
A. H. Miles (ed.). *Poets and Poetry of the Century*, 10 vols, 1891–7.
——(ed.). *Ballads of Brave Women* [?1908].
H. More. *Cheap Repository Tracts*, vol. I, 1795.
W. Morris. *Chants for Socialists*, no. I, 1885.
Sir Henry Newbolt. *Admirals All*, 1897.
Bishop Percy (ed.). *Reliques of Ancient Poetry*, 3 vols (1765) 4th ed., 1794.
——. *Bishop Percy's Folio M.S.: Loose and Humorous Songs*, ed. F. J. Furnivall, 1868.
Punch, or the London Charivari, 1841–
Sir Walter Scott (ed.). *Minstrelsy of the Scottish Border*, 3 vols, 1802–3.
Mrs M. Sewell. *Mother's Last Words* (1860) 1876.
J. W. Sharp (ed.). *The Vauxhall Comic Song Book*, ser. I, 1847.
G. K. Sims. *The Dagonet Reciter* [1909].
J. and H. Smith. *Rejected Addresses* (1812) 20th ed., 1841.
R. Southey. *Poetical Works*, 10 vols, 1837–8.
S. Spaeth (ed.). *Read 'em and Weep*, New York, 1926.
K. Stubbs (ed.). *The Life of a Man*, 1970.
A. Swinburne. *Ballads of the English Border*, ed. C. MacInnes, 1925.
Lord Tennyson. *Ballads and other Poems*, 1880.
——. *The Poems of Tennyson*, ed. C. Ricks, 1969.
J. K. Tomalin (ed.). *The World Wide Reciter*, n.d.
M. F. Tupper. *A Dozen Ballads for the Times about White Slavery*, 1854.
——. *Select Miscellaneous Poems*, 1874.
M. Turner (ed.). *Parlour Poetry*, 1967.
——(ed.). *The Parlour Song Book*, 1972.

2. CRITICAL AND BIOGRAPHICAL WORKS

M. Beerbohm. 'The Humour of the Public', in *Yet Again*, 1909.

——. 'The Blight on the Music Halls', in *More*, 1899.
M. Booth. *English Melodrama*, 1965.
M. W. Disher. *Victorian Song from Dive to Drawing Room*, 1955.
T. S. Eliot. 'Marie Lloyd' (1923) in *Selected Essays*, 3rd ed., 1951.
——. Introduction to *A Choice of Kipling's Verse*, 1941.
B. Farwell. *Queen Victoria's Little Wars*, 1973.
D. C. Fowler. *A Literary History of the Popular Ballad*, Durham, North Carolina, 1968.
A. B. Friedman. *The Ballad Revival*, University of Chicago, 1961.
G. H. Gerould. *The Ballad of Tradition*, Oxford, 1932.
R. Graves. *The English Ballad*, 1927.
G. Grigson. Introduction to *The Faber Book of Popular Verse*, 1971.
F. E. Hardy. *The Early Life of Thomas Hardy 1840–1891*, 1928.
E. Hardy (ed.). *Thomas Hardy's Notebooks*, 1955.
A. L. Hayward. *The Days of Dickens*, 1925.
——. *Green Room Recollections*,
M. J. C. Hodgart. *The Ballads*, 1950.
——. Introduction to *The Faber Book of Ballads*, 1965.
N. Jacob. *Our Marie*, 1936.
E. Lee. *Music of the People*, 1970.
A. L. Lloyd. *Folk Song in England*, 1967.
C. MacInnes. *Sweet Saturday Night*, 1967.
E. D. Mackerness. *A Social History of English Music*, 1964.
R. Mander and J. Mitchenson. *British Music Hall*, 1965.
H. Mayhew. *London Labour and the London Poor*, 3 vols, 1851; *Mayhew's London*, ed. P. Quennell, 1969.
H. Nathan. *Dan Emmett and the Rise of Early Negro Minstrelsy*, University of Oklahoma Press, 1962.
R. Nettel. *A Social History of Traditional Song*, Documents of Social History, 1969, first published as *Sing a Song of England*, 1954.
——. *Seven Centuries of Popular Song*, 1956.
G. Orwell. 'Rudyard Kipling', in *Collected Essays*, ed. S. Orwell and I. Angus, 4 vols, 1968.
R. Pearsall. *Victorian Popular Music*, 1973.
C. Pulling. *They Were Singing*, 1952.
A. Reeve. *Take it for a Fact*, 1954.
J. C. Reid. *Thomas Hood*, 1963.
H. Scott. *The Early Doors*, 1946.
C. J. Sharp. *English Folk Song: Some Conclusions* (1907) 4th ed., 1972.
L. Shepard. *The Broadside Ballad*, 1962.
——. 'Popular Broadside Ballads' in *Folk Scene*, no. 11, Sep 1965.
——. *John Pitts, Ballad Printer of Seven Dials*, 1969.
——. *The History of Street Literature*, 1973.

M. H. Spielmann. *The History of Punch*, 1895.

A. C. Swinburne. 'The Poems of Dante Gabriel Rossetti', in *Essays and Studies*, 1875.

A. Tennyson. *Charles Tennyson*, 1949.

W. Wordsworth. *Letters of William and Dorothy Wordsworth*, 1806–1820, ed. E. de Selincourt, 2 vols, Oxford, 1937.

W. B. Yeats. Introduction to the *Oxford Book of Modern Verse*, 1936.

Index

Adams, Harry, 37–41
Albert, Fred, 182, 193
amateur entertainment, 23, 28, 42, 52, 90, 106–7, 135, 217–18
Ancient Mariner, The, 6, 18
Anderson, Alexander, 64
animals, 67, 123, 124, 130–1, 181, 217, 218, 221–2
Anstey, F., 215–19
'Arethusa, The', 43, 50
Armstrong, Tommy, 93, 152, 187, 190
Arnold, Samuel, 44, 53
Auden, W. H., 252
Austin, Alfred, 50–1, 67, 128–9
'Auto-da-fé, The', 234–6
Aytoun, William Edmondstoune (*see also* Bon Gaultier), 48–9, 226, 234, 237

Bab Ballads, The, 245–50
Balfe, Michael William, 27, 43
Ballads of Policeman X, 213–15
Bard, Wilkie, 166–7, 201
Barham, Rev. Richard Harris, 210, 225–6, 229–36, 239
Barnes, William, 252
Barrack-Room Ballads, The, 74–88
Barrett, C. F., 202
Barrett, T. W., 169–70
Bateman, Edgar, 102, 190–1
Bayley, Thomas Haynes, 27
Bedford, Harry, 183
Beerbohm, Max, 99, 165, 175
Beggar's Opera, 28
'Belles of London, The', 169–70, 199
Bellwood, Bessie, 99, 103–4, 184–5
Bennett, Billie, 116
Bennett, William Cox, 51, 54, 56, 117–19
Bentley's Miscellany, 230
Billy Taylor, 25–6
'Billy's Rose', 126
Birkenhead, loss of, 69–70
Blackwood's Magazine, 228–9
Bohemian Girl, The, 27, 43
Boker, G. H., 66
Bon Gaultier, *Ballads* (*see also* Aytoun, W. E.), 225–9
Bonehill, Bettie, 193
Booth, Michael, 111–12
'Bowton's Yard', 94
Braham, John, 44
Brierley, Ben, 93
broadside ballads, 42–4, 47, 55, 56, 72, 201, 208, 244, 251
  comic, 155–6, 162–4, 185, 189–90, 195–6
  political, 12–13, 78, 119, 151–2
  propaganda, 137, 138–41, 146
  relationship with music-hall song, 24–7
  Wordworth's use of, 13–15
Browning, Elizabeth Barrett, 227–8
'Burial of Sir John Moore', 55, 210
Burnand, F. C., 33
Burns, Robert, 5, 37

Campbell, Herbert, 98
Campbell, Thomas, 53
Carleton, Will, 37, 131
Carrington, Charles, 76
Carroll, Lewis, 236–45, 247, 248, 251
Cary, Phoebe, 58–9, 66
'Casabianca', 55, 65
Catnach, James, 24

Causley, Charles, 253
Champion, Harry, 171, 174–5
'Charge of the Light Brigade, The', 31, 59–61, 66, 68, 70
Chatterton, Thomas, 60, 211
Cheap Repository Tracts, 138–41, 251
Chesterton, G. K., 45
Chevalier, Albert, 30, 93, 99–101, 105, 107, 174
'Chickaleary Cove', 98–9
Child, F. J. (*see also English and Scottish Popular Ballads*), 4, 5, 6, 7, 8–9, 10, 13–14, 20, 87, 157, 158
children, 9, 15, 140, 141, 142–3, 175–6, 224–5, 235
  heroic, 65–6
  pathetic, 109–11, 126, 127–8, 132–4, 146–7
  recitations for, 49–51, 132–4
Clifton, Harry, 95, 116
Coal Hole, 28, 97
Cohen, Leonard, 253
Cole, E. W., 37
Coleridge, S. T., 6, 13, 16, 18, 206, 210, 220
comique singers, 81–2, 98, 177, 198
'Costermonger Joe', 94
costermongers, 94, 99–104
Covent Garden, 41, 90
Cowell, Sam, 94–5, 96, 105, 166
Cowper, William, 203
'Crabfish, The', 172–3, 189
Cyder Cellars, 28, 33, 97, 182

Darling, Grace, 67, 68
Davidson, John, 252
Davidson, Peter, 96, 104
de Sola Pinto, V., and Rodway, A. E., 5–6, 195
Defence of Guinevere, 21
dialect, 92–5, 128–31, 148, 189–92, 212–19
Dibdin, Charles (the elder), 41, 42, 50, 159
Dickens, Charles, 13, 246
Dilke, Charles, 177
Disher, Maurice Willson, 42, 91, 96, 101–2, 103, 116, 145–6
Doyle, Sir Francis H. C., 38–41, 58, 64, 69, 71
Doyle, Richard, 33, 211–12
drink (*see also* temperance), 9, 29, 40, 82, 84, 110, 141, 153, 217, 222
Dryden, Leo, 43, 108–9
Durrell, L., 252
Dylan, Bob, 253

''E Talks Like a Picture-Book', 191–2
Ehrenpreis, Anne, 6
Elen, Gus, 67, 93, 97, 99–103, 156, 176, 190–2
Eliot, Lottie, 114–15
Eliot, T. S., 30, 75, 104
Ellis, Albert, 100, 194
emigration, 108–9
Empire, British, 61–2, 73, 76, 81, 83, 89
English and Scottish Popular Ballads, 4–10, 13–14, 72, 97, 157, 158, 167
'Etiquette', 248–50
Evans's, 28, 32, 33, 96
'Excelsior', 210–11, 212

Fields, Gracie, 182
'Follow the Van', 174
Fortey, W. S., 24, 43
Fowler, David, 5
Frazer's Magazine, 226
Friedman, A. B., 6, 16
Fun, 32, 209

Gardner, Martin, 244, 245
Garrick, David, 41
Gassoway, F. H., 67
Gay, John, 28, 203
Geoghegan, J. B., 178, 194
Gerould, G. H., 10
Gilbert, Fred, 102
Gilbert, W. S., 30–1, 32, 33, 193, 208, 221, 236, 241, 244, 245–50
'God Save the King', 41
Godfrey, Charles, 39–40, 62, 82, 178, 180
Goodchild, John A., 70
Gordon, A. L., 67
Gordon, Gen. Charles George, 62–3, 73, 149
Graham, Charles, 115
Graham, Dougal, 244

Graves, Robert, 4
Gray, Clifford, 185
'Green Eye of the Little Yellow God, The', 3, 52, 69, 107
Guthrie, Thomas Anstey, 215–19

Hardwick, J. H., 116–17
Hardy, Thomas, 7, 252
Harrington, J., 108, 110, 169–70, 193
Harrison, Clifford, 217
Hawker, Rev. R. S., 55
Hay, Col. John, 127–8
'Hearts of Oak', 41, 52, 53, 91
Hemans, Felicia, 37, 55
Henley, W. E., 50, 69
'Here upon Guard am I', 37–41, 63
Hill, Jenny, 104, 107, 110
Hodgart, M. J. C., 4–5, 92
Holiday, Henry, 240–1, 244
'Home Sweet Home', 90–1, 107
Hood, Thomas, 37, 96, 219–25, 228, 230, 231, 232–3, 241, 245, 247
  journalism, 31–2
Hook, Theodore, 32
Hudson, Thomas, 181–2
'Hulloa, hulloa, hulloa!', 196–201, 251
Hunt, G. W., 53, 98, 186
Hunter, Harry, 108
Hunting of the Snark, The, 236, 240–5, 247, 251
Hurley, Alec, 110–11

'I Dreamt I Dwelt in Marble Halls', 27
Idylls of the King, 19
Incledon, 41
Ingle, Charles, 100
Ingoldsby Legends, 210, 225–6, 229–36, 239
'It's a Great Big Shame', 102–3, 188

Jackson, Mrs Clement Nugent, 148–51, 251
Jerrold, Douglas, 32
Jones, Ernest, 152
Jongmans, E., 39

Keating, P. J., 76
Keats, John, 6, 16, 18–19
Kershaw, Jacob, 110
'King's Daughter, The', 20
Kipling, Rudyard, 74–88

'La Belle Dame Sans Merci', 6, 18–19
'Lady of Shalott, The', 19
Landon, Letitia F., 37
Langbridge, Frederick, 49, 51, 57, 60, 129, 133
Laycock, Samuel, 93, 94
Lays of Ancient Rome, 46–9, 59, 79, 210, 251
Lays of the Scottish Cavaliers, 48–9
Le Brunn, George, 102, 169–70, 178
Lee, Edward, 11, 96
Leigh, Percival, 32, 33, 211
Lemar, Alice, 185
Lemon, Mark, 210
Leno, Dan, 186, 194
Leo, Frank, 166–7
Lewis, Matthew Gregory, 18, 57, 204–5, 207, 232
Leybourne, George, 82, 98, 179, 182, 186, 193
lifeboats, 57, 68, 123, 128, 144–5
literary ballads, 4, 6, 12–22
'Little Billee', 3
'Little Chance', 93
'Little Jim', 134, 135
Lloyd, A. L., 26, 91, 92, 93
Lloyd, Arthur, 33, 97, 176, 192, 213
Lloyd, Marie, 3, 30, 104, 173, 174, 185, 196–200, 251
Lockhart, J. G., 45
Longfellow, H. W., 37, 66, 210–11, 236
Lord Bateman, 25, 209
Lucknow, relief of, 59, 68
Lyra Hibernica, 213, 215
Lyrical Ballads, 13–16

Macaulay, T. B., 46–9, 51, 55, 58–9, 61, 64, 79, 80, 87, 210, 251
Macdermott, G. H., 53–4, 62, 81, 177, 251
McGonagal, William, 58
McGough, Roger, 253
MacInnes, Colin, 100
Macintosh, William, 100
Mackay, Charles, 37

Mackerness, E. D., 91
Malins, Joseph, 63–4
married life, 160–2, 173–7
Marshall, A. R., 191
Martin, Theodore (*see also* Aytoun, W. E.), 225–9
Mask of Anarchy, 13
Masque of Alfred, 41
'Massacre of Macpherson, The', 228
Massey, Gerald, 68, 134
Mayhew, Henry, 25
melodrama, 14–15, 23, 97, 106, 111–12, 115, 207
Miles, Alfred, 49, 51, 52
Millais, Sir John Everett, 51
minstrels, nigger, 30, 106–9
'Mistletoe Bough, The', 27
Moore, Tom, 27
More, Hannah, 138–41, 152
Morris, William, 19, 20–1, 152–3
mothers, 9, 15, 107–8, 112, 142
mothers-in-law, 9–10, 165, 176
music halls, 27–30 and *passim*
  Canterbury, 29, 95
  Gatti's, 81
  Wilton's, 29, 30, 44–5
'My Old Dutch', 100–1
Myers, Ernest, 63

Napier, Sir Charles, 71
nationalism, 19, 20, 39–41, 45, 52, 53–4
Nelson, Horatio, 43–4, 52, 62, 63
Nettel, R., 6, 91
Newbolt, Henry, 54, 56, 65, 66, 251
Nightingale, Florence, 62, 67

'Only Us Two', 169
Orwell, G., 75–6, 188
''Ouses in Between, The', 190–1

parody, 6, 19, 47–8, 156–7, 194, 203–50 *passim*
Patti, Adelina, 96
Payne, John H., 90–1
Peacock, Thomas Love, 206–7, 220, 227, 228
Percy, Thomas, 3, 13, 16, 17, 18, 50, 172, 220
Phantasmagoria, 236–40, 243, 247
Pitts, John, 24–5
Plomer, William, 252
police, 167–9, 230
Pratt, W. W., 146
Preston, Ben, 93
'Pretty Little Sarah', 26
'Private of the Buffs, The', 38–41, 58, 63
'Proud Maisie', 18
Pull, J. J., 133–4
Punch, 24, 32–3, 118, 151, 153, 208–19, 227, 229, 230, 246, 251

Quiller-Couch, Arthur, 4

railways, 64–5, 123, 211–12
Ramsay, Allan, 28
Randall, Harry, 176
Ranking, H. M., 67
'Ratcatcher's Daughter, The', 94–5, 166, 209, 223
'Red Thread of Honour, The', 71
Reed, German, 30, 31, 32
Reeve, Ada, 26
Reliques of Ancient Poetry, 13, 16, 50, 220
'Revenge, The', 60–1, 70, 71, 251
Richardson, Thomas, 141
'Right on my Doo-dah', 171, 173, 189
'Road to Ruin, The', 114–15
Robson, Fred, 96
Rogers, E. W., 110–11, 180
Rollit, George, 196–8
Ross, W. G., 33, 97
Rossetti, D. G., 19, 20–2, 84
'Rule Brittania', 41, 53

sailors, 28, 30, 41, 42–5, 62, 72–3, 109
'Sam Hall', 97–8, 105, 124, 209
Scott, Clement, 33, 57–8, 69, 208
Scott, Sir Walter, 3, 19, 61, 87, 206, 230–2
  Minstrelsy of the Scottish Border, 17–18, 20, 45–6, 78
Sewell, Mrs, 142–3
sex, 32, 115–16, 155, 156, 159–64, 169–70, 184–8, 195–201
Sharp, Cecil, 7, 135, 252, 253
Sharp, Jack, 25–6

Shelley, Percy Bysshe, 13, 16, 18, 152, 220
Shepard, Leslie, 7, 44, 95–6
Sheppard, Jack, 97
Shields, Ella, 105
Shields, William, 41, 43
Sims, George R., 33, 37, 56, 58, 64–5, 123–33, 208, 218–19, 236, 245, 250–1
'Sister Helen', 21–2
'Sisters, The', 19–20
Sladen, Douglas, 56, 67
Sloman, Charles, 33
Smith, James and Horace, 207, 232
soldiers, 9, 37–87 *passim*, 109
'Song of the Shirt, The', 118–19, 135, 251–2
Southey, Robert, 68, 205–6, 220, 221, 231, 233, 248
Stansbury, Mary, 66–7
Stephen, Sir Leslie, 231
Stuart, Leslie, 54
Sugden, S. S., 64
supernatural, 17, 18, 219, 220–1, 231, 233, 238–40
Swinburne, Algernon Charles, 20, 21, 236

Tabrar, Joseph, 103–4, 175, 179, 186–7
temperance, 52, 137–54 *passim*
Temple, R., 176
Tennyson, Alfred, 19–20, 24, 31, 54, 59–61, 70, 77, 87, 133, 144, 244
  compared with G. R. Sims, 129–31
  literary ballads, 19–20
  parodied, 218, 236
Thackeray, William Makepeace, 32, 33, 212–15, 218–19, 221, 230
'That's Pa!', 180
Theatres Act, 1843, 29
Thornton, Henry, 138, 139
Tilley, Vesta, 40, 105, 177, 180–2
Times, The, 31, 40, 54, 60
'Tinker, The', 162–4
'Tom Bowling', 42
Tomalin, J. K., 52
Tupper, Martin Farquar, 54, 117, 120, 144
Turner, Michael, 109, 134, 144–5

Ufford, Rev. E. S., 145

Vance, Alfred, 94, 98–9, 178, 186–7
Vauxhall, 97
Victoria, Vesta, 196
'Villikins and his Dinah', 95, 96, 209, 222
Violence and violent humour, 32, 103, 158–9, 168–9, 171–3, 219, 220, 222–3, 228, 235, 245–6
'Vitai Lampada', 58, 65, 91, 251

Walker, Robert, 65
Wallace, Nellie, 185
'War Song of Dinas Vawr, The', 228
Watts, Isaac, 141
'We Don't Want to Fight', 53–4, 62, 251
'What Cheer, 'Ria', 103, 184–5
Whittier, John G., 37
Whyte-Melville, George John, 57
'Wil the Merry Weaver and Charity the Chambermaid', 195–6, 198–201
Williams, Bransby, 52, 107
Wilson, Joe, 93
Wincott, Harry, 171, 175, 183
Wolfe, Rev. Charles, 55
woman's 'maistrie', 102–3, 162, 177, 187–8
women, 9, 10, 15, 67, 103–4, 112–16, 118–19, 124–5, 159–64, 176, 184–8
Wordsworth, William, 13–16, 37, 138–9, 143, 206
Work, Henry Clay, 146
'Workhouse, Christmas Day, The', 123–4
'Workhouse Door, The', 112–13, 116, 131, 135
'Wor Nanny's a Mazer', 187

Yeats, William Butler, 252
Yule, Sir Henry, 69

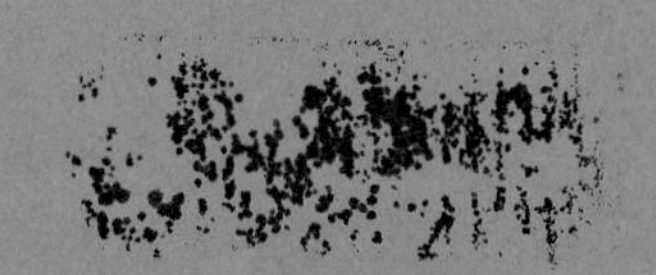